D1564699

The Role of Women's Experience
in Feminist Theologies of Atonement

Princeton Theological Monograph Series

K. C. Hanson, Charles M. Collier, and D. Christopher Spinks,
Series Editors

Recent volumes in the series:

Jeff B. Pool
God's Wounds: Hermeneutic of the Christian Symbol of Divine Suffering
Volume Two: Evil and Divine Suffering

David H. Nikkel
Radical Embodiment

William J. Meyer
*Metaphysics and the Future of Theology: The Voice of Theology
in Public Life*

Myk Habets
The Anointed Son: A Trinitarian Spirit Christology

L. Paul Jensen
*Subversive Spirituality: Transforming Mission through the Collapse
of Space and Time*

Ilsup Ahn
*Position and Responsibility: Jürgen Habermas, Reinhold Niebuhr,
and the Co-Reconstruction of the Positional Imperative*

Eliseo Pérez-Álvarez
A Vexing Gadfly: The Late Kierkegaard on Economic Matters

Gale Heide
System and Story: Narrative Critique and Construction in Theology

The Role of Women's Experience
in Feminist Theologies of Atonement

LINDA D. PEACORE

PICKWICK *Publications* · Eugene, Oregon

THE ROLE OF WOMEN'S EXPERIENCE IN FEMINIST THEOLOGIES
OF ATONEMENT

Princeton Theological Monograph Series 131

Copyright © 2010 Linda D. Peacore. All rights reserved. Except for brief
quotations in critical publications or reviews, no part of this book may be
reproduced in any manner without prior written permission from the publisher.
Write: Permissions, Wipf and Stock Publishers, 199 W. 8th Ave., Suite 3, Eugene,
OR 97401.

Pickwick Publications
An Imprint of Wipf and Stock Publishers
199 W. 8th Ave., Suite 3
Eugene, OR 97401

ISBN 13: 978-1-55635-803-6

Cataloging-in-Publication data:

Peacore, Linda D.

The role of women's experience in feminist theologies of atonement / Linda D.
Peacore.

Princeton Theological Monograph Series 131

xvi + 238 p. ; 23 cm. — Includes bibliographical references and index.

ISBN 13: 978-1-55635-803-6

1. Atonement. 2. Feminist theology. 3. Experience. I. Title. II. Series.

BT265.3 P3 2010

Manufactured in the U.S.A.

To Matt

Contents

Acknowledgments

IT IS DIFFICULT TO EXPRESS THE DEPTH OF GRATITUDE I WISH TO extend to those who played a part in the completion of this thesis. A project like this can never be done alone and rests upon the shoulders of many that helped, encouraged, and guided.

I am indebted to two groups of people represented by two institutions. First, thanks to those friends and faculty at Fuller Theological Seminary in Pasadena, California, especially Laura Schmidt Roberts and Tammy Williams, and professors William Dyrness and the late David Scholer. Each was helpful throughout the process of research and writing, reading the thesis and offering valuable and insightful critique.

The second institution is King's College London. My fellow students who were part of our weekly Research Seminars in Systematic Theology provided stimulating discussion and insights. Of that group, Demetrios Bathrellos and Shirley Martin were especially important colleagues and friends. From the faculty, Dr. Murray Rae was a tremendous resource, reading the penultimate draft of the thesis and offering wise critique. I am particularly grateful to the late Professor Colin Gunton who was my supervisor and friend during those years. His support of me (and of all his students) reflected his commitment to both the church and the academy and will be an example to me throughout my life. Needless to say, despite the perceptive comments on the part of these many readers, the final product remains my own and I take full responsibility for its shortcomings.

I would also like to thank Chris Spinks of Wipf and Stock Publishers who helped see the publishing of this thesis through to the end—his consistent support was a blessing to me. On a personal note I thank my daughters Grace and Caroline for their presence in my life, which brings such joy and keeps everything else in perspective, and my husband Matt for his unwavering faith in me.

Introduction

THIS BOOK GREW OUT OF MY FIRST ENCOUNTER, SEVERAL YEARS AGO, with a feminist attack on traditional atonement theology: "Christianity is an abusive theology that glorifies suffering."[1] These words were not easy to ignore. Such a view troubled me, as a Christian and a feminist, not simply because a harsh critique had been directed at what might be considered the core of Christian faith, but also due to the fact that I discovered such a view is common within feminist theology. I desired to see if there was a way to take feminist theological priorities seriously without discarding the traditional atonement imagery that has been at the core of Christian and biblical tradition. My subsequent examination of the subject is reflected in the content of this book. Through the course of considering the predominant critique of traditional atonement theology launched by many feminist theologians, it quickly became apparent that the notion of women's experience was crucial. This category is used widely within feminist theology and is determinative of a great deal of feminist theological reflection on Christian doctrine. The question emerged: what *is* women's experience and *how* does it affect feminist theology, specifically feminist views on the atonement? The category of women's experience is pivotal to feminist theology, and its use may lead to models of atonement that place excessive stress upon the subjective element, failing to provide an adequate account of the objective aspects of atonement.

Due to the nature of the question driving my study, it was necessary to divide the work into two parts. Part One focuses on methodological issues regarding the category of women's experience and Part Two considers women's experience specifically in the context of feminist theologies of atonement. The first chapter reviews how the category of women's experience first came to be used in feminist theology and how it has generally been defined. Critique of the definition and

---

1. Brown and Parker, "For God So Loved the World?" 26.

use of women's experience arises from various groups within feminist theology, particularly from those feminists of color who challenge the notion of universal women's experience. How shall the category be defined when there are such diverse expressions of women's experience? Furthermore, women's experience is used as a foundation in feminist theology—another aspect of the category that is challenged by feminists of color and others. Further insight into the limitations of women's experience is gained by comparing its use in feminist theology to its use in feminist epistemology, in addition to observing how a similar category of experience is used in black theology. The difficulty in defining women's experience accurately and the problems inherent in its foundational use in feminist methodology are primary weaknesses of the category. Nevertheless, despite these potential drawbacks, the category of women's experience remains valuable and necessary to the feminist theological project.

In the second chapter we examine women's experience within the context of a feminist theology of religious experience reflected in the work of post-Christian Daphne Hampson. By considering Hampson's work one begins to see the pitfalls of a theological approach that starts with experience, thus revealing similar deficiencies in feminist theology as well, since it is in many ways a theology of experience. Hampson's position is dependent upon the work of Schleiermacher, whom many consider to be the father of such theologies; therefore, Hampson's interpretation and use of Schleiermacher is considered at some length. The flaws exhibited by an experience-based theology, such as a tendency toward pantheism and a danger of relativism, are exposed and challenged.

The role of women's experience in feminist theology is next considered within the context of feminist theologies of liberation. This area of feminist theology is probably the most significant and therefore the work of three influential feminist theologians is presented: Letty Russell, Elisabeth Schüssler Fiorenza, and Rosemary Radford Ruether. Although each considers herself a feminist liberation theologian and practices a method of correlation more or less, there remain distinctions between them. We gain insight into their methodology by examining the method of correlation as it is used in Latin American liberation theology, in James Cone's black liberation theology, and, especially, in the work of Paul Tillich, with particular focus upon the ways in which correlation methodology shapes christological views. Despite its strengths, one finds drawbacks to the correlation method, specifically in Christology where the person of Jesus often functions as a symbol.

The framework established in Part One of the book provides the background for understanding the category of women's experience in feminist theology: its definition and use, its role in a feminist theology of religious experience, and its force in feminist liberation theology. Admittedly, the questions raised in the first part of the thesis are intriguing. For instance, what exactly is experience? How is experience shaped, interpreted, and defined? Such questions have great potential for further analysis; however, since matters related to the doctrine of the atonement are what prompted this study, a detailed discussion of feminist views on atonement is required. Rather than thoroughly engaging epistemological and sociological questions related to human experience, as important as those are, due to the purpose of this thesis I chose to concentrate upon one area of Christian doctrine, the atonement, to better understand how feminist views on women's experience shape feminist theology and its interpretation of Christian doctrine.

Leading off Part Two, chapter 4 presents three major feminist positions on the atonement: (1) Rita Nakashima Brock and Joanne Carlson Brown and their notion of "divine child abuse"; (2) Mary Grey and "birthing of God" imagery; (3) Rosemary Radford Ruether and the paradigm of liberated humanity in Christ. Each position offers an extended critique of classical understandings of atonement as well as presents the substance of an alternate view based on a feminist perspective. It is helpful to also note that there are some contrasting, minority views within feminist theology represented by womanists, Asian feminists, and Elizabeth Johnson in reaction to the dismissal of suffering as a valid category in many feminist views on atonement.

The role of women's experience in feminist theologies of atonement is understood further as we delve into the traditional models of atonement which come under attack from feminist theologians. In chapter 5 we examine the feminist critique of the three main views that have commonly been attacked: Anselmian/satisfaction, Peter Abelard, and *Christus victor*. Because sin and redemption are closely related it becomes necessary to consider the role of women's experience as it relates to the doctrine of sin. How has a particular view of women's experience shaped feminist understandings of sin and, therefore, views on atonement? One finds that feminist theologians endorse a subjective model of atonement largely resulting from their view of sin, which is based on an understanding of women's experience. Therefore, a discussion of a subjective view of atonement is important, returning to the work of Schleiermacher and Tillich. Although a subjective aspect of atonement is crucial to a complete understanding of the doctrine, the feminist versions are flawed due to their over-stress on the subjective, with the result that key elements of an objective understanding of atonement are not developed in feminist models of atonement.

The limitations of a subjective model of atonement are examined in greater detail in chapter 6. An emphasis upon the subjective aspect of atonement leads to a lack of engagement with Scripture and an inadequate explanation for humanity's inability to imitate Christ's example. The role of experience replaces the role of Scripture and tradition as a source for understanding our relationship to God and to each other. Therefore, it is important to consider feminist views on revelation, in particular the positions of Elisabeth Schüssler Fiorenza and Rosemary Radford Ruether. It appears that many of the apprehensions feminists have about the Bible seem to be related to the issue of authority.

In light of what has been discovered thus far, we return to the category of women's experience in the final chapter. First, it is important to recognize the benefits of women's experience. For instance, the category has served to correct the bias of male-dominated theological reflection. Furthermore, an understanding of women's experience within feminist views on atonement has provided us with a reevaluation of violent atonement imagery that has frequently been harmful to women. Feminist theologies of atonement have rightly emphasized the subjective side of atonement theology, an aspect that has often been neglected in traditional, Reformed views of the cross. The subjective element in atonement theology reminds us of the importance of contextualizing theology and of relating it to contemporary settings and communities.

However, despite their strengths, feminist atonement theologies have significant shortcomings. First, due to the variety of the content of women's experience, an attempt to apply the category to different groups of women may lead to a fragmentation between these groups and, furthermore, to a relativism where each group (or even individual) has a particular understanding of experience and, hence, of redemption as well. Second, the use of women's experience as a foundation for theological method can be seen as another form of oppression; that is, women's experience becomes determinative of theological reflection in a manner that limits the breadth and depth of Christian doctrine. Third, the lack of an objective element in feminist views on atonement means that the genuine redemption that Scripture teaches and feminists expect is not fully developed since feminist accounts understand liberation in terms of what happens between one another rather than what happens between humanity and God. Likewise, the stress on the subjective aspect of atonement, although necessary, when presented as the only aspect of redemption, fails to take human sin seriously. Such views promote an exemplarist understanding of Jesus and concentrate upon his life rather than his death and resurrection.

As a result of the limitations of feminist theologies of atonement identified in this particular study, I propose that feminist theological reflection might benefit by practicing the following: (1) further addressing the content and definition of women's experience; (2) altering the use of women's experience; (3) employing a pastoral approach to difference; and (4) giving serious attention to the gravity of sin, therefore, embracing both the objective and subjective aspects of atonement. Meaningful models that reveal God's redemptive purposes are needed in all theologies of atonement, but perhaps particularly in feminist views where the oppression of women is such a significant part of women's experience.

This thesis attempts to answer the primary question behind this study: what *is* women's experience and *how* does it affect feminist theologies of atonement? Any theological consideration of experience can easily become too broad in scope and, therefore, must have boundaries placed around it in order to provide fruitful study. Consequently, the thesis focuses on categories of understanding experience within feminist theology without delving too deeply into philosophical, linguistic, or epistemological issues related to human experience generally (e.g., considering a sociology of knowledge approach to experience). These certainly are valid and important matters that may shed further light on our understanding of the category of women's experience. Since the days of Schleiermacher, theologians have wondered what the role of experience should be in theological reflection. Although the thesis raises several issues related to experience, it is an area for further study and one that lies beyond the scope of this particular work.

A lingering concern raised by this thesis regards the rules of engagement under which much feminist theology operates. That is, one could say of feminist theology in general that the eschewal of authority, particularly a revealed authority that is part of traditional understandings of atonement that many feminists find heteronomous, is actually considered a value of the feminist approach by its advocates. In contrast, this thesis argues that traditional atonement models have strengths that the feminist models lack due in part to their understanding of what is authoritative for theology. Many feminist theologians would remain unconvinced that any such views should be reconsidered unless it is done under their conditions—with women's experience as the determining factor rather than another "outside" authority. In the concluding chapter of the thesis, I have alluded to possible ways forward that could address the feminist position while still upholding the validity of traditional perspectives. The challenge for future work lies in providing compelling reasons for a feminist to prefer "traditional" elements of atonement theory on her own terms, weaving a view of Scriptural authority and a more objective focus in atonement theology into a feminist account that has integrity for both sides. That such an aim is possible remains to be seen. The goal of the present work is to analyze the feminist theological landscape, particularly in terms of method, evaluating the function of women's experience as a source for feminist theology and how such an approach leads to certain strengths and weaknesses, soteriologically. One must clearly understand the possibilities before determining an ultimate way forward.

PART ONE

The Category of Women's Experience

1

Women's Experience in Feminist Theology

Introduction: Theology's Gender Perspective

FEMINIST THEOLOGY'S FIRST SIGNIFICANT RELATIONSHIP WITH THE category of experience is most often attributed to an influential piece written by Valerie Saiving in 1960, titled "The Human Situation." In the article Saiving criticizes, from the viewpoint of feminine experience, the estimate of the human situation made by certain contemporary theologians, primarily Anders Nygren and Reinhold Niebuhr, who represented a tendency in contemporary theology to describe humanity's predicament as rising from a separateness and anxiety and to identify sin with self-assertion and love with selflessness.[1] Saiving argues that although men and women do share common experiences, women's sin cannot be characterized as pride or will-to-power because such a doctrine of sin is based primarily on masculine experience and thus, portrays the human condition from a male standpoint. Women's sin is more accurately described in terms of underdevelopment or negation of the self.[2] Saiving's timely article drew theology's attention to the significant role of experience in the construction of theology. Jewish feminist scholar Judith Plaskow adopted Saiving's proposal in her Yale doctoral dissertation, also claiming that Reinhold Niebuhr describes sin in terms of male experience and that in order for a doctrine of sin to be relevant to women's experience it must deal with more than self-exaltation.[3] Whether or not one agrees with their conclusions about sin,

---

1. Saiving, "Human Situation," 25–26.
2. Ibid., 37.
3. Plaskow, *Sin, Sex and Grace*, 109.

3

both feminists demonstrate that to some degree experience, male or female, affects all theological reflection.

Other feminist theologians, cognizant of the need for more work in this area, began composing theology from a distinctive viewpoint. Rosemary Radford Ruether, one of the most influential feminist theologians, poignantly notes that feminist theology is not unique in its use of experience, but rather its use of "*women's* experience, which has been almost entirely shut out of theological reflection in the past."[4] In this regard, feminist theologians share a common perspective with liberation theologians by acknowledging the "standpoint-dependent" nature of theology, considering all theology to be a construction of particular persons and faith communities who confess their faith through particular metaphors and thought patterns.[5] In addition, the voices and experiences of "non-persons" are important for an understanding of God.[6] However, most theology has been written primarily by male theologians who, by neglecting the experience of half of the human race, effectively define the human condition in terms of male perspective. Such Christian theology represents a form of imperialism when it claims that white male experience is equivalent to the experience of universal humanity.[7] Ruether notes that "[a]ll the categories of classical theology in its major traditions . . . have been distorted by androcentrism. This not only makes the male normative . . . but it also distorts all the dialectical relationships of good/evil, nature/grace, body/soul, God/nature by modeling them on a polarization of male and female."[8] Consequently, contemporary feminist theology understands its task in large part as an attempt to give voice to women and to include a female perspective in the construction of theological doctrines.

My intention is not to elaborate on Saiving's argument; however, she and Plaskow represent a standard as well as persuasive feminist position which perceives most systematic theology as neglecting the standpoint of women.[9] Therefore, I am concerned to include women's

4. Ruether, *Sexism and God-Talk*, 13.

5. Russell, *Household of Freedom*, 30.

6. Ibid., 31.

7. Ruether, "Future of Feminist Theology," 704.

8. Ruether, *Sexism and God-Talk*, 37. See also Ruether, "Feminist Interpretation," 113.

9. This does not necessarily imply complete agreement with Saiving's conclusions regarding defining sin in terms of male and female perspective. That is another project

experience in theological reflection, yet I will need to examine the category of experience and, more precisely, what feminist theology means
by "women's experience." I will explore the variety of ways this category
is understood, even as it is used in a similar manner throughout feminist theology. Some feminist theologians from process and womanist
backgrounds have challenged not only these definitions of women's
experience, but their use in theological method as well. These feminists'
insightful critique raises a concern: will the category of women's experience help or hinder the feminist theological project?

What Is Women's Experience?

Any discussion of the role of experience in feminist theology is hin-
dered by the fact that it is difficult to identify precisely what is meant by
the word "experience." At first it appears to be a fairly straightforward
concept, but upon closer examination one realizes experience implies
many things.[10] There are various layers of meaning to such a term and
all pervade feminist theology to some extent.[11] However, within this
multiplicity of understandings common designations do arise that
factor into feminist theology, including: *socialized experience*, which is
what we learn about women from culture, usually defined by men and
related to the private realm; *feminist experience*, which is a response to
socialized experience and is concerned with women defining their own
experience; *historical experience*, which is related to women's activities
in the past and concerned with recovering their stories;[12] and *individual*

---

altogether—are gendered understandings of sin necessary and appropriate to theology? We do agree, however, that in general, theology has been written by males who
either explicitly or implicitly portray their perspective as applicable to the human race
without serious consideration of the particularities of gender, class, race, etc. To some
extent, all theology suffers from a similar exclusivity, including feminist theology.

10. Christ, "Spiritual Quest," 230.

11. Hence, some feminist theologians prefer speaking of feminist "theologies"
rather than "theology." We will use the singular form of the word, although it should be
understood that it by no means reflects a unified feminist theology. As in all types of
theology, there is variation.

12. See especially Schüssler Fiorenza, *In Memory of Her*. In contrast, post-Christian
feminist Mary Daly resists traditional methods of recovering women's historical experience, instead giving priority to women's contemporary experience. See Daly, *Beyond
God the Father*, 74.

experience, which acknowledges the limitations of generalized under-standings of experience.[13] In addition to these categorizations, we find women's religious, bodily, and sociopolitical experience as particularly significant to feminist theology, thus requiring further consideration.

Religious/Spiritual

Although it is not the primary way feminist theologians speak about experience, an underlying understanding of religious experience is of-ten relevant to and influential upon the theology being constructed. According to Rosemary Radford Ruether, reaction to patriarchal dis-tortions of the Christian tradition forces feminist theology to utilize the "primary intuitions of religious experience itself" as a theological resource. Ruether understands such experience to be a "belief in a di-vine foundation of reality which is ultimately good . . . and upholds our autonomous personhood as women."[14] Likewise, Daphne Hampson is a feminist theologian who emphasizes religious experience in her writing, and, although she has left the Christian tradition for what she describes as feminist and ethical reasons, her understanding of the realm of the divine shares some subtle similarities with Ruether's view. Grounding much of her thinking upon Schleiermacher, Hampson be-lieves that religious experiences are evidence that there is a dimension of reality beyond ourselves, which she calls God.[15] On a related note, Catholic feminist Catherine Hilkert contends that feminist theology's use of women's experience reveals a conviction that it can be revelatory of the divine and that the Church has excluded women's experience as part of revelation.[16] However, not all feminist theological discourse on religious experience is related to metaphysical understandings, as there is also an emphasis upon the practical realm. Feminist theology per-ceives women's piety as lived out in real life, particularly domestic life, with typical female domestic activities such as cooking, weaving, and gardening providing a perspective from which to understand female

13. Carr, "New Vision," 22–23. See also Young, *Feminist Theology*, 53–56.

14. Ruether, "Future of Feminist Theology," 710.

15. See the following chapter for detailed examination of Hampson's theism and its influences.

16. Hilkert, "Experience and Tradition," 70. Hilkert does acknowledge that it is un-clear how one determines which types of experiences count as revelatory.

religious experience as well as the imagery to describe it.[17] Moreover, religious experience for some women involves a spiritual depth and meaning seen, for example, in the reflections of a Nicaraguan Roman Catholic sister who speaks of a "paschal" experience where hope and joy in the resurrection come out of oppression.[18]

Bodily

Feminists widely accept that all experience is embodied experience, that everything we experience is at a basic, concrete level and in relation to the world.[19] Specifically, women's bodily experience has to do with the biological functions unique to women such as menstruation, pregnancy, childbirth, lactation, and menopause.[20] These functions also provide metaphors for theology and for God.[21] Related to the physical experience of being a woman are the psychological and cultural implications of those bodily functions, most significantly the role of motherhood.[22] In addition, there are other significant aspects of embodied experience such as how one perceives her body image or a fear of rape and/or assault.[23] Nevertheless, feminist theology's relationship to women and the body is somewhat ambivalent. On the one hand, much Christian theology has included a dualism between the mind and the body, elevating spirit over nature and, by associating men with the mind and women

17. Chopp, *Power to Speak*, 118–19.

18. Arellano, "Women's Experience of God," 333.

19. McFague, *Body of God*, 86.

20. Carr, "New Vision," 22. In *Essentially Speaking* (25) Diana Fuss warns against making any substantive claims based on the authority of bodily experience. Even in such cases of bodily experience as menstruation we are on shaky ground because not all women menstruate.

21. See McFague's *The Body of God*, which is a theology based upon the body as a model for God. McFague argues that such a model values rather than denigrates the body as well as unites the transcendence and immanence of God. This panentheistic understanding of God leads to an inclusive Christology and a position that promotes planetary well-being.

22. For a compelling personal reflection on motherhood see Rich, *Of Woman Born*. See also Carr and Schüssler Fiorenza, eds., *Motherhood: Experience, Institution, Theology*.

23. Young, *Feminist Theology*, 54.

with the body, has made women inferior to men.[24] This unfortunate association makes some feminists wary of drawing too close a relationship between the female and nature for fear of perpetuating the failure in theology to attribute full humanity to women. Some radical feminists disassociate themselves completely from female biological functions and malign traditional female roles related to women's physicality, particularly motherhood.[25] On the other hand, there are feminists who celebrate the relationship women have often shared with nature, claiming that women are more in tune with the natural world and, therefore, basically more interconnected and relational people than men.[26]

Sociopolitical

Despite the variations in feminist understandings of experience, feminist theologians appear united in asserting that women as a class suffer oppression by men.[27] Therefore, not surprisingly, the most widely used definition of women's experience is broadly understood in sociopolitical terms. Feminist theologians who stress this particular understanding of women's experience are often described as feminist liberation theologians, defining women's experience primarily as a struggle for liberation against patriarchy and, like Third World theologians, writing out of an experience of oppression in society.[28] In agreement with liberation

24. This position is widely accepted in feminist theology. For one analysis see Ruether, *Sexism and God-Talk*, especially pp. 54, 95. "The dualism of nature and transcendence, matter and spirit as female against male is basic to male theology. Feminist theology must fundamentally reject this dualism of nature and spirit" (ibid., 70).

25. Mary Daly would be one example of a radical feminist who appears to reject any designation of men and women based on biology. Her emphasis upon androgyny implies an elimination of sex roles. Along with such a view is an alternative social network comprised of women living in separatist communities. See Daly, *Beyond God the Father*. An extreme form of this position strives for reproduction without men. See Ruether, *Sexism and God-Talk*, ch. 9 for a discussion of radical feminism.

26. Goddess religion links womanhood with nature. Some Goddess thealogians include Carol Christ, Emily Erwin Culpepper, and Starhawk. We also see elements of this position expressed in some understandings of women's religious experience touched on above.

27. Carr, "Theological Anthropology," 123.

28. Wondra, *Humanity Has Been a Holy Thing*, 47. See also Russell, *Human Liberation*, 21. However, women's experience of oppression in the Third World is not simply characterized by patriarchy but is multi-faceted. Third World theology is influ-

theology, feminist liberation theologians maintain the conviction that a position of neutrality is impossible to achieve and, therefore, one must adopt an explicit advocacy stance on behalf of the oppressed; in the case of feminist theology this means women. Such advocacy involves exposing sources of oppression and working toward its end, thus, protest against the suffering caused by sexism is foundational to liberation feminist theology.[29] Included in an understanding of women's experience as an experience of oppression is the identification of liberation and resistance as important elements of the response to that experience.[30] The word "struggle" is characteristic of such theology, pointing to the desire for liberation and vindication of women, the promise of which is a source of hope.[31]

Experience in Womanist Theology and Asian Feminist Theology

In addition to the various ways of understanding women's experience presented above, there are feminists of color who express views on women's experience that vary in some considerable ways. Since most feminist theology is written by white women from middle-class, educated, North American or European backgrounds, it becomes important to consider the viewpoints of women from outside that particular group in order to gain a more inclusive perspective of women's experience. The work of two particular feminists of color will be discussed primarily, as they each have fairly wide exposure and represent influential views from their respective settings: Asian (Korean) feminist Chung Hyun Kyung and womanist Delores Williams.[32]

---

enced by the major experiences of its authors, which are socioeconomic and political with roots in classism and racism. See Oduyoye, "Reflections," 28.

29. Johnson, *She Who Is*, 29.

30. Schüssler Fiorenza, *In Memory of Her*, 36. Schüssler Fiorenza does not want women's history to be solely represented by oppression, but wants to include liberation as part of our theological heritage.

31. Russell, *Human Liberation*, 50.

32. Although these two have been somewhat controversial in specific contexts, they are good representations of Asian feminist and womanist approaches. Due to the focus of this thesis we have chosen to limit our discussion of non-white feminist theology, highlighting the work of those who are most influential and relevant to our study and touching upon the work of others. *Mujerista*, African, and Latin American feminist

In contrast to white feminist theology, which tends to reject suffering as a meaningful experience for women, Asian feminist theology considers suffering an important part of Asian women's self-understanding and one that allows women to identify with Jesus Christ.[33] According to Chung, Asian women suffer from oppression at many levels (e.g., economically, politically, culturally) simply because they are women.[34] Needless to say, many Asian women experience a lack of full humanity, a perception that is exacerbated by such practices as the wish for sons instead of daughters, and extensive prostitution.[35] More specifically, Chung describes the core experience of oppressed Korean women as characterized by a feeling of abandonment by God, hopelessness, pain and sorrow (known as *han* in the Korean language).[36]

Womanist theology, like much white feminist theology, characterizes black women's experience as fundamentally one of oppression; however, the concrete ways this oppression is lived out may be distinct. Black women's experience has a complexity of oppression not found in white oppression.[37] Williams identifies surrogacy as a primary example of black women's experience. Coerced surrogacy was seen in social role exploitation during the period of slavery in America where black female slaves operated in nurturing roles in white households (e.g., "mammy"), replaced male energy with female energy in field labor, and provided sexual gratification. This type of surrogacy continued beyond this period in "voluntary" but similarly exploitative roles. In addition, a "wilderness experience" is, negatively and positively, important to womanist theology as it relates to black women's experience of trying to find

---

theologies have not been as significant to our presentation in part because there is not a large volume of work represented by these groups due to their more recent development.

33. Chung, *Struggle to Be*, 54. "Because Asian women's life experience is filled with 'suffering and obedience,' it seems natural for Asian women to meet Jesus through the experience that is most familiar to them." Jesus becomes Messiah through suffering and service, not by the domination of others. Chung does acknowledge the danger of finding meaning in suffering, recognizing suffering as both a source of liberation and oppression.

34. Ibid., 24.

35. Ibid., 39, 46.

36. Ibid., 42.

37. Williams, *Sisters in the Wilderness*, 202.

their way in the world amidst various forms of oppression as well as their religious experience of meeting God in a sacred space.[38]

The Essence of Woman

Why is there such diversity in definitions of women's experience? Besides the obvious differences between individual women and, hence, their experiences, the response to such a question seems related to the subject of anthropology—how one understands "woman."[39] Generally speaking, feminists have two views: either they endorse something of an essentialist position, which understands there to be a certain "essence" of woman which is distinct from men; or they understand there to be a common humanity and that distinctions between women and men are the result of psychological and/or cultural factors, rather than the result of innate, biological differences.[40] A position such as Elizabeth Johnson's could be considered to reflect the dominant mainstream feminist position; that is, she accepts only one human nature, but recognizes an interdependence of multiple differences, which should be celebrated.[41] Most feminists do reject essentializing "woman," but this becomes less clear when considering "experience."[42] For instance, Johnson acknowl-

38. Ibid., 60. Williams sees the biblical story of Hagar as analogous to black women's experience of both surrogacy and the wilderness, forming what Williams describes as a "survival/quality-of-life tradition of African-American biblical appropriation" (ibid., 6).

39. O'Neill, "Nature of Women," 730.

40. Fuss, *Essentially Speaking*, 37. Fuss discusses the complexities of essentialism and that the notion is not necessarily in clear opposition with constructionist positions. She claims that there is no essence to essentialism and that constructionism may operate as a more sophisticated form of essentialism. While every other category (i.e., experience, identity, self) may be displaced, *politics* is not and arguably becomes the essence of feminism.

41. O'Neill, "Nature of Women," 734.

42. Jones, "'Women's Experience,'" 171; Chopp, *Power to Speak*, 116. Chopp wants to distinguish a pragmatic approach from phenomenological ones that study the essence of experience. Feminist pragmatics opens sources of direct experience such as narrative and descriptive sources rooted in the realm of the practical (Chopp, "Feminism's Theological Pragmatics," 248). Judith Plaskow notes in *Weaving the Visions* (3) that feminists of color have shown that white feminists can no longer speak of women's experience as if it were some Platonic form. One notable exception to the non-essentializing position would be Mary Daly. See also Greene-McCreight, "Gender, Sin and Grace," 420. Greene-McCreight claims most feminists oppose essentialist definitions of women, but continue to operate with totalizing concepts.

edges no universal norm of female experience and yet she identifies experiences of suffering and resistance as distinctive.[43] Furthermore, her claim that women's moral, psychological, epistemological, and relational ways of being are marked by an interconnectedness, unlike the male ideal, reveals essentialist leanings regarding her understanding of women's experience.[44] Serene Jones presents similar tendencies in a helpful article where she notes that although most of the feminist theologians she examines reject essentialist understandings of "woman," they do tend to universalize experience.[45] For instance, process thinkers Rita Nakashima Brock and Catherine Keller attach a particular notion of relational ontology to experience.[46] Evidently, there is a tension in contemporary feminist scholarship, that is, women's claims to experience run up against the prevailing opinion that men and women are not that different.[47]

Concern to avoid essentialist definitions of woman has led some feminists to ponder the source of gender differences. If not biology, then what? Many rely on the work of psychologists Nancy Chodorow and Carol Gilligan, who began to study gender development after recognizing the lack of psychoanalytic research on women's development. Neither Chodorow nor Gilligan make absolute claims about the source of gender differences, and both reject an essentialist understanding of gender. They conceive gender differences as arising in social contexts

43. Johnson, *She Who Is*, 61–62.

44. Ibid., 68.

45. Jones, "'Women's Experience.'" The theologians (and the texts) Jones considers are: Elizabeth Johnson (*She Who Is*), Catherine Mowry LaCugna (*God for Us*), Rita Nakashima Brock (*Journeys by Heart*), Catherine Keller (*From a Broken Web*), Delores Williams (*Sisters in the Wilderness*), Sallie McFague (*The Body of God*), Kathryn Tanner (*The Politics of God*), Ada María Isasi-Díaz (*En la Lucha*), Rebecca Chopp (*The Power to Speak*). Jones sees the work of Johnson, LaCugna, Brock, Keller, Williams and McFague as "the rock"—stable, but perhaps unable to accommodate those experiences of women on the margins. Tanner, Díaz, and Chopp are examples of "the hard place"—avoid universalizing tendencies, but lacking in substance (stable enough to be a hard place, but not a rock).

46. Jones, "'Women's Experience,'" 176. Specifically, Brock understands experience similar to process thinkers Whitehead and Hartshorne for whom experience is interpreted through creative synthesis, which occurs through the energy provided by erotic power. This erotic power is called the "Heart of the Universe," a life-giving love, God. Brock, *Journeys by Heart*, 39.

47. O'Neill, "Nature of Women," 739.

with various power and social forces, which combine with biological factors to shape gender identity.[48] As object-relations theorists, they are occupied with how relationships shape a sense of self, seeing family and culture as crucial factors. Therefore, to see men and women as qualitatively different is to deny these relations.[49]

The Function of Women's Experience in Theological Method

Regardless of the diversity of feminists' understanding of women's experience, as it relates to method, the category operates uniformly within feminist theology. Most feminists agree that women's experience is difficult to define and that it is part of a method that involves many elements.[50] Yet, writing ten years after the publication of Christ's and Plaskow's feminist volume, *Womanspirit Rising*, Plaskow claims that women's experience is still central to feminist theology in spite of the expansions in its definition.[51] Just how central is it?

Source and Norm

Within North American feminist theological circles in particular, it has become well known that women's experience is "both the source for theological reflection and the norm for evaluating the adequacy of any theological framework."[52] Experience is necessary to supply the raw

---

48. Gilligan, *In a Different Voice*, 2.

49. Chodorow, *Feminism and Psychoanalytic Theory*, 113. Saiving's conclusions about an appropriate understanding of the doctrine of sin for women bears much in common with such work. Research on mothering attempted to determine the ways that boys and girls identified with their mothers (most often the primary caregiver) and thus learned to become either more individuated and separate or connected and related. Simply put, girls seemed to have an easier time identifying with their mothers and then adjusting to their adult roles, whereas boys struggled to differentiate themselves and develop a sense of self in adulthood. Saiving understands this struggle as leading boys to become concerned with matters of authority and independence, which then leads to a specific interpretation of sin as pride and a will-to-power (Saiving, "Human Situation," 36–37).

50. Johnson, *She Who Is*, 10. Women's interpreted experience is diverse.

51. Introduction to *Weaving the Visions*, 3.

52. Davaney, "Limits of the Appeal," 31–32. See also Chopp, "Feminism's Theological

material for theological reflection as well as the means by which other sources are incorporated and/or excluded. In other words, as source, experience provides the substance of theology, and as norm it functions as the criterion.[53] Although, women's experience may function as the *primary* source for feminist theology, most feminists would resist claiming experience as the *sole* source.[54] For instance, Sallie McFague does not presuppose one source for theology; rather she views embodied experience as one part.[55] McFague wants her theology to be judged by a combination of criteria: postmodern science, compatibility with experience, and ecological insights.[56] Likewise, Letty Russell does not see experience as the only source for Christian theology; indeed it is part of a network of sources, such as biblical and church tradition, which are related to one another.[57] While it may be determined that women's experience cannot be the sole criterion for judging theological adequacy, it is considered crucial.[58]

Because androcentric theology has for so long neglected the perspective of women, it becomes essential to the feminist theological task to include lived experience as a resource.[59] Therefore, related to the use of experience as source and norm, experience in feminist theological reflection is pragmatic, revealed by an appeal to concrete, lived experience. Much feminist theology understands its purpose as *praxis*, meaning action in relation with reflection that then leads to new actions and reflections.[60] A focus on the practical realm also involves the anticipa-

---

Pragmatics," 241; Wondra, *Humanity Has Been a Holy Thing*, 121; O'Neill, "Nature of Women," 738.

53. Such a view is in keeping with James Cone's understanding: "The sources are the relevant data for the theological task, whereas the norm determines how the data will be used" (Cone, *Black Theology*, 21). He goes on to cite Paul Tillich and Karl Barth as examples of theologians who have similar ideas about the primary source (Bible) but differing ideas about the norm.

54. Culpepper, "Contemporary Goddess Thealogy," 52. Culpepper presents one's own experience as the primary source for Goddess religion.

55. McFague, *Body of God*, 85.

56. Ibid., 163.

57. Russell, *Household of Freedom*, 33.

58. Young, *Feminist Theology*, 67.

59. Johnson, *She Who Is*, 61.

60. Russell, *Human Liberation*, 55. See also Chopp, "Feminism's Theological Pragmatics," 242.

tion of change. This pragmatic emphasis is evident in feminist theology's focus upon embodied, particular experience as well as its desire to maintain liberation as a product of women's experience of oppression and evidence of potential transformation.

Foundation

Although many feminists speak of multiple sources and criteria for theological construction, we must ask, is there an underlying dependence upon experience as the most important source and/or criterion? Does women's experience actually operate as a foundation for feminist theology? Mary McClintock Fulkerson is but one feminist theologian who recognizes a tension in feminist theology in that it tends toward an anti-foundationalism, but then uses women's experience as a foundation for theological construction.[61] Broadly speaking, foundationalism in feminist theology is an effort to provide an ultimate standard, related to the Enlightenment attempt to establish a single principle of truth.[62] Both Rosemary Radford Ruether and Elisabeth Schüssler Fiorenza note that experience is the "starting point" for hermeneutics and feminist reflection.[63] Similarly, Carter Heyward outlines human experience as the fundamental source for theology, also calling it her starting point, and Daphne Hampson states explicitly that experience is the "basis" for theology.[64]

These are a few examples of feminist theologians who incorporate some form of foundationalism into their theological method. In fact, most of the feminist theologians mentioned so far, despite their acknowledgement of a variety of sources, appear to operate with women's experience as the ultimate source for theological reflection, the last word. We observe similar usage in Asian feminist and womanist

---

61. Fulkerson, *Changing the Subject*, 16.

62. Woodhead, "Spiritualising the Sacred," 199.

63. Ruether, *Sexism and God-Talk*, 12; Schüssler Fiorenza, *Jesus*, 12. Schüssler Fiorenza insists that this experience must be systematically reflected upon. The nature of experience in the theology of both Schüssler Fiorenza and Ruether will be discussed in a later chapter, including their foundationalist tendencies.

64. Heyward, *Redemption of God*, 13. Specifically, Heyward utilizes the experience of human relatedness as her core theology concept. See also Hampson, *After Christianity*, 10.

theology as well. Chung Hyun Kyung understands concrete, historical experience of Asian women to be the final test for her theology, that is, religious teaching and practice that provides life-giving power to Asian women is teaching and practice that they may consider "good news," gospel.[65] Related to this concept is the common reference to experience as the "lens" through which one does theology.[66] Delores Williams, for instance, intends black women's experience to provide the lens through which theological sources are viewed as well as the issues that will form the content of theology.[67] Experience is functioning as the filter through which other sources must pass in order to be included in theological doctrine.[68] Nevertheless, if a multiplicity of sources is utilized, as feminists claim—and it remains unclear how these sources are evaluated, except for their accordance with some understanding of women's experience—then it seems reasonable to conclude that experience operates as the norm or foundation for feminist theology. In other words, women's experience is the *ultimate* source.

The Limitations of Women's Experience as a Theological Foundation

Although feminist theology appears fairly unified in employing women's experience as a foundation for its theological method, this use is not without criticism from within feminist circles. In recent years, feminists have grown more aware of the shortcomings of such an approach. A predominant criticism is the identification of feminist theologians' use of experience as an attempt to establish an authoritative foundation upon which to construct theology, not so unlike what occurred in nineteenth- and twentieth-century theologies wherein claims to experience

---

65. Chung, *Struggle to Be* , 6.

66. Russell, *Household of Freedom*, 32.

67. Williams, *Sisters in the Wilderness*, 12.

68. Johnson, *She Who Is*, 15. Johnson claims that the account of God can be judged by how well it integrates experience to itself.

were essentially claims to authority.[69] Whether it is acknowledged or not, feminist theology is a thoroughly modern theology in this regard.[70]

Process Feminist Critique

One major critic is process feminist theologian Sheila Greeve Davaney. Davaney sees the influence of modern theology upon feminist theology as propelling it toward a quest for sure foundations and argues, despite efforts to the contrary, that most feminism ends up with an implicit foundationalism.[71] She considers the work of Rosemary Radford Ruether, Elisabeth Schüssler Fiorenza, and Mary Daly in particular. Although Ruether and Schüssler Fiorenza acknowledge the historicity of truth and the particularity of experience, it appears that ultimately the feminist view is normative for them, and Davaney wonders why this is so. It seems that each feminist theologian associates her view of women's experience with a notion of divine reality, with "the way things are," so to speak. In Davaney's estimation, "the feminist principle is normative both because it reflects a commitment to women and because it corresponds to the nature and purposes of the divine."[72] Ruether aligns a notion of the full humanity of women with divine reality, while Schüssler Fiorenza claims that the feminist viewpoint is more valid than other positions. Ruether identifies the Old Testament prophetic tradition and the life of Jesus as providing the principle of liberation for contemporary women struggling against patriarchy. This principle is in line with divine purposes, giving it a validation and normativity. For Schüssler Fiorenza, God is revealed in women's struggle against patriarchy, there-

---

69. Allik, "Human Finitude," 67. Use of women's experience is search for epistemological certainty. See also Cooey, *Religious Imagination*, 42–43. Of course, such claims to experience are subject to conceptual problems. See also Davaney, "Limits of the Appeal," 48 n. 1. The relationship to Schleiermacher's post-Enlightenment turn to experience is evident.

70. Martin, *Feminist Question*, 164: "[F]eminism relies on precisely that mode of thought that is responsible for the situation it wishes to change"—modernity. See also Woodhead, "Spiritualising the Sacred," 197; Reno, "Feminist Theology," 406. The feminist project is related to modern theology in how it values ethical criteria over the dogmatic, distrusts the tradition and has confidence in contemporary experience upholding a vision of theology as saving the tradition from error and irrelevance.

71. Davaney, "Problems with Feminist Theory," 92.

72. Ibid., 88.

by making women's perspectives normative, having more weight than male viewpoints. More explicitly than Ruether and Schüssler Fiorenza, Daly argues for the authority of the feminist vision on the grounds that it corresponds to ultimate reality, suggesting that women have a capacity to participate in the divine.[73] Daly roots normativity in the experience and consciousness of women who have stepped outside the boundaries of patriarchal tradition into separate communities. In all three feminists we observe an association of women's experience with divine reality, which is supposed to give the category of experience more weight, according it some epistemological and existential normativity.[74] According to Davaney, these feminist theologies assert that "feminist experience and consciousness yield a more accurate rendering of reality, including the nature and purposes of what might be termed the 'divine.' Hence, they can claim greater ontological validity."[75]

There are some feminists who oppose Davaney, accusing her of a relativism or nihilism which would be harmful to feminist theology, and also alleging that a diminishment of the category of experience might effectively lessen the significance of particular experiences.[76] In particular, Carol Christ responds to Davaney expressing concern that Davaney's postmodernism leaves her with no objective, universally valid knowledge.[77] Christ understands positions like Schüssler Fiorenza's as providing a more helpful approach. As a theological subject, Schüssler Fiorenza understands truth claims to be rooted in contemporary women's experience, providing a framework of meaning for those who already do or are willing to share her assumptions. This perspectival understanding of feminist theology is not persuasive for Davaney who holds a more detached stance regarding truth claims.[78] In contrast, Christ believes that one escapes a thoroughgoing relativism by taking a position such as Schüssler Fiorenza's that is not detached from religious commitment and acknowledges the perspectival nature of truth

73. Ibid., 90–91.

74. Davaney, "Limits of the Appeal," 35.

75. Ibid., 42.

76. Thistlethwaite, *Sex, Race and God*, 15. She is primarily concerned with the experience of violence against women.

77. Christ, "Embodied Thinking," 7.

78. Ibid., 11.

claims.[79] Davaney concludes that relativism can be avoided through a pragmatic approach. This pragmatism would evaluate the repercussions of different theological visions rather than base their validity on how "truthful" they are.[80] Moreover, by no longer appealing to ontological reality, female and male perspectives would share equal status and their validity would not be judged by which is "closer to reality" but upon "the pragmatic grounds of what kind of existence these visions permitted or inhibited."[81]

Having noted Christ's challenge to Davaney's relativism, however, it remains unclear how Christ herself avoids relativism by merely grounding truth claims in particular perspectives. It appears that her position leads to a different type of relativism than Davaney's, but a relativism just the same. We could argue that Davaney questions the validity of *any* religious truth claim, while Christ seems to find truth in *every* position. Nevertheless, Davaney, along with others, has identified the debt feminist theology owes to modern theology's Enlightenment influences, most clearly expressed in the understanding of women's experience as the foundation for theological construction.[82] Women's experience is normative for feminist theology, revealing that although feminist discourse began in part as a critique against all male-defined theology, it nevertheless retained one of modern theology's central assumptions since Schleiermacher, that theology proceeds out of experience.[83]

Womanist Critique

Perhaps the strongest and most significant critique of the role of experience in feminist theology is demonstrated by womanist thinkers who accuse white feminism of perpetuating the idea of white humanity

79. Ibid., 13–14.

80. Davaney, Introduction to *Theology at the End of Modernity*, 13.

81. Davaney, "Problems with Feminist Theory," 93.

82. In addition to those mentioned above (e.g., Martin, Reno, Woodhead) see Schner, "Appeal to Experience," 45. Schner describes the appeal of experience as a displacement of authority from the dominant community to particularized groups in the community; a move extending from the Enlightenment. See also Greene-McCreight, *Feminist Reconstructions*, 44: "The appeal to experience within feminist theology seems less of an opportunity for women to claim their own voice and rather a foundationalist warrant or grounding for the theological position being recommended."

83. Briggs, "History of Our Own," 167.

as the model of all female humanity.[84] Beginning with Betty Friedan's influential feminist book of the 1960s, *The Feminine Mystique*, and extending into contemporary feminist theology, one can observe white, middle-class feminists essentially making their condition universal for all women.[85] Ironically, what results is that much feminist theology makes the same mistake as patriarchal theology, that is, promoting a particular understanding of experience as universal. Whereas male theology contains an understanding of male experience which is then rendered, either explicitly or implicitly, as representative of the whole of humanity, feminist theology extends a view of women's experience that is intended to be representative of all women.[86] Racism replaces patriarchy.[87]

Consequently, the notion of "generic woman" functions as "generic man" did in Western thought.[88] Feminists have been as sloppy in their descriptions of women's condition as philosophers have been describing the human condition, seeming to forget that a person's identity is constructed in concert with racial, ethnic, and class identity.[89] The description of women's experience of sexism must attend to many factors, for the sexism one experiences as a woman cannot be separated from the particular woman she is, including her racial and class identity. By merely claiming that all women suffer sexism and that black women suffer racism in addition, one ignores the differences in contexts between white and black women's experience of sexism.[90] Clearly, the sexism all women may experience will not be the same.[91]

84. Williams, *Sisters in the Wilderness*, 184.

85. Hooks, *Feminist Theory*, 2.

86. Thistlethwaite, *Sex, Race and God*, 78. For example, Saiving's analysis of sin does not necessarily relate to the experience of black women.

87. Ibid., 101.

88. Spelman, *Inessential Woman*, ix.

89. Ibid., 9, 192 n. 29. Spelman notes that Chodorow's work on mothering and gender identity recognizes mothering's relationship to class and race. See also Zappone, "'Woman's Special Nature,'" 92. Zappone recognizes race and class as significant to gender development.

90. Spelman, *Inessential Woman*, 125.

91. Ibid., 14.

Women's Way of Knowing

The limitations of the category of women's experience might be further demonstrated by considering the use of women's experience in the area of feminist epistemology. An analysis of experience easily leads to the topic of knowledge, for the two are inextricably linked. What one knows of the world is only received and/or interpreted within the context of some human experience, be it bodily, intellectually, emotionally, linguistically, or more accurately, a combination of all these levels and more.

Feminist theological writings have given some attention to the subject of feminist epistemology, although the majority of the discussion has been handled outside feminist theology within the area of philosophy of science. Within that field feminist epistemology has been described as the study of how contingent historical factors color scientific theories and practices, which have led to the often sexist metaphors in which scientists conceptualize their work. It tries to reinvigorate values and emotions in our account of cognitive activities, arguing for the contribution of emotions to knowledge, and attacks various sets of dualisms characteristic of Western philosophical thinking, such as reason/emotion, culture/nature, universal/particular.[92] Beginning in the 1970s, distinctive feminist theories of knowledge emerged claiming that conceptual schemes in social sciences and biology that purported a notion of objectivity were actually distorted.[93] The critique in science focused on how the discipline has been done as a "totalizing theory" that excludes women as worthy knowers.[94] We are able to see the similarities between the feminist critique of the sciences and the feminist critique of theology out of which two basic views emerge (i.e., there is either a *women's* way or a *human* way), thus raising the same types of questions and having similar limitations. Much like their feminist colleagues in the sciences, feminist theologians who argue for an understanding of *women's* experience would also most likely argue for a *women's* way of knowing.[95]

---

92. Narayan, "Project of Feminist Epistemology," 257.

93. Solberg, *Compelling Knowledge*, 6.

94. Ibid., 25.

95. For a discussion of feminist epistemology in theology that highlights similar issues see Wilson-Kastner, *Faith, Feminism, and the Christ*.

Feminist Standpoint Epistemology

Fundamentally, feminist standpoint epistemology has its roots in the understanding that women have a social location such that they can perceive and comprehend aspects of the world that challenge the male bias of existing perspectives.[96] Generally speaking, in societies where experiences are primarily differentiated by sex/gender and result in a politics of an oppressed group and privileged group, "a sound perspective on social and political life is possible only for members of the oppressed group."[97] Although there are differences in feminist standpoint epistemologies, all share some general insights similar to the "metatheoretical" claim outlined by Nancy Hartsock, whose article "The Feminist Standpoint" many consider to be the standard piece on the subject. Upon a methodological base provided by Marxist theory, Hartsock attempts to develop an important epistemological tool for understanding and opposing all forms of domination, that is, a feminist standpoint.[98] Marx's metatheoretical claim that a correct vision of class society is only available from one of the two major class positions in capitalist society provides the basis for Hartsock's position. She suggests that there are epistemological consequences for claiming that women's lives are different structurally than those of men (analogous to Marx's claims that the proletariat had a privileged vantage point), thus grounding her critique of "phallocratic institutions and ideology which constitute the capitalist form of patriarchy" on women's vantage point.[99] Hartsock believes that female experience meets the criteria for such a standpoint, which carries the "contention that there are some perspectives on society from which, however, well-intentioned one may be, the real relations of humans with each other and with the natural world are not visible."[100] A feminist standpoint based on "women's relational self-definition and activity is intended to expose the world which men have constructed as partial and perverse."[101] Although Hartsock is not speaking from a theological perspective, we recognize the parallelism between her posi-

96. Narayan, "Project of Feminist Epistemology," 256.

97. Nelson, *Who Knows*, 271.

98. Hartsock, "Feminist Standpoint," 283.

99. Ibid., 284.

100. Ibid., 285.

101. Ibid., 303.

tion and much of what we find in feminist theology, that is, women are able to know and experience things as they really are.

However, it seems that both feminist theologians and feminist philosophers are aware of the weaknesses in such an unqualified stance. As in feminist theology, critique often begins by feminists of color who are quick to expose the flaws in speaking about a universal understanding of women's knowledge or women's experience. Indian feminist Uma Narayan stresses that the notion of a feminist standpoint should not be dismissed entirely, although it does pose particular problems for non-Western feminists. She offers two reasons for taking seriously the claim that oppressed groups have an "epistemic advantage": (1) the possible failure to understand the concerns of an oppressed group, and (2) the important need for such groups to be able to control the means of discourse about their own situations.[102] The oppressed are seen to have an epistemic advantage because they operate with two sets of practices in two contexts that may lead to critical insights because each framework provides a critical perspective of the other. For example, indigenous people learn the language of their colonizers.[103] However, she argues, feminist theory must be temperate in the use of such "double vision" as the relation between the two contexts is not straightforward and it is difficult to carry out a dialectical synthesis that preserves the advantages of each context.[104] Furthermore, Narayan does not consider that the commitment to the contextual nature of knowledge necessarily means that those who do not inhabit certain contexts can never have any knowledge of them. Nevertheless, this commitment does "permit us to argue that it is *easier* and *more likely* for the oppressed to have critical insights into the conditions of their own oppression than it is for those who live outside these structures."[105]

In addition to Narayan's non-Western critique, there are other feminists who also find Hartsock's theory useful but finally unsatisfactory. Terri Elliott considers Hartsock's approach beneficial in challenging repeated patterns of oppression, but lacking in adequately capturing the experience of marginalized people. She claims that Hartsock speaks

102. Narayan, "Project of Feminist Epistemology," 265.

103. Ibid., 266.

104. Ibid., 268.

105. Ibid., 264.

too ironically of epistemic privilege; that what the oppressed experience is hardly a privilege, rather it is the manifestation of their oppression.[106] The problems in feminist standpoint theory are analogous to what we observe in feminist theology. The category of woman is in danger of becoming essentialized because it reflects assumptions about women's knowledge and/or experience.[107] Do women know things that men cannot know? Do women experience things that men cannot experience? Lynne Nelson doubts that such a chasm exists, but also does not deny that feminists have unique insights. Feminists have a contribution to make, one which is able to be shared with others.[108] Like Narayan and Elliott, Nelson finds value in feminist standpoint theory, but is concerned about the epistemological distance such a view assumes.[109] Given recent research, Nelson considers it the reasonable view that "women" and "men" are neither exclusively biological nor sociological categories. They are historically and culturally relative and related in endless ways to other cultural practices and categories.[110]

It appears that most feminist thinkers are aware of the limitations of an exclusive feminist epistemology and acknowledge the complex issues involved in any epistemology due to the fact that knowledge is socially constructed. For instance, Mary Hesse contends that no one is arguing that gender is the overriding factor in claims to knowledge; this is not what is meant by feminist epistemology. She argues that what has been intended is a critique of the existing epistemological tradition and the philosophy of post-seventeenth-century science which largely structured it.[111] Contemporary feminists understand that there is an objective and subjective aspect to knowledge: subjective because it is

---

106. Elliott, "Making Strange," 424–33.

107. Code, *What Can She Know?*, 260. See also Baber, "Market for Feminist Epistemology," 419. Baber believes thinking about women and men as being different leads to a vicious circle whereby feminist epistemologies perpetuate myths about gender difference.

108. Nelson, *Who Knows*, 8.

109. Ibid., 41.

110. Ibid., 190. Therefore, speaking to her particular field, Nelson claims that male biology is not the source of androcentrism in science.

111. Hesse, "How to be Postmodern," 445. Hesse supports a view of epistemology that allows for a plurality of languages to express it, but which does not deny that rational arguments in the human sciences can take place, including ways to distinguish good explanations from bad ones.

marked by specifically located subjects, objective because the constructive process is constrained by reality.[112]

Regardless of the awareness of potential weaknesses, it remains that discussions of feminist epistemology in the sciences are based upon a similar foundation as feminist theology, that is, experience.

> What counts as knowledge must be grounded on experience. Human experience differs according to the kinds of activities and social relations in which humans engage. Women's experience systematically differs from the male experience upon which knowledge claims have been grounded. Thus the experience on which the prevailing claims to social and natural knowledge are founded is, first of all, only partial human experience only partially understood: namely, masculine experience as understood by men. However, when this experience is presumed to be gender-free—when the male experience is taken to be the human experience—the resulting theories, concepts, methodologies, inquiry goals and knowledge-claims distort human social life and human thought.[113]

Algerian sociologist Marnia Lazreg persuasively argues against the conception of experience as the source of knowledge. She contends that the general understanding of women's experience that is put forth does not adequately examine the relationship between objectivity and subjectivity. Likewise, although experience is utilized as the vantage point for a feminist critique, the term is seldom defined in any systematic way. These concerns lead Lazreg to ponder how such an elusive and diverse concept like experience can be the building block for a new epistemology.[114] Any claims that women's experience is the source of true knowledge as well as the substance of the world to be known places feminists on the brink of committing the very fallacies of which they accuse others.

112. Longino, "In Search of Feminist Epistemology," 475; Code, *What Can She Know?*, 256. Code is critical of the book *Women's Ways of Knowing* (Belenky et al.) because it is too subjective, thus obscuring the need for critical interpretation and reinterpretation, both of women's experiences and of the "real" world. On the subjective and objective nature of scientific knowledge see Polanyi, *Personal Knowledge.*

113. Harding, "Why Has the Sex/Gender System Become Visible Only Now?" x. See also Stanley and Wise, *Breaking Out.* Stanley and Wise consider feeling, belief, and experience as the basis for knowledge.

114. Lazreg, "Women's Experience," 50–51.

Feminist Epistemology in Feminist Theology

Feminist theologians typically do not discuss epistemology in as much depth as many feminist philosophers of science; however, we will consider briefly two feminist theologians who give some extended attention to epistemology within a feminist theological context: Mary McClintock Fulkerson and Patricia Hill Collins. Their positions reflect elements of standpoint epistemology, presented above, and the feminist concern to address the need for particularity in experience and knowledge without falling into relativism.

MARY MCCLINTOCK FULKERSON

Fulkerson claims that by virtue of its appeal to women's experience, feminist theology/theory is in danger of invoking a universal subject; therefore she argues for an approach to difference that takes seriously the way in which subjects are constructed out of social relations that feature various forms of gender oppression.[115] According to Fulkerson, feminist theology needs a liberation epistemology that moves beyond inclusionary strategies and respects difference. Such an epistemology is about the relation between social relations, discourse, interests, and oppression-liberation, investigating how certain kinds of subjects are produced. It should be concerned with the relationship of social location to the oppressive effects of discourse and to the possibilities of liberation.[116] A feminist liberationist perspective employs women's experience in order to contest the male as "false universal" as well as to display a commitment to the located character of all knowledge.[117] Fulkerson finds some elements of standpoint epistemology better than a mere sociology of knowledge approach. Due to its liberationist commitment, feminist appeals to experience might be better described as feminist standpoint theory than a social constructionist version (related to sociologists Peter Berger and Thomas Luckmann) because feminist standpoint theory implies that the "position of oppression gives women (the subject) a special vantage on reality, something the sociology of

---

115. Fulkerson, *Changing the Subject*, 7.

116. Ibid., 18–19.

117. Ibid., 52.

knowledge does not entail."[118] Like many feminists, Fulkerson is aware of the dangers with standpoint theory, but is not willing to dispense with such an approach altogether. She may not find such a theory fully adequate, but its use of experience does move us away from experience as a universalizing category.

PATRICIA HILL COLLINS

Collins develops an Afrocentric feminist epistemology that accesses knowledge claims using standards that are consistent with black women's criteria for substantiated knowledge and methodological adequacy.[119] Such an Afrocentric consciousness includes a core African value system and a common experience of oppression. An Afrocentric feminist epistemology reflects elements of epistemologies used by African Americans and women as groups, while also containing features that may be unique to black women, utilizing black women's experience to examine points of contact between Afrocentric and feminist perspectives.[120] However, she does not find helpful a standpoint approach that basically considers that the more oppressed the group, the purer its vision. Collins believes the distinction between wisdom and knowledge is important to an Afrocentric feminist epistemology. The use of experience provides the edge whereby the subordinated gain essential wisdom for survival. Stories, narratives, and Bible principles are symbolic representations of a whole wealth of this experience.[121] Another significant aspect of an Afrocentric epistemology is black institutions, churches, and families, which are primarily women centered. Within these institutions the value of connectedness is expressed, for example, in the call-and-response discourse which is a part of them.[122] Within the black community where such connectedness and caring is experienced,

118. Ibid., 53. See Berger and Luckmann, *Social Construction of Reality.* Their basic assertion is that reality is socially constructed and the purpose of the sociology of knowledge is to analyze the process by which this occurs. Their view of the nature of social reality is greatly influenced by Durkheim, though his view has been modified by a dialectical perspective derived from Marx and an emphasis on the constitution of social reality through subjective meanings derived from Weber (ibid., 28–29).

119. Collins, *Black Feminist Thought,* 206.

120. Ibid., 207.

121. Ibid., 208–10.

122. Ibid., 212–13.

black women find a support for their type of knowing; in contrast to their denigration by white, male-controlled institutions, they find empowerment within their own families and churches.[123]

Oppression as Fundamental Experience

The role of women's experience within feminist theology and feminist epistemology leads us to consider further women's experience as oppression, an understanding which is basically accepted as fundamental, informing most feminist theory and influencing nearly all definitions of experience.[124] What is meant by oppression? Although not expressly defined in much feminist theology, oppression is comprised of sexism, in which women are not accorded full humanity and equal status with men, combined with an exclusion of women from theological reflection and disregard for their particular voice and contribution. Some appeals to experiences of oppression are characteristic of feminist standpoint theory, including the belief that the oppressed have a special perspective on reality (as discussed above).[125] Harvard scholar bell hooks defines oppression as the absence of choices.[126] In light of Hooks' definition, it seems apparent that oppression would be experienced differently by different women, and, furthermore, would not be an experience associated solely with women.

Evidently, it must be accepted that women are present in every oppressed and oppressing group.[127] This fact has been incisively raised by feminists of color who question white feminists' ability to understand the particularity of non-white women's experience. Womanists doubt that the tyranny women suffer as a gender is really sufficient to create a common bond between them. They perceive no reason to believe that white women are more concerned about black women than are black

---

123. Ibid., 217.

124. Oppression as a component of experience is especially significant for feminist liberation theologians (e.g., Schüssler Fiorenza, Ruether, Johnson, Russell). These feminist theologians are concerned with systems of domination and resistance to these, primarily on a sociopolitical level.

125. Fulkerson, *Changing the Subject*, 53–54.

126. Hooks, *Feminist Theory*, 5.

127. Grant, *Fundamental Feminism*, 29.

men and, in fact, find evidence to the contrary.[128] Black women have suffered oppression at the hands of white women and, therefore, are rightly suspicious of any description of oppression that only accounts for oppression of women by men and not other forms of oppression.

Clearly, the understanding of experience as oppression is not free from complications. Making oppression the primary category of feminist liberation theology essentially makes it a universal category and such universals do not account for the complexities of identity formation.[129] Perhaps there is a need to reassess patriarchy as the definitive description of female oppression in order to discover a more adequate approach that ceases to focus on "men as the enemy" and better addresses systems of domination.[130] Feminists are right to be concerned with oppression as a significant aspect of women's experience. However, due to the intricacies related to oppression at many levels within our society, a more comprehensive view is needed.[131] The opposition of women and men is insufficient to account adequately for the many layers of domination experienced by all people.

Lessons from Black Theology

As we seek to understand the problems of feminist theology's use of experience, further insight might be gained by engaging with black theory, specifically, Victor Anderson's study *Beyond Ontological Blackness*. His critique of ontological blackness has certain parallels with the category of women's experience and its use in feminist theology. Anderson describes ontological blackness as "a covering term that connotes categorical, essentialist, and representational languages depicting black

128. hooks, *Feminist Theory*, 4. See also Grant, *White Women's Christ*, 145–46.

129. Fulkerson, *Changing the Subject*, 58.

130. Morgan, "Race and the Appeal," 23. There is the genuine concern that making sexism and oppression the paradigm of evil reduces the significance of racism (21). See also hooks, *Feminist Theory*, 25–26.

131. Most feminist theologians are aware that race and class are issues in any understanding of women's experience as oppression. However, these matters often get brief consideration. See Davaney, "Limits of the Appeal," 42. Mary Daly represents a position that is not atypical in feminist theology, where sexism is viewed as the basic model and source of oppression. Daly responds to racial concerns by suggesting that if we can solve the problem of sexism then we can address other problems such as racism and the plight of the poor (Daly, *Beyond God the Father*, 190).

life and experience."[132] In particular, Anderson believes that ontological
blackness distorts many of the conditions of African-American life and
experience in the United States as well as fails to meet the demand for
a new cultural politics of black identity that meaningfully relates to the
conditions of postmodern North American life.[133] Anderson considers
the use of ontological blackness problematic for a full understanding
of African-American identity and prefers what bell hooks has termed
"*postmodern blackness*," which recognizes the permanency of race as an
effective category in identity formation. However, this understanding
also recognizes that "black identities are continually being reconstituted
as African Americans inhabit widely differentiated social spaces and
communities of moral discourse."[134]

Anderson devotes one chapter of his book to the application of
ontological blackness in black theology. It is here that one may more
clearly perceive the similarities between the problems the category
poses for black theology and the problems the category of women's
experience causes for feminist theology. Black theology, with James
Cone as its foremost theologian, basically incorporates a correlational
method that seeks to identify black experience and life with traditional
theological categories.[135] For Anderson the dilemma arises when blackness signifies ontology and corresponds with black experience where
black experience is defined as an experience of suffering and rebellion
against whiteness. According to Anderson, black suffering and rebellion
are ontologically created and provoked by whiteness as a necessary condition of blackness. Thus, whiteness appears to be the ground of black
experience and, hence, of black theology. Therefore, while black theology justifies itself as radically oppositional to whiteness, it nevertheless
requires whiteness, white racism, and white theology for its legitimacy.
In this way, black theology effectively renders whiteness identifiable with

---

132. Anderson, *Beyond Ontological Blackness*, 11. Anderson considers such thinkers as Cornel West, bell hooks, Toni Morrison, Alice Walker, Henry Lewis Gates Jr.,
Houston Baker Jr., Darlene Clark Hine, Wilson J. Moses, Michael Dyson, and Joe Wood
as proponents of his position.

133. Anderson, *Beyond Ontological Blackness*, 15.

134. Ibid., 11.

135. Ibid. 86. "The black theology project seeks to disclose the essential meanings
of black faith in the black God revealed in the black Christ from the perspective of the
black experience" (88).

what is of ultimate concern.[136] Similarly, womanist theology is bound by ontological blackness by making oppression the defining experience of black women. Womanist theology suffers the contradictions of ontological blackness because it proposes the privilege of self-definition, and yet ontological blackness binds the discourse almost exclusively and exceptionally to suffering and resistance.[137] The promise of cultural transcendence proffered by the womanist theologian's self-defining discourse appears subjugated under ontological blackness.[138]

Although this author is not particularly qualified to comment on the specifics of Anderson's racial theory, it is evident that certain aspects of his discussion are relevant to feminist theology. In this chapter we have attempted to show that, against better intentions, there is effectively an understanding of women's experience that functions as a foundation for feminist theological method. This understanding of women's experience is to a great extent an essentialist one, described in terms not unlike Anderson's account of ontological blackness. The category of women's experience is fundamentally conceived as oppression under and resistance to patriarchy, similar to black experience being defined by oppression and rebellion. Just as black experience is ontologically created, as Anderson argues, so also it seems the case with women's experience. The essentialist tendencies in a variety of feminist theologians reveals an understanding of female experience as ontologically distinct from male experience. Furthermore, as black experience, understood in terms of ontological blackness, means the necessity of whiteness for black theology, so women's experience requires patriarchy for feminist theology, thus making maleness and patriarchy the ground of women's experience and feminist theology. It becomes what is of ultimate concern. Moreover, it is difficult to see how such a theology is able to transcend the culture and to provide substance for women's identity, comparable to the situation for black theology. If women's experience is primarily characterized by oppression and resistance, it lacks a transformative aspect that allows women to define themselves beyond the confines of patriarchal society.[139]

136. Ibid., 91–92.
137. Ibid., 111.
138. Ibid., 112.
139. Woodhead, "Spiritualising the Sacred," 199. Woodhead wonders if the association with oppression too closely links women's experience with victimhood. Such an

If Anderson's argument is persuasive, it seems that feminist theology should regard his insights concerning ontological blackness as an indication of the need for a reconsideration of women's experience as a helpful category for feminist theological construction. However, one must take care in such matters. Although Anderson recognizes the problems with a category such as ontological blackness, he also shares a concern for racial identity and the need for some categorization. Likewise, feminist theology wants to speak of women and their experience without discarding the category altogether. In Anderson's words: "Can womanist theology transcend the aporias of ontological blackness and, at the same time, hold to the transcending openings that . . . womanist connotations commend?"[140] We pose essentially the same question: Can feminist theology transcend the limits of women's experience while maintaining an understanding of woman that makes space for diversity as well as allows for the self-definition necessary for women to establish their own identity?

Conclusion: Feminism Needs Women

It seems that our discussion has brought us to the subject of universal categories and their necessity. We have defined various understandings of women's experience utilized in feminist theology. We have also seen that regardless of the diversity of these definitions feminist theology consistently incorporates the category into its theological method, where experience acts as the source and norm, and perhaps more accurately, the foundation of theological reflection. As other feminists have recognized, this usage is problematic by repeating Enlightenment mistakes of foundationalism and neglecting to understand adequately the perspectives of all women, especially those women in minority groups whose views are often overlooked. In its universalizing tendencies the essentialist definition of woman underlying much feminist theology neglects the particularities of women and reduces the participation of women in producing their story.[141] However, is the solution to be found by discarding the category of women's experience? Even the crit-

association leaves women with few resources to establish their own identity or means for changing their situation.

140. Anderson, *Beyond Ontological Blackness*, 117.

141. Spelman, *Inessential Woman*, 158–59.

ics would be reluctant to adopt such an approach, including Anderson, who recognizes the value of black women's experience and the need to have some terminology for defining it.[142] Women and women's experience are crucial to feminist theology, which is a valuable enterprise because it integrates feminism into the theological task, transforming it in the process.[143] Without speaking about women as women we will lose the core of feminism.[144] If we want to preserve feminism as an effective political force, it seems that an approach is required that values the particular experiences of women and at the same time maintains a notion of women that is non-universalizing.[145] Is there a way to take differences seriously enough without undermining the category of women which feminism requires?[146]

Since we acknowledge a variety of women's experience, it seems that a definition of women's experience will need to include space for variety, and yet, enough cohesiveness to be a stable category. The challenge will be to conceptualize a multiplicity of female experiences while maintaining some notion of woman without falling into individualism.[147] In addition, we need to utilize the category in a way that avoids foundationalism, whereby feminist theology is built upon grounds that are outside the tradition, lacks a comprehensive view of the nature of human experience, and fails to take into consideration the various resources Christian theology incorporates. We have seen that a focus on gender without adequate consideration of race and class is no foundation for feminist theory.[148] A consideration of just how experience comes to be defined, evaluated, and understood is also essential—how does experience affect our knowledge of God, how should revelation relate to experience, and finally, what is authoritative for theological construction?

142. Anderson, *Beyond Ontological Blackness*, 111. Anderson commends womanist theology for reminding us of the complexity of black women's experience and for disclosing sources of black women's subjugation.

143. Woodhead, "Spiritualising the Sacred," 208.

144. Spelman, *Inessential Woman*, 172.

145. Grant, *Fundamental Feminism*, 91.

146. Spelman, *Inessential Woman*, 79.

147. Grant, *Fundamental Feminism*, 91.

148. Hooks, *Feminist Theory*, 14.

At this stage we are only beginning to ponder these questions. One preliminary way of addressing the matter might be to return to the issue of source and norm. It has been shown that women's experience is used in feminist theology as a primary source and norm for theological construction. The problem becomes apparent when the category is no longer considered *a* source, but the foundational or most important source and a norm by which theological adequacy is determined. Using experience in such a way determines the shape of theology; in other words, we get what we start with.[149] However, experience can, and, in fact, should be used in theological method, but for the Christian feminist theologian this use should possibly include an active skepticism.[150] It is with such skepticism that we will consider the role of women's experience in feminist theology further, attempting to develop an understanding helpful to Christian feminist theologians whose decisive norm should be a Christian norm.[151]

Nevertheless, despite its complications, the feminist understanding of experience arguably offers a distinct improvement over a modern theological approach because of its stress upon mutuality, corporality, and future orientation rather than an emphasis upon the individual, moral will, and orientation to the present.[152] By appealing to pragmatic, ethical foundations and by placing experiences of communities rather than individuals at the core of feminist theology, the radical relativism implied by individualistic understandings of experience may be limited.[153] It may be that the category of women's experience itself is not harmful to feminist theological construction and, in fact, actually enriches the feminist theological project. Thus, it is quite possible that feminist theology will ultimately contribute to a reformation of Christian theology by its weaving together of experience and tradition.[154]

---

149. Woodhead, "Spiritualising the Sacred," 204.

150. Riley, *"Am I That Name?"* 113.

151. Carr, "New Vision," 22.

152. Chopp, "Feminism's Theological Pragmatics," 252.

153. Hogan, *From Women's Experience*, 170.

154. Chopp, "Feminism's Theological Pragmatics," 256.

2

A Feminist Theology of Religious Experience

Introduction: A Post-Christian Perspective on Christian Theology

THE VOICE OF NON-CHRISTIANS HAS OFTEN BEEN USEFUL TO CHRISTIAN theology and contemporary feminist theology is no exception. For feminists this non-Christian challenge might be best represented by the work of post-Christian feminist theologian Daphne Hampson. In her first book, *Theology and Feminism*, Hampson explains why, intellectually and emotionally, she must reject Christianity as incompatible with feminism and modern scientific truth.[1] In particular, Hampson identifies the area of Christology as raising the most notable problems for feminists since it gives a male human being a status given to no woman.[2] Hampson challenges Christian feminists who have tried to redeem Christology from this dilemma, asserting that one cannot solve the problem by establishing a "non-gendered cosmic Christ" on the one hand, nor by emphasizing Jesus' humanity on the other.[3] Either way a divine person is bonded to male human nature. Hampson is especially critical of those feminists who try to redress the situation by distin-

1. Ruether, "Is Feminism the End?" 391. Ruether accepts Daphne Hampson's critique of the Christian view of scripture as normative, but accuses her of exercising the very absolutist exclusivism of which she accuses the Christian tradition is guilty.

2. Hampson, *Theology and Feminism*, 76.

3. Hampson specifically addresses what she calls the "high" Christology of Patricia Wilson-Kastner, claiming that in Wilson-Kastner's *Faith, Feminism and the Christ* she minimizes human distinctions and emphasizes the common things of humanity, for example, seeing gender as a distinction like race (Hampson, *Theology and Feminism*, 60).

guishing the human Jesus from the cosmic Christ in order to separate him from his male human nature. She rightly argues that what results is a "type" Christology, which leads to a Jesus who is no longer the unique savior of the Christian faith.

Hampson's point is well taken. Maintaining a Christian position means that one proclaims Jesus as unique. If Jesus is *a* Christ or *a* prophet, then the theologian professing such a view is not a Christian, according to Hampson.[4] This first book of Hampson's offers significant points of criticism for the Christian tradition and especially for those who consider themselves to be Christian feminist theologians. Although the book is primarily critical rather than constructive, it does provide a first glimpse of the source of Hampson's theological method. Hampson claims that there can be no particular revelation in a certain age such that that revelation and tradition become normative for others, therefore, "methodologically the place where theology arises must be out of our own experience of God."[5]

Hampson continues her critique of sexism in the Christian tradition in her second book, *After Christianity*, where she develops her particular brand of "theism" based explicitly upon human experience, an experience of a dimension of reality she names God.[6] Uncovering how she understands and utilizes this category of experience will provide much of the content of this chapter, in an effort to determine whether Hampson's approach contributes toward a proper development of the role of experience in theological method.

Hampson is significant for a discussion about experience in theological method for several reasons. As mentioned above, Hampson is a post-Christian feminist, an informed outsider so to speak, who offers

4. Citing Rudolf Bultmann as an example, Hampson argues that belief in a unique Jesus does not necessarily include an orthodox position. Moreover, she maintains that feminists such as Rosemary Radford Ruether should be considered post-Christian since Jesus is not portrayed as unique, but one savior among others (Hampson, *Theology and Feminism*, 50). Ruether understands Christ as a redemptive person, not once-for-all in the historical Jesus, but continued in the Christian community (Ruether, *Sexism and God-Talk*, 138).

5. Hampson, *Theology and Feminism*, 150.

6. By "theism" Hampson means "a conviction that there is more to reality than meets the eye; that there are powers on which we may draw; that we are profoundly connected with what is in excess of what we are" (Hampson, *After Christianity*, 253; see also p. 10).

important critique of the Christian tradition and of how Christian feminist theologians interpret what are perceived as problematic Christian doctrines. Furthermore, Hampson understands religious experience in a manner similar to some Christian feminist theologians. Rosemary Radford Ruether is one example of a Christian feminist theologian who holds a view of religious experience not unlike Hampson's. Ruether perceives the primary intuitions of religious experience as a belief in a divine foundation of reality which is ultimately good and which affirms the autonomous personhood of women.[7] If Hampson's views are somewhat representative of a general feminist understanding of religious experience that explicitly or implicitly influences Christian feminist theology, then we must consider her thought at some length.

Religious Experience in Daphne Hampson and Friedrich Schleiermacher

Hampson on Schleiermacher

Hampson makes experience the foundation of her theological method.[8] Why? A number of issues concern her, not the least of which are feminist interests and problems with how patriarchy has damaged Christianity. All these factors are ultimately connected to the notion of autonomy. According to Hampson, religion based on human experience is a more ethical position, allowing persons to maintain authority over their own lives, as opposed to a religion based on a particular revelation of God, which requires allegiance to an other outside the self.[9]

In a chapter titled "A Future Theism," Hampson sets out her position, which is dependent upon the work of F. D. E. Schleiermacher. Before considering Hampson's use of Schleiermacher, let us summarize the chapter's main points.[10] In agreement with Schleiermacher,

7. Ruether, "Future of Feminist Theology," 710.

8. What exactly is meant by "foundation"? The term is often understood as a prolegomenon—a necessary theoretical foundation to be established in order to do theology. In reference to Hampson it is interpreted generally as the ultimate criterion upon which a particular theology is grounded.

9. Hampson, *After Christianity*, 38.

10. We have focused principally upon this particular chapter of *After Christianity* as it is where Hampson relates her theism to Schleiermacher's thought as well as develops the substance of her position.

Hampson asserts that the question of the nature of the membrane between the self to that which is beyond the self is the kernel of theology,[11]
but whereas Schleiermacher grounds his theology in an immediate
awareness of God, Hampson wants only to utilize his *conception* of
the self and its relation to that which is outside the self.[12] Although
she acknowledges an immediate awareness of God, Hampson does
not wish it to be the foundation of her theism, rather she grounds her
position upon evidence of religious experience, bringing it to bear on
Schleiermacher's interpretation of the self. In considering the evidence
for such a dimension of reality, Hampson looks not to Schleiermacher,
but to what has essentially been an Anglo-Saxon tradition: the study of
religious experience.[13]

Because Hampson is shaped significantly by the Enlightenment
and science, she regards a methodology based upon evidence from experience as the kind of objectivity needed in theology.[14] She does not
believe in divine interventions and considers it an "*a priori* that theology
can have no quarrel with the fact that nature and history form a causal
nexus."[15] While Hampson rejects miracles or divine interventions for
scientific reasons, she nevertheless acknowledges that there are some
"phenomena" that reveal a reality beyond ourselves, what she would
identify as religious experiences. Schleiermacher's understanding is
useful to Hampson by indicating that reality which lies beyond the self,
but rational evidence is required if one is to make it the basis for theology. Therefore, Hampson recognizes two types of evidence as support
of the belief in a dimension of reality she calls God: first, a power that
allows mental and physical healing, and second, what we may call "intuition or clairvoyance."[16] To corroborate her claim, she refers to several
anecdotes from her own life and historical situations as well as reports
from the Oxford Religious Experience Research Unit.[17]

11. Hampson, *After Christianity*, 212.

12. Ibid.

13. Ibid., 213.

14. Ibid., 257.

15. Ibid., 223.

16. Ibid., 226.

17. The chapter includes several illustrations of what some might call "coincidenc-
es," but which Hampson cites as evidence of the dimension of reality she calls God. One
example is a story in which she describes herself stranded in her car in the countryside

Furthermore, what Hampson finds most important about Schleiermacher is what she calls a "lack of the possibility of any heter-onomy in the human relation to God."[18] Hampson supplies a general description of Schleiermacher's thought found in the early pages of his *The Christian Faith*.[19] She refers to his understanding of an antithesis of feeling between freedom and dependence, and that in feeling dependent we understand ourselves to be derived from and related to God. We do not relate to God as an "object" the way we relate to others in the world; rather, by intuiting ourselves, we sense ourselves immediately connected to that which is more than ourselves, to God.[20] Following this, Hampson concludes that Schleiermacher understands there to be no heteronomy in the relationship to God.[21] She refers to §4.4 of *The Christian Faith* to emphasize the point: God is not an "object," a "given" like other parts of the world; anything outwardly given could be considered an object on which we could effect our influence. "Precisely because God is not, for Schleiermacher, such an 'object' and does not exist within the realm of reciprocity, the relationship to God cannot by definition, be heterono-mous and our responsibility towards the world remains unqualified."[22] Inasmuch as our relation to God is of an entirely different order from our relation to others in the world, it is acceptable to describe it as one of absolute dependence, which is a way to understand God as our sense of "whenceness" or being.[23] In other words, as reciprocal relations, objects (or human beings) exercise influence in one way or another upon other objects. Since God is not understood as an object in this sense, there is

---

outside St. Andrews on her way to catch a train for an important meeting. The only available telephone was out of order and her attempts at knocking on doors for assis-tance failed to rouse anyone. At the very moment the situation seemed desperate, a taxi drove up the road and she was able to make her appointment. It is an instance where Hampson's openness to God was demonstrated in a tangible way (ibid., 235).

18. Ibid., 213.

19. Hampson refers chiefly to the introduction of *The Christian Faith*. Karl Barth has perceptively noted, contrary to Schleiermacher's assurances that the introduction is only an entrance to the real dogmatics, that the whole of the nineteenth century found the true content of dogmatics only in relation to this opening analysis (Barth, *Theology of Schleiermacher*, 211).

20. Hampson, *After Christianity*, 216–17.

21. Ibid., 217–18.

22. Ibid., 219.

23. Ibid., 220.

no reciprocity and the issue of the heteronomy of God, of God standing over and against us, becomes irrelevant, a non-issue.

Schleiermacher on Schleiermacher

Has Hampson accurately interpreted Schleiermacher? Let us first consider some general elements of his thought. The Enlightenment's emphasis upon reason was a concern of Schleiermacher's. It seemed that much of Christian doctrine was at odds with what science and reason taught, therefore, he sought to establish a basis for Christian faith that would avoid these pitfalls: "I thought I should show as best I could that every dogma that truly represents an element of our Christian consciousness can be so formulated that it remains free from entanglements with science."[24] At the same time, he opposed how Kant had dealt with the age of reason by dividing the human moral agent into a duality of phenomenal and noumenal, leaving theology to speak of God only in a speculative manner.[25] Schleiermacher resisted such speculative theology and developed a phenomenological approach of religion that would unite the phenomenal and noumenal selves—we can know something of God and the basis for this is in personal experience, a feeling of absolute dependence.

In agreement with Kant, Schleiermacher was against maintaining an external authority as a guide for questions of morality and religion, hence his reliance upon the inner experience of the individual (though not the individual understood as an isolated self). Although metaphysics and morals have the same object as religion (i.e., the universe and the relationship of humanity to it), the latter must be differentiated from the previous two;[26] therefore, Schleiermacher makes a distinction between feeling, knowing, and doing. Piety, or religion, belongs to feeling and

24. Schleiermacher, *On the Glaubenslehre*, 64. One instance of Schleiermacher reconciling Christian doctrine and reason can be seen in the area of Christology. Schleiermacher is willing to maintain the traditional christological formulas, as long as they are in agreement with the Christian self-consciousness. He shows little regard for such traditional formulas as the two natures of Christ, which seemed incoherent in an age of reason. Accepting the physical resurrection and ascension of Christ would also be of little relevance to his Christology (see Gerrish, *Prince of the Church*, 28).

25. Schleiermacher, *On Religion*, xxi–xxiii. See also Berkhof, *Two Hundred Years of Theology*, 30–31.

26. Schleiermacher, *On Religion*, speech 2, p. 19.

takes place in a subject who is completely receptive, stimulating knowing and doing, which are more active, and passing beyond the purely receptive self.[27] Piety has its locus in feeling and feeling is specified as an immediate self-consciousness of absolute dependence by which we experience ourselves as absolutely dependent upon God. These are the moments of religious self-consciousness.[28]

This understanding of the meaning of the religious self-consciousness in Schleiermacher provides the background to Hampson's analysis of him. It is difficult to articulate adequately this conception of religious experience, mainly because it is considered a precognitive experience that precedes our language to describe it. Nevertheless, our purpose at this point is to consider further their understandings of heteronomy and autonomy.

Heteronomy and Autonomy

The first obstacle we encounter is that Schleiermacher does not use the terms autonomy and heteronomy as does Hampson; therefore, our strategy will be to identify certain terms that Schleiermacher uses that are associated with issues of heteronomy, such as the independence, will, omnipotence, holiness, and justice of God. In addition, Schleiermacher explains the freedom of the individual, which corresponds to the concept of autonomy to which Hampson refers. Before continuing, let us clarify how Hampson understands heteronomy and autonomy. She defines heteronomy as one ruling another, involving a subjection of one to another and limiting his or her freedom and self-determination. In contrast, autonomy is self-rule and is the appropriate way for adults to live; heteronomy is for children.[29] Furthermore, Hampson perceives the Christian God to be heteronomous: "It follows that if God is an other and is God, the relationship to God must ultimately, by definition, be heteronomous."[30]

Hampson is correct in identifying that such a description of heteronomy conflicts with Schleiermacher's conception of God's relationship

---

27. Schleiermacher, *Christian Faith*, §3.
28. Schleiermacher, *Two Letters to Dr. Lücke*, 10.
29. Hampson, *Swallowing a Fishbone?*, 1.
30. Ibid., 9.

to human beings, likewise, she recognizes his emphasis on freedom and reciprocity. Schleiermacher understands the total self-consciousness as made up of the feeling of dependence and the feeling of freedom and that both together make up a "*[r]eciprocity* between the subject and the corresponding Other."[31] However, "the immediate self-consciousness is not characterized by a reciprocity of receptivity and activity on the part of the self, but by sheer receptivity."[32] God is not given to us as other objects are given. God is not an object upon which we can exercise our influence, nor does God's existence in any way spring from our activity.[33] Even so, Schleiermacher maintains that this concept of human receptivity does not destroy human freedom.[34] The feeling of absolute dependence does not place persons in a servile state and allows free interactions with the finite world.[35] Schleiermacher's stress on human freedom and reciprocity applies to an understanding of human activity within the natural world and with other human beings, but not with God.

If God is not understood to be an object, as are other humans, then the opportunities for influence or activity over and against this object are nonexistent. Schleiermacher's concern with human freedom relates to moral freedom rather than freedom to affect or influence God. At the same time, this inability to influence God does not entail some sort of heteronomous or tyrannical relationship between God and humanity. Similarly, Hampson describes human agency in relation to God as somehow "prompted" by what is more than we are, yet avoiding either/ or questions about who has the agency, God or ourselves.[36] God does not limit human freedom in the world, but allows humans to be free agents in reciprocal relation with the world. Thus, Hampson stands in agreement with Schleiermacher in understanding the self as both determinate and also posited.[37]

---

31. Schleiermacher, *Christian Faith*, 14.

32. Schleiermacher, *Two Letters to Dr. Lücke*, 15.

33. Schleiermacher, *Christian Faith*, 15, 18.

34. Schleiermacher, *Two Letters to Dr. Lücke*, 43.

35. Ibid., 17.

36. Hampson, *After Christianity*, 231.

37. Ibid., 233.

Despite this aspect of agreement between Schleiermacher and Hampson regarding the nature of the freedom of the self, if Hampson were to take Schleiermacher's dogmatics a step further he would no longer provide support for an understanding of heteronomy and autonomy that she would find acceptable.[38] Schleiermacher maintains a sense of God as other, including traditional attributes that presumably Hampson would reject. The sections of *The Christian Faith* that discuss God's attributes include most of the traditional attributes, which Schleiermacher describes based upon "abstraction from the definite feeling-content of our God-consciousness."[39] Briefly, some of these attributes are: God's will as Creator and sustainer where everything is absolutely willed by God (§54); God's omnipotence related to the will of God in that everything is founded upon divine causality "as affirmed in our feeling of absolute dependence" (§54);[40] God's independence meaning that there is no ground for God's being, no determining cause outside God (§54); God's holiness associated with divine causality and the need of all human conscience for redemption (§83); and God's justice, understood corporately, which punishes sin and rewards good (§84). Looking beyond exactly how Schleiermacher arrives at these attributes, but at the attributes themselves as he describes them, it appears that God as a creator and a holy judge would stand in stark contrast to the kind of God Hampson is trying to construct. Moreover, by asserting God as creator, Schleiermacher preserves a sense of the "creatureliness" of human beings, which Hampson would also reject. Though they seem to have a similar starting point, preserving reciprocity and human freedom, ultimately Schleiermacher's God resembles a transcendent, Christian God, quite at odds with Hampson's conclusions.

38. Hampson admits to taking Schleiermacher "beyond anything of which [he] conceived" by claiming that "in being most fully ourselves we are also realizing God in the world." She acknowledges where Schleiermacher is no longer useful to her purpose while retaining key elements of his thought as significant to her methodology (ibid., 250.

39. Schleiermacher, *Christian Faith*, 731.

40. "As Schleiermacher sees it, "God to be God must be understood as doing everything, not as simply watching for occasions to act sometimes. God's omnipotence does and causes everything" (Gerrish, *Prince of the Church*, 57).

Schleiermacher and Other Religions

This affinity to a Christian God found in Schleiermacher's theology is a result Hampson challenges, questioning how he could move from the presupposition of universal religious experience to the particularity of Christianity.[41] In contrast, Hampson considers that she more accurately follows through with the implications of his thought, acknowledging that it is likely he would disagree with her.[42] Schleiermacher concludes that Christianity is the superior form of religion. Even beginning with *On Religion*, Schleiermacher does not intend to establish an understanding of universal religion and then move from that to Christianity: "I wish to lead you, as it were, to the God who has become flesh."[43] He considers a description of universal religious knowledge as nothing other than an abstraction from what is Christian[44] and declares that the aim of *The Christian Faith* is to describe the consciousness characteristic of Christianity.[45] Rather than trying to explain Christian piety on the basis of a universal human consciousness of piety, Schleiermacher states that he is attempting to "specify the distinctive place Christianity occupies among the various possible modifications of that common consciousness."[46]

How does Schleiermacher arrive at such a conclusion? He begins with the feeling of absolute dependence, the immediate self-consciousness of being in relation to God, understood as an essential element of human nature.[47] All human beings have the capacity for this experience. The next point falls under his discussion of monotheism, polytheism and idol worship found in §8 of *The Christian Faith*. He views monotheism as superior to the other forms of religion because the latter two are a confusion of the self-consciousness. Since we are absolutely dependent upon one God there is no plurality as the source of this feeling; no dis-

---

41. Hampson, *After Christianity*, 222. On this point she agrees with Karl Barth who observed that there was not an opposition between God and humanity in Schleiermacher as there should be in Christianity.

42. Hampson, *After Christianity*, 212.

43. Schleiermacher, *On Religion*, speech 5, p. 96.

44. Schleiermacher, *Two Letters to Dr. Lücke*, 52.

45. Ibid., 58.

46. Ibid., 76.

47. Schleiermacher, *Christian Faith*, 26.

unity or difference. At this stage he determines that Christianity is the superior form of monotheism. Of the three great monotheistic faiths, Judaism, Christianity, and Islam, Christianity best avoids tendencies toward either polytheism or idol worship, and is therefore preferred. Although Schleiermacher displays a tolerance in his work, nearly adopting a version of relativism that refuses to legislate a person's relationship to that which is beyond, he still builds a heavy Christian bias into his account of religions, preferring it as his own choice, religion raised to a higher degree.[48] Ultimately, Schleiermacher fails Hampson because he proposes the Christian faith and the Christian God as the superior expression of religious experience. Our feeling of absolute dependence is none other than that of the Christian God and is related in all its facets to the redemption accomplished by Jesus of Nazareth (regardless of how exactly Schleiermacher understands Jesus and redemption).[49]

Our purpose here is not to determine whether Schleiermacher's account of other religions is correct or valuable, but rather to consider Hampson's use of Schleiermacher to construct a theism based upon evidence of religious experience that begins with an acknowledgment of the relation of the self to that which is beyond the self, a concept gained primarily from the work of Schleiermacher. Although there are areas of agreement between the two, their purposes and conclusions are vastly different and finally incompatible.

The Pitfalls of a Theology of Experience

We have taken account of Hampson's understanding of Schleiermacher and how she uses his thought in service of her own theism. How helpful to theology, particularly feminist theology, is her approach? Before answering that question, we will examine a few weaknesses found in Hampson's theism: (1) a tendency toward pantheism; (2) a danger of relativism; and (3) problems with the category of religious experience. Throughout the discussion of each of these, Schleiermacher's thought and Hampson's use of it will also be presented.

---

48. One sees evidence of this open-mindedness in *On Religion* where Schleiermacher acknowledges that there are other elements of religion that another may experience that are different from one's own (*On Religion*, speech 2, p. 27; see also p. xxxvi).

49. Schleiermacher, *Christian Faith*, 52.

Tendency toward Pantheism

Theologies of experience may contain pantheistic tendencies and often come across as some form of natural religion. Hampson denies any pantheism in her position: "I am in no way suggesting that matter is God and I am not a pantheist."[50] By upholding the self as centered and complete, yet somehow connected to that which is more than the self, Hampson keeps aligned with Schleiermacher, thus trying to avoid accusations of pantheism. However, both she and Schleiermacher reveal tendencies toward pantheism that are not easily avoided, and in Hampson's case in particular, not sufficiently defended. Stating that God is not matter is insufficient to dispel the pantheistic tendencies evident throughout her theism.[51] Hampson conceives of God as intrinsically a part of who we are as human beings, and as a dimension of all there is, explaining that "God, we and the world are inter-related."[52] Moreover, she argues that there is a goodness, beauty, and harmony in the world which she identifies with what she calls God and which can be postulated of the whole.[53] God is not external to us, but intimately tied with what we are.[54] Finally, Hampson does not understand God as the creator of all there is, but rather as interwoven with creation.[55]

Perhaps in an effort to avoid pantheism, she does not explicitly state that God *is* all there is, rather she maintains that God is a dimension, a part of the whole. However, other assertions contradict this understanding of God, making her position seem rather ambiguous. Is God merely a part of the whole such as we are? Is God represented by ideals that permeate all of creation? What exactly does it mean that God is inter-related to the world and interwoven in creation? Despite these fuzzy boundary lines between human beings, the world, and God, Hampson clearly describes an immanent rather than a transcendent

50. Hampson, *After Christianity*, 231.

51. "Historically, pantheism has tended to lapse into materialism, but this was in the days when a now obsolete conception of matter held the field, and would not be true today, when it is understood that matter is no mere aggregation of inert particles but a highly complex energy structure" (Macquarrie, *Twentieth-Century Religious Thought*, 439).

52. Hampson, *After Christianity*, 214, 231.

53. Ibid., 245.

54. Ibid., 252.

55. Ibid., 239.

God. This emphasis upon immanence (or might we say *de*-emphasis on transcendence?) leads to a pantheistic interpretation of her theism in which everything finite is submerged in the whole. Such theism portrays an impersonal God who is not a divine being. God does not exist independently of creation and is not the creator of all else.[56] Regardless of efforts to the contrary, it remains that significant elements of Hampson's theism leave her vulnerable to the accusation of pantheism. The stress on immanence and the dubious nature of God's relation to us and the world make it difficult to determine just where the world ends and where God begins.

Furthermore, there is an idealism present in Hampson's view that is not incompatible with pantheism. Hampson claims that her concept of God performs a transcendental (not transcendent) function, by which she means that it provides purpose and meaning to life.[57] Essentially, God is the unity which lies behind the world, perceived as ideals (e.g., goodness, beauty, harmony) by which our lives should be guided. This idealism is further evident in an apparent disregard for particular history. Hampson defends herself against accusations of being ahistorical, yet takes steps to discredit such feminists as Elizabeth Schüssler Fiorenza who work to reclaim women's history in the early church.[58] Likewise, Hampson professes an optimism about human nature that is also characteristic of idealism: she has "more faith in humanity's ability to stand on its own feet" than in a mindset that chooses allegiance between one Lord or another.[59] This idealism revealed in Hampson's theism goes hand in hand with the pantheism contained in her position.

How does Schleiermacher fare under similar charges? Like Hampson, he denies that his theology is pantheistic, citing his intent to write a Christian dogmatics for Christians, not a philosophical account of religion.[60] However, there are elements of Schleiermacher's position which contribute to a pantheistic tenor. Schleiermacher makes the religious experience a universal aspect of human nature, which leads toward an

56. Ibid., 245.

57. Ibid., 244–45.

58. As a woman with civil rights undreamed of two thousand years ago, Hampson asks, "How then should the lives of women in the ancient world be relevant to me?" (ibid., 72).

59. Ibid., 38.

60. Schleiermacher, *Two Letters to Dr. Lücke*, 51.

understanding of God as immanent with the world.[61] Moreover, God is not an "object" in the sense of a personal God with whom one can interact. Schleiermacher uses the word "God," but the content of the word and the relation to humanity is arguably impersonal.[62] Our awareness of absolute dependence is not an awareness of absolute dependence upon God: "Feeling is not itself God; nor does it relate to God as an independent 'object.' Rather, feeling signifies a *relation* to God."[63]

As seen in Hampson's approach, an overemphasis upon the immanence of God and the lack of understanding of God as a personal object leads to a pantheistic interpretation. However, what keeps Schleiermacher from ultimately being considered pantheist is the christological emphasis of his dogmatics. James Wm. McClendon claims the tendencies toward either a blind particularity in a "confirmed Jesus-faith" or a bland theism that blends into pantheism can be avoided by a christological center of the doctrine of God.[64] Schleiermacher's system of Christian dogmatics as a whole is shaped by Christology, keeping him from falling into an utterly immanent, and therefore utterly impersonal, understanding of God.[65] Schleiermacher conceives of a Christian God who is in some sense an other, standing outside humanity. It is a God to whom humanity needs to be reconciled and redeemed, which is the work of Jesus Christ. Due to his developed Christology, Schleiermacher is spared from being understood as fully promoting pantheism.[66]

Danger of Relativism

Another area that could be considered a weakness for theologies such as Hampson's and Schleiermacher's that are based upon religious

---

61. Schleiermacher, *Christian Faith*, 26. Richard Niebuhr notes in *Schleiermacher on Christ and Religion* that in Schleiermacher's thought, the world and God cannot be confused, or the one reduced to the other (188). However, "the appearance of immanentism in Schleiermacher's thought remains," (191).

62. Barth, *Theology of Schleiermacher*, 218.

63. Schleiermacher, *Two Letters to Dr. Lücke*, 19.

64. McClendon Jr., *Doctrine*, 322–23.

65. Gerrish, *Prince of the Church*, 45.

66. Gerrish notes that Schleiermacher leaned toward the pantheistic side of a pantheism/atheism debate current in Germany. He opposed a deism that claimed that some events fall outside divine activity as well as a pantheism taht spoke of divine activity as adding nothing to an understanding of natural events (ibid., 52).

experience, is a relativism in which theology is based upon an individual's experience, thus making theology something that varies with the instance of each person's experience. Related to a tendency toward relativism is a theology with an undeveloped conception of community or context. Hampson seems aware of these problems, defending Schleiermacher against those who allege that it is impossible to have a religious experience that is unpolluted by concepts and could form an epistemological starting point for theology.[67] According to Hampson, understanding him this way is a misreading of Schleiermacher. She perceives Schleiermacher as valuing the role of language and culture in the formation of religion and acknowledges that he does not consider the awareness of God as independent from the world.[68] Hampson herself offers little defense for her own position, perhaps because she regards her association with Schleiermacher, who she believes does not have a context-less theology, as sufficient to fend off any charges of her own relativism.

Although there is warrant to challenge Schleiermacher on the point of relativism, it is true that he does not have a context-less theology. Schleiermacher begins *The Christian Faith* with a claim that a foundation for dogmatics cannot be established outside the church (§2). In speaking

67. Hampson, *After Christianity*, 221. In a footnote (315 n. 20) Hampson states her disagreement with Wayne Proudfoot who has challenged such conclusions on religious experience: "The religious consciousness is said to have the immediacy and independence from thought which are characteristic of sensations, and yet to include an intuitive component whose object is the infinite . . . It is not dependent on concepts or beliefs, yet it can be specified only by reference to the concept of the whole or the infinite. This combination, required for Schleiermacher's program, is an impossible one. If the feeling is intentional, it cannot be specified apart from reference to its object and thus it cannot be independent of thought." See Proudfoot, *Religious*, 11. William Alston criticizes Proudfoot on this very point. He argues that just because we use concepts to identify something it does not follow that what we are identifying involves concepts and judgments (e.g., pain—to identify a state as pain one must employ a concept, but it is mistaken in supposing pain is conceptual). "To be sure, it may well be that Schleiermacher cannot, consistently with his other key views, maintain that the 'feeling of absolute dependence' is free from concepts . . . But if so, this will be because of his *characterization* of the states, not because he uses concepts to classify them in a certain way" (Alston, *Perceiving God*, 41). It seems the question remains: Does one even have (not merely identify) an experience, religious or otherwise, without interpreting it and hence, utilizing concepts (e.g., regarding pain—the experience of pain seems meaningless without some knowledge by which it can be interpreted)?

68. Hampson, *After Christianity*, 220–21.

of a particular religion, we are referring to a "church" whose religious affections form the foundation of its communion (§6). Religious communion is essential for Schleiermacher's understanding of the religious consciousness because, although each person has the potential for an awareness of absolute dependence, it is first awakened by the power of communication and utterance.[69] Furthermore, this self-consciousness leads one to be in religious fellowship where a cycle of self-renewing occurs and a propagation of religious emotions is organized such that one can tell which individuals belong to this fellowship and which do not. This concept is what is designated as "Church."[70] This understanding of church lies in distinction from natural religion, which Schleiermacher claims is never a basis for religious communion.[71] Natural religion basically does not extend beyond what we mean by humanity's natural tendency for religious emotions.[72] By his interpretation of church, Schleiermacher does not intend that the church is a slave to doctrine. Rather, we could say that doctrines serve the church; doctrines must be tested for adequacy by the inner life of her members.[73] Schleiermacher is not concerned with acts of cognition as distinct from piety, but with piety itself, which is the original and underived basis for theological reflection.[74] This understanding is exemplified in the very structure of *The Christian Faith*, where Schleiermacher strictly adheres to a method whereby doctrines are constructed in light of the feeling of absolute dependence experienced by the Christian person.

69. Schleiermacher, *Christian Faith*, 27.

70. Ibid., 29.

71. Part of Schleiermacher's defense against natural religion was due to his opposition to Enlightenment views, which held religion to be indeterminate. Natural religion had an indeterminate form with no unity of a specific view for its religious intuition (*On Religion*, speech 5, p. 109).

72. Schleiermacher, *Christian Faith*, 48.

73. Gerrish, *Prince of the Church*, 24. This concept of validating doctrine by way of religious experience is not so unlike what some feminists promote. Schüssler Fiorenza describes the "women-church," the movement of self-identified women and women-identified men in biblical religion, as the "hermeneutical center" of feminist biblical interpretation. The Bible is subjected to feminist scrutiny and the theological authority of women-church, which assesses the oppressive and liberative elements of the biblical texts. In other words, doctrine is dependent upon the experience of the members of women-church (see Schüssler Fiorenza, *Bread Not Stone*, 13–14).

74. Schleiermacher, *Two Letters to Dr. Lücke*, 20.

A concept of some form of faith community is one aspect of Schleiermacher that Hampson might consider adopting. There is minimal development of an understanding of community within Hampson's theism. This lack is partly revealed by the evidence of religious experience presented, which focuses on individuals including herself. Hampson is assuredly not anti-community and refers to the Quakers as a particular community that cultivates some of the virtues her theism advocates. However, it remains that a notion of community and its relationship to experience is inadequately explored, thus contributing to a sense of relativism in that it is unclear if Hampson is suggesting that each particular context should develop its own theism, as she has done for her particular context, or if her theism is appropriate for people in other social locations. If individual experiences are the basis for the evidence of the dimension of reality she calls God, who is to say that one's experience is more valid than another's? Without an understanding of the community's role in experience, an individualistic view of experience prevails.

Alternatively, there are some aspects of Hampson's position that point away from the conclusion that she is a relativist. For instance, she rejects some elements of Eastern spirituality as harmful to women and clearly rejects Christianity, therefore appearing to draw some boundaries between what is acceptable and unacceptable theology. Furthermore, she claims that she writes legislatively, not simply descriptively. She believes her theism to be morally acceptable whereas others (i.e., Christianity) are not.[75] Although Hampson suggests a universal understanding of religious experience that is rather individualistic, based on each person's experience of that dimension of reality within the self, she simultaneously condemns some understandings and expressions of religious experience as harmful and immoral. Perhaps this is not the voice of a relativist after all.

It seems that both Schleiermacher and Hampson develop a theology of experience that very well may lead to a form of relativism, yet both claim certain boundaries for what is proper theology and what is not.

75. Hampson, *After Christianity*, 250, 248.

Problems with the Category of Religious Experience

Finally, we must consider the general category of experience as a component of theology. Hampson bases her theism upon evidence of a religious experience, what she describes as an awareness of a dimension of reality upon which we can draw and which she names God. Rather than providing a precise definition of religious experience, Hampson presents evidence of such experience by way of anecdotes and illustrations, many based upon the work of the Religious Experience Research Unit in Oxford.[76] It could be assumed that Hampson understands religious experience in much the way Schleiermacher does, however, Schleiermacher is quite descriptive of the content of religious experience (the feeling of absolute dependence or piety) and its meaning. Hampson does not want to place too much emphasis upon experience itself because she is aware of how subjective a category it is. As we have already mentioned, rather than utilizing religious experience as a basis for her theism, Hampson goes for a more scientific orientation by bringing evidence of such experiences as the grounds for her position. This approach seems a bit incongruous in that she challenges many of the beliefs within Christianity because of her understanding of the scientific world (miracles such as water becoming wine are impossible) and then goes on to use empirical evidence in support of experiences for which there is no explanation (where healing occurs). Hers is a scientific approach that seeks to provide knowledge about the connection and order of phenomena, and yet it is essentially a neo-Kantian positivism that results in a metaphysical spirituality. This ambiguity within Hampson's theism makes it difficult to determine exactly where she stands. For centuries, rationalists have objected to Christianity's lack of

76. Since the term is used widely, often with little definition, it may seem that religious experience is a commonly accepted and understood concept. However, there are a number of possible, related definitions: (1) "a roughly datable mental event which is undergone by a subject and of which the subject is to some extent aware" (Davis, *Evidential Force of Religious Experience*, 19); (2) "an experience that seems (epistemologically) to the subject to be an experience of God (either of his just being there, or doing or bringing about something) or of some supernatural thing" (Swinburne, *Existence of God*, 246); (3) a survey from the Religious Experience Research Unit asked respondents to identify with one of three quotations regarding a certain type of religious experience. These three generally were described as a "force" or "power" that helps (Beardsworth, *Sense of Presence*, vii). Each of these definitions of religious experience could be considered in general agreement with what we find in Hampson.

scientific evidence to support it, and here we find Hampson providing such evidence in spite of being an evidentialist objector herself.[77]

Despite the questions that arise regarding Hampson's use of evidence, there are other concerns related to the category of religious experience as a basis for theology. There are limitations in speaking about experience at all which Hampson neglects to address. Without a particular culture and language, one cannot articulate or interpret experience. Doubtless Hampson acknowledges a role for such factors as culture and language, however, in agreement with Schleiermacher, she still maintains that there is an immediate awareness of that which is beyond ourselves, that dimension of reality she calls God.[78] Although she defends Schleiermacher, and presumably herself as well, against a Derridean critique by maintaining that such a position does not equate with a detachment from the world or particular context, it seems that a Wittgensteinian position is more persuasive. As George Lindbeck has argued, religion is shaped by our experiences, life, and thought and makes possible description and formulation of realities and beliefs. Religion "shapes the subjectivities of individuals rather than being primarily a manifestation of those subjectivities."[79] If by its very definition the criterion of religious experience is that one believes it to be produced by God or the unity of the whole, or whatever idea of the transcendent, then it cannot be independent of language or thought. It is not immediate, precognitive, prereflexive. Hampson takes religious language to be expressive and receptive, but neglects the fact that it "also plays a very active and formative role in religious experience."[80] What we get in Hampson (not so much in Schleiermacher who develops the role of the faith community as contributing to religious experience) is a fairly one-sided understanding whereby the evidence from religious experience is brought to bear upon theology, but religious concepts are not brought to bear on experience.[81]

---

77. "No religion is acceptable unless rational, and no religion is rational unless supported by evidence. That is the evidentialist challenge" (Wolterstorff, *Faith and Rationality*, 6).

78. Hampson, *After Christianity*, 217.

79. Lindbeck, *Nature of Doctrine*, 33.

80. Proudfoot, *Religious Experience*, 40.

81. Davis, *Evidential Force*, 165.

Hampson provides evidence of those phenomena that lead us to speak about God and to consider how we conceptualize God, believing that the conception of God she is constructing is more true to the experiential evidence than how we have understood God in the past.[82] What do we, in fact, learn about God, based upon the evidence Hampson presents? It appears that God is a dimension of reality beyond us, a power that can bring physical and mental healing, protect us from danger, and bring a sense of wholeness to our lives. More explicitly, Hampson says, "[w]e may understand God as that which gives us illumination, which allows us to heal in ourselves, and which passes between us and those whom we love. God is both that which connects me to the greater whole and that which enables me to be my true self."[83] Ultimately, for Hampson God is an extension of ourselves, equivalent to becoming our true self and being in touch with our deepest self. God is one with our self-realization.[84] This kind of rhetoric bears little to distinguish it from much popular self-help and New Age spiritualities. Why call it a theism or talk about God at all? Hampson admits that the primary reason she maintains the words "God" and "spiritual" is as an act of subversion, a way to jettison the Christian myth she sees to be co-opted by men.[85]

This leads us to the primary reason that a theology of experience such as Hampson's is problematic. Such a theism is not actually about God at all, but about humans. "A theology of experience, as I [Hampson] have called it, places the human self centre-stage. God is known with and through the self."[86] Feuerbach leveled an impressive critique against theology, claiming that belief in God is merely a projection of the human mind. In the case of Hampson's theism, his critique seems fitting: "Consciousness of God is self-consciousness, knowledge of God is self-knowledge. By his God thou knowest the man, and by the man his God; the two are identical."[87] With a theology centered on the experiences of the human being, it is reasonable to conclude that some sort of anthropology rather than theology is being developed. Karl Barth

82. Hampson, *After Christianity*, 248.

83. Ibid., 251.

84. Ibid., 284.

85. Ibid., 283.

86. Ibid.

87. Feuerbach, *Essence of Christianity*, 12.

charges Schleiermacher with a similar problem, claiming that he made the pious person the criterion and content of theology.[88] Barth finds Schleiermacher in close proximity to Feuerbach, asking how the feeling of absolute dependence, which is not oriented toward any object, can still objectify itself in certain ideas. The only explanation must be the power of the imagination.[89] In bringing Barth into the discussion, we are in direct opposition to Hampson who refuses to consider a theology based upon revelation. Although there are significant similarities between Schleiermacher and Hampson in their development of a theology of experience, and Barth's criticisms of Schleiermacher would apply equally well to both, at some point the conversation breaks down. Against Barth, Hampson believes starting with a revelation of God is not objective, but that objectivity in theology can only be found in the evidence of the dimension of reality we call God.[90] It appears we are at an impasse.

Conclusion: Foundationalism and a Theology of Experience

We do not want to appear opposed to an understanding of religious experience nor to its value for the theological project. On the contrary, religious experience is undeniably a significant element of theological method as well as to the Christian faith tradition (Paul on the Damascus road springs to mind). Indeed, religious experience is crucial. What we do object to, however, is the way Hampson has used evidence of such experience as an "objective" and seemingly indubitable foundation for theism. The methodological tools Hampson utilizes in constructing her theism are not particularly innovative, in fact, her approach is a good example of Western, Enlightenment foundationalism.

Foundationalism refers to the "conviction that knowledge as a true and justified belief is based on foundations." A foundation is neither justified by nor based upon other beliefs. It provides support for all other beliefs and presupposes basic truths that can be described

---

88. Barth, *Theology of Schleiermacher*, 271.

89. Ibid., 217.

90. Hampson, *After Christianity*, 257.

as either self-justified or irrefutable.[91] To put it another way, a classical foundationalist maintains that propositions are rational and can be held as immediate grounded upon two criteria: (1) the proposition is self-evident (e.g., 1+1=2), and (2) the proposition is incorrigible, that is, based upon a state of consciousness (e.g., I am dizzy). This basic strategy exemplifies the epistemological tradition of the Enlightenment, and Wolterstorff claims that most contemporary philosophers no longer find this approach tenable.[92] Furthermore, beliefs that meet the above criteria are considered properly basic beliefs and become the foundation upon which other beliefs are built. In order to accept a belief as rational which is not already properly basic, there must be evidence provided that traces back to properly basic beliefs.[93]

What is (are) Hampson's foundation(s)? Evidence from religious experience or something else? Hampson states that her starting point is found in two areas, one epistemological and the other ethical.[94] First, she claims that our conception of God must not incompatible with what we know about the nature of the world. It is further explained that reasons for speaking about God in the first place are based upon the presented evidence which reveals a power for healing beyond ourselves and a notion of clairvoyance and/or intuition. Second, our conception of God must be morally tenable. Although Hampson affirms an immediate awareness of a dimension of reality she calls God, she objects to belief in God without some rational evidence. Hampson emphatically does not want theism grounded upon our immediate awareness of God because it is not adequately scientific, whereas evidence such as that from the Religious Experience Research Unit is the

---

91. Fiorenza, *Foundational Theology*, 285. Fiorenza goes on to argue that experience cannot function as foundational but only in consideration with other factors (298). In theory, most feminists would likely agree, and yet it seems that experience still functions as a foundation and it is unclear what "other factors" are considered and what order of priority these would have.

92. Wolterstorff, *Faith and Rationality*, 3–4.

93. Plantinga, "Reason and Belief in God," 48. In this essay, Plantinga argues that belief in God should be considered a properly basic belief. Although it is an interesting and compelling argument, it is not our focus. What we endeavor to utilize is his understanding of basic beliefs and his challenge to those like Hampson, who hold certain propositions as properly basic, as representing a flawed position.

94. Hampson, *After Christianity*, 234.

objective resource she requires.[95] It appears that Hampson includes certain presuppositions prior to considering the evidence of religious experience, presuppositions about what is moral and immoral, the nature and experience of women (and men), the reliability of scientific evidence, the nature of religious experience, and the virtues that contribute to an awareness of God.

It could be argued that Hampson stands in the tradition of classical foundationalism as described by Wolterstorff and Plantinga.[96] It would be accurate to consider that the epistemological and ethical criteria she suggests function as the properly basic beliefs upon which she builds her theism. However, these two criteria are not really properly basic beliefs. As we have described, the criteria for basic beliefs are that they are self-evident and incorrigible; therefore it seems reasonable to conclude that the epistemological and ethical foundations of Hampson's theism are not properly basic beliefs at all—her reasons for speaking of God, scientific knowledge of the world, and appropriate morality are not self-evident or incorrigible.[97] Hampson might respond to such a charge by claiming that these properly basic beliefs are supported by certain arguments that establish their proper basicality. For instance, she opposes a view that allows any divine interventions because it obviously violates what we know scientifically of the world. In addition, it seems that she takes for granted the reliability of the evidence of a power beyond ourselves and a notion of intuition. She takes more effort to establish what is morally tenable based upon a feminist position that emphasizes the autonomy of individuals. However, it remains that these arguments about science, religious experience, and feminist ethics are

95. William James offers an insightful challenge to the notion of objectivity: "But practically one's conviction that the evidence one goes by is of the real objective brand, is only one more subjective opinion added to the lot. For what a contradictory array of opinions have objective evidence and absolute certitude been claimed!" (James, *Classical and Contemporary Readings*, 204).

96. Hampson is not opposed to being associated with Enlightenment thinking. She believes "[t]he Enlightenment has come to stay" (*After Christianity*, 2).

97. Fundamental to Hampson's project is belief in equality of women, which is considered a "self-evident truth." However, she "makes no philosophical enquiry into her central value, in the light of which Christianity is found to be sadly inadequate" (West, "Justification by Gender," 100). In response to West's review, Hampson argues that her use of equality as self-evident compares to the American Constitution (Hampson, "Reply to Angela West," 116).

not themselves properly basic beliefs and, hence, do not provide adequate support for the theistic criteria upon which she relies. Hampson has particular starting points for her theism that are intended to lend a certain credibility and objectivity, but one must ask, what are the starting points for the starting points? How does one determine what should be considered religious experience? How does one determine what is scientifically reliable? How does one determine exactly what is morally tenable? To make conclusions on these matters, a whole set of factors come into play, based upon one's social location, culture, education, and yes, experience. It is not a stable foundation upon which to build a system of thought and reveals the difficulties inherent in a foundational approach.

Like most modern theology, Schleiermacher is also foundational in his approach to theology in that his dogmatics builds upon one basic development, that is, an understanding of the feeling of absolute dependence. However, he is not foundational in the sense that he goes outside theology for support, but rather, from within theology he attempts to establish reasons for speaking about God. Still, one may challenge Schleiermacher because although he rejects Descartes' dichotomy between the subject and object, he makes the mistake of creating a dichotomy between the direct apprehension of God and a subsequent articulation of this in terms of a religious tradition.[98] The use of religious experience as a foundation for knowledge about God is a mistake of much modern theology and those theologies, like Hampson's, which follow in its footsteps. In this chapter we have identified how Hampson's and Schleiermacher's theologies of religious experience use experience as a foundation for theology, and the general problems inherent in such approaches.

No Genuine Hope for Redemption

One final aspect of Hampson's theism that is particularly troubling is her neglect of the subject of individual and communal sin. Hampson describes domination of other life as a vice contrary to true spirituality, but does not speak of sin explicitly, although she does discuss

---

98. Martin, *Feminist Question*, 171.

Schleiermacher's concept of sin and the theodicy issue.[99] She understands Schleiermacher to be unconcerned with theodicy in the way
those who understand God as transcendent would be concerned with
it. In addition, she claims that for Schleiermacher religion is more about
rising above the pain of reality than dealing with questions of human
suffering and God's relationship to that suffering. Schleiermacher's dogmatics does contain a notion of sin. In §66 of *The Christian Faith* he
describes sin as an inner state in which the development of the God-
consciousness is arrested or as a moment in which it is not active in
us. This experience determines our self-consciousness as pain rather
than pleasure. Furthermore, there is a relationship between sin and
evil understood communally (§77). Related to sin and evil is a need
for redemption, which Schleiermacher considers present in all religious communities. Redemption can mend this condition of the God-
consciousness (§11). Barth notes that Schleiermacher's understanding
of sin and redemption contradict what we learn in scripture, limiting
sin and redemption merely to states of consciousness rather than corresponding to our reality as physical people.[100]

For Hampson, the theodicy issue is even less of an issue than for
Schleiermacher in that she does not understand God as a creator, so
the question of why God did not create the best of all possible worlds
is not a concern of hers. Hampson places more emphasis upon human
responsibility and the possibility of humans being in touch with that
which is beyond themselves in a way that raises up the good within
and overcomes evil.[101] While Schleiermacher's understanding of sin and
redemption is insufficient, we nevertheless recognize that his dogmatics
develops these concepts. Despite her claims to take human responsibility quite seriously, Hampson undervalues it by not addressing how it is
that humans with an innate ability to experience that which is God in
them fail to do so, and actually are the perpetrators of egregious offenses
against one another. There is no need of redemption in Hampson's view,
and this is what is so disheartening. It seems that feminists in particular should address the issue of redemption since they defend women
against the multiple oppressions they have experienced living in a

99. Hampson, *After Christianity*, 259.
100. Barth, *Theology of Schleiermacher*, 196.
101. Hampson, *After Christianity*, 238.

patriarchal society. Within Hampson's scheme is there no redemption for these women and for those who have oppressed them? In order to achieve newness of life are they simply to try harder to rise above their limitations and discover the good within them? The idealism within Hampson's theism is a feature of modern theology as it emphasizes that the divine is best communicated to the mind while disregarding the particular issues and perils of physical existence. If there is no source of redemption beyond ourselves, no opportunity to become more than who we are, in what rests our hope? Is not Hampson telling us to merely hope for that which is God in us?

Perhaps there is a Christian theology of experience that offers more than what we find in Hampson's post-Christian perspective. However, if Schleiermacher is the father of the theology of religious experience, it has been shown that his position is inadequate. Although Barth considered Schleiermacher the greatest theologian since the reformers, he believed his theology led to a dead end.[102] We might say the same of Hampson, that she leads feminists to a dead end. Despite her insightful critique of the Christian tradition, Hampson's theism fails to address the complexities of religious experience or to provide Christian feminist theology with a constructive and hopeful direction.

102. Barth, *Theology of Schleiermacher*, 259.

3

Feminist Liberation Theology and the Method of Correlation

Introduction: Feminist Liberation Theology

ANY CONSIDERATION OF WOMEN'S EXPERIENCE MUST INEVITABLY DEAL with the subject of oppression. Nearly all feminist theology understands women's experience to be characterized by oppression of various forms and degrees. For feminist liberation theologians in particular, such an understanding of experience is predominant and a critical component of their theological method. At the very roots of the feminist theological project one finds what is arguably the most significant branch of feminist theology, feminist liberation theology, which includes some of the most prolific and influential feminist theologians. Elizabeth Johnson provides a helpful description of Christian feminist liberation theology as reflection on "religious mystery" from an *a priori* option for "human flourishing of women."[1] Generally speaking, the task of feminist liberation theology is to change unjust structures and distorted symbol systems, making possible a new community of women and men in harmony with each other and the earth.[2]

Although there are important similarities between them, feminist liberation theologians are distinct from one another in various ways. The work of three feminist liberation theologians, Letty Russell, Elisabeth Schüssler Fiorenza, and Rosemary Radford Ruether, will concern us in this chapter as they are extremely influential and provide a good example of the range of theological perspectives within feminist

1. Johnson, *She Who Is*, 17.

2. Ibid., 31.

liberation theology. We will explore their theological method, including how they understand and use the category of experience, as well as touch on their Christology, in order to gain insight into each position. In addition, it will be important to consider influences upon these three, particularly that of Latin American liberation theology and a correlative method developed primarily in the work of Paul Tillich. Problems within this method will need to be addressed, including how feminists fall victim to its limitations in their own theological systems. Where does use of such a method leave feminist theology?

Feminist Liberation Theologies

Russell, Schüssler Fiorenza, and Ruether have contributed to feminist theology in valuable ways and continue to provide leadership for the feminist theological project. Likewise, each would consider herself a liberation theologian. Letty Russell might be considered the more "biblical" of the three because she attempts to retain a positive relationship to Christian scripture and tradition more explicitly than the other two. Although Elisabeth Schüssler Fiorenza is a biblical scholar working primarily in the area of feminist hermeneutics, her position is influential for feminist theology in general. She has developed a particular approach to scripture, attempting to uncover the history of women in the early Christian tradition that lies behind the text. Rosemary Radford Ruether also values the biblical tradition, although is not bound to it as her only source for theological reflection. Let us consider each of these feminists further.

Letty Russell

Russell considers feminist theology by definition to be liberation theology: "*Liberation theology is an attempt to reflect upon the experience of oppression and our actions for the new creation of a more human society.*"[3] Feminist theology is written out of women's experience of oppression, finds its reference point for understanding liberation in the biblical stories of the exodus and the resurrection, and is driven by an longing for

3. Russell, *Human Liberation*, 20.

freedom in women's experience in today's world.[4] According to Russell, feminist liberation theologies do not begin with theory and then move to practice, rather they begin with communities of faith and struggle to ask how experience leads to new questions and ways of thinking.[5] By finding the basis for understanding liberation and oppression within the biblical narrative, Russell reveals a reliance on the Bible, which she understands to have a relationship to the life of the Christian community. Interpretations of the gospel are tested by the experience of Christian communities, and the actions of communities are tested by the biblical witness to the meaning of human liberation.[6] Hers is an inductive method where material for reflection is drawn from life experience and then related to the gospel.[7] This practical theology which brings action and reflection together is dependent upon the corporate support of the community of faith where thinking about God in light of concrete oppressive experiences is done with the intention of finding ways to express God's plan for human liberation.[8]

Russell is an example of a feminist theologian who draws theological norms from Christian theology and women's experience.[9] Like liberation theologians, Russell values the relationship of scripture and tradition, seen particularly in her conviction that biblical promises of liberation are important to theological reflection.[10] However, Russell seems aware that such a stance places her in some tension with other feminist positions:

> In the women's liberation movement there has been a lot of rejection of the Bible as the basis for theology because of the patriarchal, cultural attitudes that it reveals. Yet those who would do Christian theology cannot abandon the story of Jesus of Nazareth. They find instead that they must use the best tools of scholarship to wrestle with the texts, and to find how liberation

4. Ibid., 27.

5. Russell, *Household of Freedom*, 88.

6. Russell, *Human Liberation*, 50–51.

7. Ibid., 53.

8. Ibid., 56.

9. Young, *Feminist Theology*, 40. Young lists other feminists who work with a similar perspective: Anne E. Carr, Virginia Ramey Mollenkott, Elisabeth Moltmann-Wendel, and Patricia Wilson-Kastner.

10. Russell, *Human Liberation*, 56.

and universality apply to their own experience of longing and groaning for freedom.[11]

She is not interested in demolishing the biblical and church tradition as a source of life, but desires to "build a new house of authority" using the tools of critical analysis as well as tools for rediscovering our theology while continuing to live in the "old house."[12]

Despite the importance of the biblical tradition to Russell's system, she maintains experience as an authoritative source for theology, a position she bases upon biblical passages such as Galatians 3:28, where a community of freedom is a present experience foreshadowing God's intentions for the world.[13] Russell reminds those in the white male theological establishment who may find this appeal to experience troubling that feminist theologies, like other liberation theologies, recognize the importance of experience and context in the development of all theologies as well as in the formation of scripture, tradition, and paradigms of rationality.[14] According to her, women add their piece of experience to all the other pieces so that theology becomes more holistic and comprehensive.[15] She notes that the Christian community has always had a pattern of criteria for what is an authoritative witness to God in Jesus Christ that has included resources of scientific knowledge and human experience as well as scripture and tradition; hence Russell claims that her inductive approach to theology, which includes experience as authoritative, is no less logical or scientific than other theologies.[16]

At this point a difficulty in Russell's position begins to emerge regarding how she judges between the various authoritative sources. While she acknowledges experience as significant, the relationship of experience to other theological sources remains ambiguous: "experience, tradition, biblical witness, and intellectual research enrich each other in a rainbow of ordered (but not subordinated) diversity, in a synergetic perspective of authority in community."[17] Clearly, experience

11. Ibid., 58.

12. Russell, *Household of Freedom*, 64.

13. Ibid., 20.

14. Ibid., 17.

15. Russell, *Human Liberation*, 53.

16. Russell, *Household of Freedom*, 31.

17. Russell, "Authority and the Challenge of Feminist Interpretation," 145–46.

does not appear to be the independent grounds or sole source for her theology since she advocates "critically reflected experience" in relation to the Christian community.[18] Moreover, Russell criticizes Schüssler Fiorenza for using women's experience as a single critical principle rather than understanding both the biblical texts and women's reality as possible loci of revelation.[19] Nevertheless, it remains unclear how the many sources within Russell's position (e.g., community, biblical witness, experience, tradition) function together. Is it possible to have multiple sources that contribute to theological reflection equally without any subordination between them? Ultimately, for Russell the pattern of criteria of a particular church is not what is authoritative, but the "connection of that pattern with the divine self-revelation of God that gives it authority and limits its claims."[20] It seems that Russell wants to avoid valuing one theological source over another since she supports a coordination of many theological sources, including experience, yet desires to maintain the normativity of the Bible.[21] Russell rightly draws attention to the significance of experience for the theological project, though she does not rule out other authoritative sources, nor does she adequately explain the nature of authority, which she contends both the text and experience possess. Her integrative approach is a strength, but how the various elements operate within her system is somewhat ambivalent.

CHRISTOLOGY

Russell is less comprehensive on the topic of Christology than Schüssler Fiorenza or Ruether. Like Ruether, she finds the question of Jesus' maleness to be of central concern for Christology. According to Russell, there has always been a "scandal of particularity" associated with the cross; however, for women the scandal is not seen just in Jesus' Jewishness, but most importantly in his maleness.[22] She asks, "How is it possible for this male to be the bearer of God's togetherness with women and

18. Russell, *Household of Freedom*, 33.

19. Ibid., 68.

20. Ibid., 24.

21. Russell, "Authority," 40. Russell would rather live with the paradox of struggling against the Bible as patriarchal yet use the Bible as the source of liberation.

22. Russell, *Household of Freedom*, 137.

men when he represents only one half of the human race?"[23] Russell identifies proposed solutions, for example, one could cast off Jesus completely and look for a female savior, or merely acknowledge Jesus as a "good person" but not as representative for all of humanity.[24] Rejecting these alternatives, Russell argues that such positions appear to think of Christ in terms of his male sex alone and are a reversion to a *biological determinism*, which affirms that the most important aspect of a person is their sex or gender. Russell believes the most important aspect of ourselves is that we are accepted as subjects and persons, with biological differentiation only operating as a secondary element of who we are.[25] In distinction from many common feminist approaches, she reinterprets the meaning of Christ as the representative, asserting "that the relationship by which we also become representatives of new humanity is that of servanthood." Christ's representation frees us to be representatives of true humanity by working toward new forms of partnership.[26]

Elisabeth Schüssler Fiorenza

Fundamentally speaking, the resources for Schüssler Fiorenza's theology are women's experience and praxis. Her influential theology, principally biblical hermeneutics, starts with women's experience and ensures that texts and traditions usually considered normative are evaluated in the light of their liberative or oppressive potential.[27] Schüssler Fiorenza describes her particular perspective as a critical feminist theology of liberation that, like traditional liberation theology, addresses experience primarily in sociopolitical terms, recognizing that issues of power and domination in the world are experienced at this level.[28] Schüssler Fiorenza considers liberation theology in Latin America to attend insufficiently to the fact that the majority of the world's poor are women and children under the care of women; therefore, she argues, a different

---

23. Ibid., 137–38.
24. Ibid., 138.
25. Ibid., 139.
26. Ibid., 153.
27. Hogan, *From Women's Experience*, 100.
28. Schüssler Fiorenza, *Jesus*, 37.

theoretical framework is required.[29] According to Schüssler Fiorenza, biblical interpretation for liberation should engage in critical analysis of the "politics of otherness" inscribed in the Christian scriptures.[30] She is critical of feminist theologies that emphasize interpersonal interpretation and connectedness to the detriment of the struggle against sociopolitical, kyriarchal structures of domination.[31] By kyriarchy she means the rule of the emperor/master/lord/father/husband over his subordinates. This is not to imply that all men dominate and exploit all women without difference to culture or economic status. Whereas patriarchy implies an opposition between male and female, Schüssler Fiorenza incorporates an understanding of domination and oppression that goes beyond this; in other words, kyriarchy and patriarchy are two separate and significant terms, but kyriarchy is intended to be more comprehensive.[32] According to Schüssler Fiorenza, a sociopolitical emphasis does not exclude the specific category of *women's* experience since she understands women to share a common historical experience as an oppressed group struggling to become full human subjects. For her, this experience of solidarity as a social group is not based on biological distinctions, in contrast to Russell and Ruether, who, she insists, highlight gender dualism rather than the androcentric symbolic tradition; patriarchy rather than kyriarchy.[33]

In addition to the various differences beginning to emerge within feminist liberation theology, Schüssler Fiorenza notes a fundamental distinction between many feminist writers and liberation theologians:

29. Schüssler Fiorenza, "Politics of Otherness," 311.

30. Ibid., 312. She understands a "politics of otherness" as rooted in the Western political system whereby patriarchal domination and subordination of others is legitimated. See also Ruether, "Feminist Interpretation," 116. Similar to Schüssler Fiorenza, Ruether argues that we find patriarchy in the Bible as well as contemporary and historical Christian culture and thus demands that the patriarchal bias of scripture be judged.

31. Schüssler Fiorenza, *Jesus*, 50–53. Specifically, the work of Carter Heyward, Mary Grey, and Rita Nakashima Brock exemplify the relational approach she criticizes.

32. Schüssler Fiorenza, *Jesus*, 14. In spite of this inclusive definition, Schüssler Fiorenza speaks primarily in terms of women's oppression.

33. Schüssler Fiorenza, *In Memory of Her*, 15–17. See also Schüssler Fiorenza, "Politics of Otherness," 316–17. She advocates a feminist self-understanding that involves an "interstructuring" of sex, race, class, culture, and religion in systems of domination. Patriarchy must be understood as an "historical political system of interlocking dominations."

the use of God and the Bible in theological method. Liberation theologians are generally more optimistic than feminists, seeing the God of the Bible as a God of the oppressed and the Bible as a weapon in the struggle for liberation.[34] Schüssler Fiorenza stands in agreement with black theologian James Cone who considers the Bible and biblical faith as sources alongside other sources, these being our political situation and experience.[35] Possessing a liberationist perspective while at the same time having difficulty accepting liberation theology's view of scripture, Schüssler Fiorenza believes a feminist hermeneutic is required which shares in the critical methods of historical scholarship on the one hand and the theological goals of liberation theologies on the other.[36] As liberation theology stresses God's liberating activity in history and singles out the Exodus narrative as a canon within a canon, so feminist liberation theologians seek to identify a liberating theme, tradition, text, or principle as a hermeneutical key in order to reclaim the authority of scripture for their task.[37] The particular brand of critical feminist hermeneutic of liberation Schüssler Fiorenza seeks to create incorporates a mode of biblical interpretation that "can do justice to women's experiences of the Bible as a thoroughly patriarchal book ... as well as to women's experience of the Bible as a source of empowerment and vision in our struggles for liberation."[38] She opposes such post-biblical feminists as Daphne Hampson and Mary Daly who place more emphasis on contemporary religious experiences of women rather than the Christian past, finding that their position devalues women's authentic history within the biblical tradition and negates positive experiences contemporary women have in biblical religion.[39]

While women as a group share a common experience, Schüssler Fiorenza concedes that the individual perception and interpretation

---

34. Schüssler Fiorenza, *Bread Not Stone*, 52.

35. Ibid. See below for further explanation of Cone's position.

36. Schüssler Fiorenza, *In Memory of Her*, 77.

37. Schüssler Fiorenza, "Politics of Otherness," 314.

38. Schüssler Fiorenza, *Bread Not Stone*, 5. Schüssler Fiorenza describes her position as a "feminist critical theology of liberation." This definition grows out of her experience as a Catholic Christian woman who is indebted to historical-critical scholarship, critical theory, and political as well as liberation theology. See also ibid., xii.

39. Schüssler Fiorenza, *In Memory of Her*, xlix.

of women's experience varies considerably.[40] Therefore she insists that this experience must be systemically reflected upon if it is to become the starting point of feminist theology.[41] Feminist liberation rhetoric must adopt a systemic analytic that is adequate to critically explore the diverse everyday experiences of "wo/men."[42] She also roots this understanding of experience in a form of community, what she considers her hermeneutical center for feminist biblical interpretation. She names this community the *ekklēsia of women*, or "women-church," which she describes as a radical democracy of self-identified women and women-identified men in biblical religion.[43] In a sense, her understanding of experience both acknowledges variations as well as tries to maintain some order to the concept by reflecting systemically upon it and grounding this reflection in the community of women-church. Within the context of women-church, personally and politically reflected experience of oppression and liberation becomes the criterion of appropriateness for biblical interpretation and evaluation of biblical authority claims.[44] Therefore, she concludes that "only the nonsexist and nonpatriarchal traditions of the Bible and the nonoppressive traditions of biblical interpretation have the theological authority of revelation if the Bible is not to continue as a tool for the oppression of women."[45]

By observing what is authoritative for Schüssler Fiorenza's biblical hermeneutics, one sees her reliance upon experience for interpretation. Experience is the ultimate authority for what is considered to be the Word of God, that is, the experiences of women under oppression as well as experiences of God among women struggling for liberation, considered systemically from within the context of women-church, determine which biblical texts are to be used in theology. The litmus test for "invoking the Scripture as the Word of God must be whether or not biblical texts and traditions seek to end relations of domination and exploitation."[46] Yet, it remains unclear what Schüssler Fiorenza

40. Ibid., 3.

41. Schüssler Fiorenza, *Jesus*, 12.

42. Ibid., 61. For her use of the term "wo/men" see 191 n. 1. The word is meant to be inclusive of all women and oppressed and marginalized men.

43. Schüssler Fiorenza, *Bread Not Stone*, xiv.

44. Schüssler Fiorenza, *In Memory of Her*, 32.

45. Schüssler Fiorenza, *Bread Not Stone*, 60.

46. ibid., xiii. This central point raises the question of why issues of domination make up the criteria for acceptability. What is the source and authority for such criteria?

means by a systemic analytic and precisely how the community will function in her hermeneutical system. From what we can gather, Schüssler Fiorenza's position is not so different from what we find in Ruether in that she finally rejects those biblical texts that conflict with the experience of women under kyriarchal social systems, thus creating a canon within a canon. Like Ruether, she considers some texts usable and others unusable based upon experience.[47] In line with such a hermeneutic, Schüssler Fiorenza understands the Bible not as a timeless archetype, but as a structuring prototype that is open to its own critical transformation.[48]

CHRISTOLOGY

As mentioned above, Schüssler Fiorenza is critical of some feminist theologians who emphasize a relational framework, particularly in the area of Christology. While she supports the move from an individualistic or "heroic" Christology to a more communal understanding, she insists that it be conceptualized in sociopolitical categories rather than personalistic terms.[49] Moreover, she considers the question, "Can a male savior redeem women?" to be the wrong question, based upon a frame of reference that assumes femininity and masculinity are ontologically predetermined.[50] According to her, such views are caught up in the dynamics of a sex/gender system that fails to understand the concept of "humanity" and reinscribes the kyriarchal frame of reference which understands gender as a biological given.[51] Consequently, Schüssler Fiorenza finds inspiration for her Christology from a speech given in 1852 by Sojourner Truth, "Ain't I a Woman?" She argues that Truth applies a critical evaluation to those people who have articulated christological doctrine (Schüssler Fiorenza would advocate a critical evaluation of the doctrine itself as well) and roots her christological understanding upon her own experience of liberation as a source of

47. See Schüssler Fiorenza, ed., *Searching the Scriptures*. This work reflects an openness to utilizing sources outside the traditional canon, although it remains unclear precisely which sources she would employ.

48. Schüssler Fiorenza, *Bread Not Stone*, xvii.

49. Schüssler Fiorenza, *Jesus*, 54–55.

50. Ibid., 45.

51. Ibid., 47.

empowerment. Truth experienced Jesus as present in her greatest hour of need, thus anchoring "the articulation of christology in the revelatory struggle of women for survival and well-being."[52] Although Truth does not call for a development of a women's Christology in place of a kyriarchal Christology constructed by male clerics, she insists that the best response is a praxis of liberation.[53] Therefore, Schüssler Fiorenza understands a feminist liberationist exploration of Christian scriptures as beginning not with the biblical text but with a critical articulation and analysis of the experiences of wo/men.[54] Rather than extensively developing her own christological construction, Schüssler Fiorenza provides insight into how a feminist liberationist must approach the biblical text from which any Christology might be developed.

Rosemary Radford Ruether

Extremely influential upon the whole of feminist theology has been the work of Rosemary Radford Ruether. Her contribution to the field spans decades and her numerous writings make her work a necessary part of feminist theological discussion. Ruether's position reflects a correlationist method that places the full humanity of women in critical relationship with the practices of the historic Christian tradition.[55] Her theology utilizes a prophetic-liberating tradition, rooted in scripture, which understands women as one of the oppressed whom God will liberate and vindicate, thereby making the critical principle of her feminist theology the "promotion of the full humanity of women."[56] Ruether is intensely critical of what she describes as the patriarchalization of Christianity and how it has led to the exclusion of women from the shaping of theology as well as to the diminishment of their full humanity. In light of these factors, the role of experience becomes crucial to her theology. More precisely, *women's* experience: "It is this process of the critical naming of women's experience of androcentric culture that

---

52. Ibid., 59.

53. Ibid., 60. See also Boff, "Methodology of the Theology of Liberation," 10. At the root of liberation theology's method is a *"nexus with concrete praxis."*

54. Schüssler Fiorenza, *Jesus*, 61.

55. Fulkerson, *Changing the Subject*, 36.

56. Ruether, *Sexism and God-Talk*, 24, 18.

we refer to when we say that women's experience is an interpretive key for feminist theology."[57]

What is meant by *women's* experience? Ruether maintains that biological differences are not irrelevant; however, in speaking of women's experience biological differences in themselves are not meant, but rather, women's experiences created by the social appropriation of these differences in a male-dominated society.[58] Though there are cross-cultural differences within women's experience which Ruether acknowledges, she asserts that patriarchy provides enough of a common body of experiences for women from different cultures.[59] In contrast to traditional Christian theology, which has claimed the white male experience as universal for humanity, Ruether maintains a common understanding of women's experience in conjunction with a sensitivity to the variety of experience expressed in feminist theology.[60]

Ruether's understanding of patriarchy and its distortion of the Christian tradition influences her understanding of theological sources, thus leading to a particular perception of interpretation. In accordance with a liberationist perspective, Ruether contends that so-called objective sources are not unaffected by human experience:

> Just as the foundational revelatory experience is available only in a transformative dialectic between experience and accumulated interpretive keys, so it, in turn, becomes an interpretive key which interacts with and continues to be meaningful through its ability to make ongoing experience of the individual in the community meaningful.[61]

For Ruether, all religious texts and traditions are finally experiential in that primary revelatory experiences become codified in particular texts and traditions. Therefore, sources such as scripture and tradition are considered "codified collective human experience."[62] Forms of codified tradition reach back to their roots in human experience and are renewed

57. Ruether, "Feminist Interpretation," 114.

58. Ibid., 113.

59. Ibid., 115.

60. Ruether, "Future of Feminist Theology," 704.

61. Ruether, "Feminist Interpretation," 112.

62. Ruether, *Sexism and God-Talk*, 12. See also Hogan, *From Women's Experience*, 106.

through the test of experience. This experience includes an experience of the divine as well as of oneself in relationship with the world.[63]

Ruether grounds her theology upon sources that promote the full humanity of women and considers a religious tradition to be vital as long as its "revelatory pattern can be reproduced generation after generation and continues to speak to individuals in the community and provide for them the redemptive meaning of individual and collective experience."[64] If a particular religious symbol no longer speaks to experience, it is dead and should be discarded or altered.[65] Ruether does not cast off Christian scripture completely, rather, she sees scripture as normative, not in the sense of infallible truths disclosed beyond human experience or as unique experiences incomparable with other experiences, but as foundational memory such as any foundational collection of stories, laws, and ethical norms found in any community.[66] The role of experience in Ruether's theology is significant, serving as the basis for what stays and what remains as viable sources for the construction of theology. Her book *Womanguides* is a collection of various sources that she deems usable, thus creating a new canon for theology.[67] This book includes sources that coincide with women's experience in such a way that the full humanity of women is promoted, thereby including texts from within and outside the Christian tradition. Although she acknowledges Christian scripture as normative in some way, Ruether states that what is ultimately normative for feminist theology is the redemptive future.[68]

If the redemptive future is ultimately normative (over Christian scriptures or other religious traditions) from what sources is such a future perceived and developed? If her criterion for what is usable is that which promotes the full humanity of women, how does she determine

---

63. Ruether, "Feminist Interpretation," 111.

64. Ruether, *Sexism and God-Talk*, 15–16.

65. Ruether, "Feminist Interpretation," 111.

66. Ruether, "Is Feminism the End?" 397.

67. Ruether, *Womanguides*.

68. Ruether, "Is Feminism the End?" 398. See also Ruether, *Women and Redemption*. Ruether sees herself as similar to Letty Russell who she describes as working from the perspective of redemption or New Creation (*Women and Redemption*, 212). It is a working from the "other side," from the vision of the redemptive transformation of creation (ibid., 222–23).

what is promotive of full humanity? Such a position regarding usable and unusable sources could lead to relativism, at least regarding how sources are determined and, like Hampson, where a particular set of sources are not considered conclusive.[69]

CHRISTOLOGY

Ruether's essay "Can a Male Savior Save Women?" has been important for feminist Christology, alleging that the problems in Christology for feminist theology are primarily related to the issue of the maleness of Jesus Christ. Because she understands Christology to have been affected by the system of hierarchy inherent in the early church, Ruether first considers the validity of alternative Christologies that developed at that time, androgynous and spirit Christologies, neither of which are finally satisfactory to her.[70] In light of the problems with these alternative Christologies, what can feminists do? Ruether suggests a re-encounter with the Jesus of the Synoptic Gospels: "Once the mythology about Jesus as Messiah or divine *Logos*, with its traditional masculine imagery, is stripped off, the Jesus of the synoptic Gospels can be recognized as a figure remarkably compatible with feminism."[71] She emphasizes Jesus' message expressed in his ministry rather than his biological particularities and identifies Jesus as the iconoclastic prophet.[72] Jesus renews the prophetic vision whereby existing social and religious hierarchies are overturned; Jesus revises God-language by calling God the familiar *Abba*; Jesus speaks of the Messiah as a servant instead of a king; and

69. See Ruether, *Womanguides*, xi–xii. This volume is a collection of various sources, which Ruether states is not definitive. She recognizes that another person may have put together a similar volume differently.

70. Ruether, *Sexism and God-Talk*, 130–35. The trouble with androgynous Christologies is that the androgynous Christ still is associated with the male Jesus. Moreover, whether they identify woman with the lower material nature or with the higher spiritual qualities, androgynous Christologies fail to attribute to woman a full human potential. Spirit Christologies involve seeing Christ as a power that continues to be revealed in persons, both male and female. Ruether refers to the Montanists as one example of this type of Christology, illustrating a possible downfall of these Christologies in that they may come to be viewed as revolts against Christianity because they split off the historical Jesus from the ongoing work of the Spirit.

71. Ruether, *Sexism and God-Talk*, 135.

72. Ruether, *To Change the World*, 53: "The messianic prophet proclaims his message as an iconoclastic critique of existing elites, particularly religious elites."

Jesus' interaction with women shows the significant role they play in the vindication of the lowly and oppressed (e.g., Samaritan woman, Syrophoenician woman).[73] According to Ruether, Jesus is able to speak as liberator not because he is male, but rather because he renounces the systems of domination. Therefore, theologically speaking, Jesus' maleness has no ultimate significance. Ruether states that it does have social significance in the sense that Jesus manifests the *kenosis of patriarchy* by announcing a new humanity that discards hierarchical privilege and speaks on behalf of the lowly.[74] Elizabeth Johnson also identifies *kenosis of patriarchy* as what the cross symbolizes: the self-emptying of male dominating power in favor of the new humanity of compassionate service and mutual empowerment.[75]

The significance of Christ is related to Ruether's eschatological vision, given partial form in the exemplary prophet (Jesus) who manifests the shape of the new humanity. Christ is a paradigm of liberated humanity that challenges us to liberate others, and the Christian community continues Christ's identity. In Ruether's understanding, liberation and redemption come through Christ, not once for all, but rather, through the human community throughout time identifying with Christ who calls us to yet incompleted dimensions of human liberation.[76] "To encapsulate Jesus himself as God's 'last word' and 'once-for-all' disclosure of God, located in a remote past and institutionalized in a cast of Christian teacher, is to repudiate the spirit of Jesus and to recapitulate the position against which he himself protests."[77]

Liberation Theology

We have gained some insight into the theological systems of three important feminist liberation theologians. Let us now consider the influences upon these women, starting first with that which gives the sociopolitical perspective inherent to their positions, that is, liberation theology. Liberation theology was born in the slums of Latin America

73. Ruether, *Sexism and God-Talk*, 136.

74. Ibid., 137.

75. Johnson, *She Who Is*, 161.

76. Ruether, *Sexism and God-Talk*, 138.

77. Ibid., 122.

nearly thirty years ago and has found expression in the First World in various forms, including in those feminists who are expressly liberation theologians as well as many other feminist theologians who operate from a liberationist perspective to some degree, thereby driving us to consider the methodology of liberation theology in order to understand how these feminist theologians are influenced by liberation theology and employ its methodology within their own systematic theology.[78]

Latin American Liberation Theology

Liberation theology originates with the poor, interpreting the Christian faith out of the experience of the poor and oppressed of this world.[79] Liberation theologian Juan Segundo considers the specific approach of liberation theology to require a special methodology, which is described as the *hermeneutical circle*.[80] Segundo outlines two preconditions for such a circle: questions and suspicions arising out of our real, present situation; and new interpretations of the Bible resulting from

---

78. Some feminist theologians are critical of traditional liberation theology for neglecting women's issues. This criticism may be justified in that most liberation theologies have tended to focus specifically upon the plight of the poor without regard to gender issues. However, more recent liberation theology expresses a wider concern about other forms of oppression besides economic, such as cultural, religious, and gender. See the preface by Jon Sobrino in *Systematic Theology: Perspectives from Liberation Theology* and the revised introduction in Gutiérrez, *Theology of Liberation*. Both acknowledge the intolerable situation of women and the need for liberation theology to address it. Related to this concern is the specific role of Latin American feminists (a notable example is Elsa Tamez) who tend to place the women's agenda within an overall liberation context. It does not compete with economic or political liberation. See also Berryman, *Liberation Theology*, 173. Berryman finds Ruether more radical than Latin American feminists because she questions scriptural symbols themselves as well as theology and church practice. He believes such a radical approach reflects the deep-seated nature of patriarchy over against imperialism and class oppression (178).

79. Berryman, *Liberation Theology*, 4. See also Sobrino, *Systematic Theologyy*, ix: "So long as oppression exists, there must be a theology of liberation." William Dyrness notes the distinction between various liberation theologians: (1) radical theologians who are professors and academics and are more open to Marxist categories; (2) moderates who are pastoral theologians like Gutiérrez, Segundo, and Leonardo Boff and are concerned with daily life of the people and take seriously the scriptures; and (3) populists who are critical of both Marxism and capitalism and emphasize popular religiosity (Dyrness, *Learning about Theology*, 82).

80. Segundo, *Liberation of Theology*, 8.

these questions and suspicions. In addition to these preconditions,[81] he describes four "decisive" factors of the circle: (1) there is an *experience* of reality that leads to ideological suspicion, followed by (2) the *application* of this suspicion to theology out of which flows (3) a new *experience* of theological reality that leads to the suspicion that prevailing interpretations of scripture have not accounted for important data. Finally, the hermeneutical circle is complete in (4) the "new *way* [hermeneutic] of interpreting the fountainhead of our faith (i.e., scripture) with the new elements at our disposal."[82] Similarly, Gustavo Gutiérrez describes the hermeneutical circle of liberation theology as beginning with *praxis*, specifically, a Christian practice of commitment and prayer in the formula of Augustine—we believe in order that we may understand—and then moving to the second stage of *reflection* upon that praxis. This circular relationship is crucial to liberation theology and underscores the unity of orthodoxy and orthopraxis.[83] One must keep in mind that this hermeneutical circle arises out of a particular experience and context, that of the oppressed and poor in Latin America; therefore, liberation theology intends the necessary starting point of theological reflection to be primarily the destructive poverty resulting from unjust structures, which creates a poor social class that must be liberated from its plight.[84] The commitment of faith referred to in Gutiérrez's understanding of the hermeneutical circle is, in fact, participation in the process of liberation and commitment to the oppressed.[85] In the words of Gutiérrez, whom many consider the father of liberation theology,

> The theology of liberation attempts to reflect on the experience and meaning of the faith based on the commitment to abolish injustice and to build a new society; this theology must be

81. Not unlike Rudolf Bultmann, who argued that there were pre-theoretical factors that influence interpretation, liberation theologians understand there to be a pre-theoretical commitment which for them is a precommitment to liberation. However, distinct from Bultmann, for whom the play was between scripture and one's own existential self-understanding, liberation theology holds that the circle is between past readings of scripture and those of the present. Dyrness, *Learning about Theology*, 86, 88.

82. Segundo, *Liberation of Theology*, 9 (italics added).

83. Gutiérrez, *Theology of Liberation*, xxxiii–xxxiv. For liberation theology, truth is discovered only in practice. See also Dyrness, *Learning about Theology*, 88.

84. Dyrness, *Learning about Theology*, 80–81.

85. Boff and Boff, *Introducing Liberation Theology*, 22.

> verified by the practice of that commitment, by active, effective
> participation in the struggle which the exploited social classes
> have undertaken against their oppressors.[86]

More recent analysis of liberation theology describes the methodology in terms of two viewpoints. The first, and ultimately the root of
liberation theology, is "objective" faith, that is, revelation, God's word.
The second is "subjective faith," which is the viewpoint of the oppressed
and is connected to the first.[87] With these two viewpoints in mind,
liberation theology attempts to develop a distinct starting point that
combines theoretical and practical elements: faith is the *formal* starting
point and praxis is the *material* starting point. In other words, this starting point combines the hermeneutic principle and the raw material.
However, these starting points are not at odds with each other. "There
is no contradiction here, but only an interrelationship of distinct 'in-
stances' standing in reciprocal relation and duly ordered."[88] Such an
approach necessitates a dialectical logic which is reflected in the critical concept of the hermeneutical circle, existing between the poor and
the Word, relating past and present, where people find their experience
reflected in the Bible, understand the Bible in terms of that experience,
and interpret that experience in terms of biblical symbols. There is a
movement from experience to text, then back to experience.[89] Within
this circle, the continuing changes in biblical interpretation are dictated
by continuing changes in present-day reality.

Another way to describe the hermeneutical circle might be as a
movement from new reality, to the Bible, to a changed reality, to the
Bible, and so on.[90] Very much in keeping with Segundo's position,
Schüssler Fiorenza describes biblical interpretation in liberation theology as beginning with an experience or analysis of the social reality
that leads to suspicion about our real situation and the application of
this ideological suspicion to other structures, then to experiencing our
theological reality in a different way, which leads to the suspicion that
the prevailing interpretation of the Bible has not taken into account

---

86. Gutiérrez, *Theology of Liberation*, 174.

87. C. Boff, "Methodology," 2.

88. Ibid.

89. Berryman, *Liberation Theology*, 60.

90. Segundo, *Liberation of Theology*, 8.

important pieces. These insights are then brought to bear on our interpretation of scripture.[91]

Liberation theology gives particular preference to those biblical themes most appropriate for the poor, such as the Exodus narrative and the Beatitudes. Nevertheless, liberation hermeneutics seeks to interrogate the Word without dictating a response. It is open to new and challenging messages because the primacy in its dialectic belongs undeniably to God's word (primacy of value and methodological primacy).[92] A later emphasis of liberation theology, this openness is achieved because there is a posture of contemplation before God that is prior to action and combines with action as a response to the oppression of the poor, from which all theology is derived.[93] Likewise, a tenet of liberation theology, stemming from Gutiérrez, maintains theology not as the primary datum, but rather, as expressing a fundamental spiritual reality, a biblical sense of the Spirit as the principle of life.[94] Gutiérrez's book *We Drink from Our Own Wells* is an elaboration of liberation spirituality that challenges the notion that liberation theology is merely a political movement. Such spirituality is an experience of Christians who are committed to the process of liberation and is part and parcel of the purpose of liberation theology.[95]

James Cone's Black Liberation Theology

It may be helpful to consider briefly a North American version of liberation theology besides the feminist perspective, one that Segundo claims is an example of theology that completes the hermeneutic circle.[96] James

91. Schüssler Fiorenza, *Bread Not Stone*, 50. Although her approach is very similar to the methodology developed by Segundo, Schüssler Fiorenza would not adopt his term "fountainhead of our faith" to describe the Bible. Thus, she reveals a key distinction between Latin American liberation theologians and feminist liberation theologians.

92. C. Boff, "Methodology," 16.

93. L. Boff, "Originality," 40–41. See also Gutiérrez, *God of Life*, 145: all "talk about God presupposes practice, that is, the silence of contemplation and commitment." This spiritual aspect expressed in more recent liberation theology, has not been influential upon feminist liberation theology, which took its lead from earlier works.

94. L. Boff, "Originality," 40.

95. Gutiérrez, *We Drink from Our Own Wells*, 1.

96. Particularly in Cone, *Black Theology of Liberation* (Segundo, *Liberation of Theology*, 25).

Cone was the first to develop a black theology of liberation, and, like his Latin American colleagues, he sees the central message of the Bible as the proclamation of liberation.[97] Although the sources of scripture and tradition bear witness to the higher source of revelation particularized and universalized in Jesus Christ, Cone considers sources such as the history and culture of oppressed peoples to have equal or greater weight.[98] The Bible is the indispensable witness to God's revelation in Jesus, and is therefore a primary source for Christian thinking. However, revelation is incomprehensible without the "concrete manifestation of revelation in the black community as seen in black experience, black history, and black culture."[99] Because Cone's fundamental ontology originates in a view of the "black oppressed" and their struggle for being against the force of non-being, he employs a method of correlation that seeks theological answers to the experience of suffering specific to black people, incorporating scripture and contemporary existence as corroborative and correlative authorities.[100]

While Cone believes black theology must take black experience as its starting point, he does not necessarily intend the starting point to be understood as an indubitable foundation.[101] For Cone, the starting point is dialectically related to experience and divine revelation gives it validity.[102] "Revelation is God's self-disclosure to humankind *in the context of liberation*. To know God is to know God's work of liberation in behalf of the oppressed."[103] In other words, because Cone has identified

97. Cone, *God of the Oppressed*, 37.

98. Ibid., 9. Other sources Cone uses for understanding black experience are black sermons, spirituals, and tales. For further discussion of Cone's sources for black theology see *Black Theology of Liberation*, 23–35. Segundo describes Cone as beginning with the experience, the history, and the culture of black people rather than scripture, fully realizing "that this will scandalize academic theology which has a long tradition of proceeding quite differently. But he is not alone in such an approach, and he can cite Tillich in his favor" (Segundo, *Liberation of Theology*, 30).

99. Cone, *Black Theology of Liberation*, 29.

100. Stewart, "Method of Correlation," 32–34. Stewart's identification of Cone's ontology of the "black oppressed" reveals similarities to Anderson's discussion of "ontological blackness." Cone's ontological emphasis is also in keeping with a Tillichian understanding of theological language as symbolic: "blackness is an ontological symbol" (*Black Theology of Liberation*, 7).

101. Cone, *God of the Oppressed*, 17–18; *Black Theology of Liberation*, 23.

102. Cone, *God of the Oppressed*, 82.

103. Cone, *Black Theology of Liberation*, 45.

the central message of scripture to be God's liberation for oppressed people, and due to the fact that he understands the core of black experience to be suffering, the God of the Bible makes the experience of black people a valid place to start theological reflection. His system gives due weight to revelation; however, he argues that an appeal to the objectivity of revelation ultimately fails because all theological talk about God's revelation is filtered through human experience.[104] Consequently, based on these two aspects of his theology, black experience and God's revelation in scripture, Cone considers the Christian theologian's hermeneutical task to be defined by the oppressed's struggle for liberation, while seeking to "adhere to the delicate balance of social existence and divine revelation."[105]

The Method of Correlation

We have examined liberation theology in its feminist and Latin American expressions, finding that it employs a method of correlation as part of its theological system evident in the drive to correlate human experience to the biblical tradition. In feminist liberation theology, the principle of women's experience is utilized as the predominant component in a correlative method that seeks some reciprocity between the horizon of the investigator today and the teaching of the textual expression of tradition.[106] Furthermore, this correlation consists in establishing a reciprocal relationship between present experience and some aspect of Christian tradition that then becomes normative for interpreting the whole of that tradition.[107] Specifically, we find Russell describing her own method as correlating the promise of mended creation with the feminist search for human wholeness and partnership in all creation.[108] Schüssler Fiorenza works with women's present experience of oppression and the reconstructed history of the social context of the Bible. In other words, she correlates experience and reconstructed history.[109]

---

104. Cone, *God of the Oppressed*, 43.

105. Ibid., 98.

106. Martin, *Feminist Question*, 210.

107. Ibid., 216.

108. Russell, *Household of Freedom*, 68.

109. Martin, *Feminist Question*, 216. Although Schüssler Fiorenza would object to Martin's identification of her method as correlative, he argues that she develops an

Ruether has a liberationist model that correlates experience and the text, identifying the correlation between biblical and feminist critical principles in the prophetic-messianic tradition.[110] Though widely used and accepted in a variety of theological styles and projects, the method of correlation is most commonly associated with Paul Tillich, who developed it in an effort to rediscover the lost religious dimension of cultural life.[111] Therefore, we must consider Tillich's work in more detail.

The Method of Correlation in Paul Tillich

An attempt to connect religion and culture places the method of correlation in the service of apologetic theology, illustrated by Tillich's concern that the Christian message be expressed so as to offer some answers to present-day questions.[112] Tillich even calls apologetic theology "answering theology," that is, it answers the questions implied in the human situation with the means provided by that situation.[113] He claims that systematic theology has always, more or less consciously, used the method of correlation as a necessary part of an apologetic view.[114] Therefore, Tillich considers correlation as old as theology and

---

analysis of women's experience as an adequate correlate and uses this to establish the "facts" of history. See also Tolbert, "Defining the Problem," 124. Tolbert is critical of any reconstruction acting as the basis for Christian faith. According to her such an approach is ultimately unreliable. It is for this very reason that Martin prefers Ruether since he considers her position more tied to the biblical text than Schüssler Fiorenza's. However, although Ruether seeks a correlation between experience and the text, her conclusions about what is usable and unusable scripture are similar to Schüssler Fiorenza's such that their positions do not seem to differ significantly. We recall that Schüssler Fiorenza's *Searching the Scriptures* advocates an openness to using sources outside the biblical canon, and Ruether has edited a collection of sources for feminist theology that includes several non-biblical materials. Perhaps Martin is right to judge any correlation that links experience and texts as superior to one that merely links experience to a reconstructed history, but the end result in the cases of Ruether and Schüssler Fiorenza are rather alike, despite any differences in their articulated approaches.

110. Ruether, "Feminist Interpretation," 117.

111. Clayton, *Concept of Correlation*, 5. Tillich's approach echoes Schleiermacher's own effort to develop an alliance between religion and culture.

112. Kelsey, *Fabric of Paul Tillich's Theology*, 4.

113. Tillich, *Systematic Theology*, 1:6.

114. Tillich, *Systematic Theology*, 1:68.

believes he is doing nothing original, but rather, understands his task as making explicit the implications of older, apologetic theologies.[115]

Tillich's earlier thought could be considered somewhat dialectical, and it is this dialectical method which was an important first step toward an eventual method of correlation.[116] In contrast to Karl Barth, whose dialectic theology Tillich describes as a supernatural theology that seeks "to protect the divinity of the event from being diluted with human possibilities," Tillich argues for a true dialectic theology that maintains that the "*question* about the divine possibility is a human possibility."[117] In other words, for a person to be able to ask about God means that one must experience God as the goal of a possible question. His dialectical approach is influenced by Hegel and entails the identification of polarized alternatives and a third way between them, a process characteristic of Tillich's whole system.[118] Most often the principle of correlation is associated with creating a relation between philosophy and theology whereby philosophy makes an analysis of the human situation from which existential questions arise and theology provides the answers. However, this is only one instance of correlation. It can also occur between faith and reason, history and revelation, humanity and God.[119] The inclusive character of correlation means there is a relationship between religion and culture generally and not just between theology and philosophy.[120]

In its most basic sense, Tillich's method of correlation is a way of uniting the message and the situation, trying to "correlate the questions implied in the situation with the answers implied in the message."[121] Correlation is a unity of the dependence and independence of two factors, or to put it another way, an interdependence of two independent factors.[122] In using the method of correlation, systematic theology makes an analysis of the human situation out of which existential questions arise and then demonstrates symbols of the Christian mes-

---

115. Tillich, *Systematic Theology*, 2:18.

116. Clayton, *Concept of Correlation*, 169.

117. Tillich, "What Is Wrong?" 109–10.

118. Heron, *Century of Protestant Theology*, 138.

119. Mondin, *Principle of Analogy*, 128–29.

120. Clayton, *Concept of Correlation*, 16.

121. Tillich, *Systematic Theology*, 1:8.

122. Ibid., 2:14.

sage as answers to these questions. Although question and answer are independent of each other, there is mutual dependence between them. In other words, with respect to content, answers are dependent on the revelatory events upon which Christianity is based, and with respect to form, on the structure of the questions.[123] Moreover, question and answer are also independent in that it is impossible to derive one from the other, that is, existential questions are not the source of revelatory answers.[124] For instance, Tillich describes the human situation as one characterized by finitude, estrangement, and non-being. He believes religion must respond to the existential situation; thus, Tillich identifies "God" as the answer to the questions implied in human finitude.[125] Religion is about that which concerns us ultimately, that is, our being. This is the first criterion of theology for Tillich, that the object of theology is what concerns us ultimately.[126] The second criterion is that the ultimate concern determines our being or non-being, where being is not taken in the sense of existence, but in terms of what is ultimate, total, infinite.[127] God is identified as "being-itself" or the "ground of being."[128] Hence, ontologically speaking, the idea of God is the correlate of our existential awareness of finitude.[129] This concept is extended in

123. Ibid., 1:70–72.

124. Ibid., 2:14–15.

125. Ibid., 1:234.

126. Ibid., 1:15. Tillich claims that his "ultimate concern" is rather near to what Schleiermacher meant by "feeling of absolute dependence" (47). Scholars disagree on how closely Schleiermacher and Tillich actually are. Clayton understands Tillich to describe the concept of "ultimate concern" as a phenomenological description of religious commitment in the sense that it describes the sort of commitment the religious person exhibits toward the object of his commitment. It says nothing of the content of the object. Clayton finds this concept quite distinct from Schleiermacher's feeling of absolute dependence (Clayton, *Concept of Correlation*, 109). On the other hand, McKelway sees similarities between the two. Tillich's criterion of theological statements, "ultimate concern," is parallel to Schleiermacher's use of "feeling of absolute dependence." Since both concern human self-interpretation, we could say they start with anthropology (McKelway, *Systematic Theology of Paul Tillich*, 20).

127. Tillich, *Systematic Theology*, 1:17.

128. Ibid., 1:261, 264. "The religious word for what is called the ground of being is 'God'" (173). There are radically immanental themes in Tillich's doctrine that lead to confusion on his understandings of immanence and transcendence. See Taylor, *Paul Tillich*, 23.

129. Macquarrie, *Twentieth-Century Religious Thought*, 371.

Tillich's *The Courage to Be* where he describes God, being-itself, as the ultimate source of power for a self-affirmation or courage that is able to resist non-being and meaninglessness.[130]

Tillich's method of correlation involves many sources for theology (e.g., Bible, church history, history of religion, and history of culture), but Tillich considers the basic source to be the Bible as it contains the original witness of the revealing events.[131] As the setting for the theologian and the primary source of the existential questions, the broadest source is culture.[132] While the human situation plays an important role in Tillich's system as one half of correlation, it is distinct from human "experience." Tillich considers experience to be the medium through which theological sources speak to us, and just about anything can serve as a medium of revelation, such as nature, persons, history, and words.[133] Feminist theologian Judith Plaskow understands Tillich as distinguishing experience from the content of theology. According to her, in Tillich's system, experience is a medium through which the contents of theology are received; therefore, the contents are only meaningful to one who participates in them through experience. Sources are given to experience, not created by it, nor does experience add up to Christian revelation. The medium may color the interpretation but never intentionally.[134] In addition to the sources and medium for theology, Tillich recognizes the necessity of a norm, which he considers to be the "New Being in Jesus as the Christ as our ultimate concern."[135] The norm stands over the sources and medium as the criterion of each.[136] The content of this norm is derived from the Bible, and collective and individual experience are the mediums through which the norm is received and

130. Tillich, *Courage to Be*, 166–67. Tillich's characteristic approach is reflected in this work where he identifies two alternatives, the courage to be as oneself and the courage to be as a part, and devises a third way between them by reuniting the two sides (90).

131. Tillich, *Systematic Theology*, 1:41; Kelsey, *Fabric of Paul Tillich's Theology*, 2. See also Thomas, "Method and Structure," 95. Thomas wonders why Tillich does not refer to the Bible more often and more explicitly if it is indeed his basic source.

132. McKelway, *Systematic Theology of Paul Tillich*, 51.

133. Tillich, *Systematic Theology*, 1:46, 131–39.

134. Plaskow, *Sin, Sex and Grace*, 97. See also Thomas, "Method and Structure," 93–94.

135. Tillich, *Systematic Theology*, 1:56.

136. McKelway, *Systematic Theology of Paul Tillich*, 56.

interpreted. The norm grows within the medium of experience, but at the same time is the criterion of any experience.[137] Experience receives, not produces the event of Jesus as the Christ.[138] Simply put, answers are contained in revelatory events and are taken by systematic theology "*from* the sources, *through* the medium, *under* the norm."[139]

CHRISTOLOGY

To understand the purpose of Jesus Christ in Tillich's scheme, we must assess the state of the human being, which Tillich understands to be that of estrangement, implying much of what is meant by sin.[140] The Christ brings a new state of affairs as the "New Being."[141] In Christ the "Essential God-Manhood" appeared in existence, was subjected to its conditions, yet without being conquered by them overcame estrangement.[142] Tillich understands the church to mediate this type of courage by preserving its concrete symbols and through preaching "the Crucified who cried to God who remained his God after the God of confidence had left him in the darkness of doubt and meaninglessness."[143] The reality of the New Being which conquers existential estrangement makes faith possible because faith is the experience of this power.[144] Therefore, to experience New Being in Jesus as the Christ is to experience the power in him and in everyone who participates in him.[145] Consequently, the atonement is the effect of New Being on those grasped by it in their state of estrangement.[146] Being drawn into the power of New Being in Christ

137. Tillich, *Systematic Theology*, 1:59.

138. Ibid., 1:52.

139. Ibid., 1:72.

140. Ibid., 2:51–53; Plaskow, *Sin, Sex and Grace*, 115–16. Plaskow finds Tillich's doctrine of sin as providing some categories that are more likely to be associated with women than with men. For instance, "uncreative weakness" characterizes sin as a contradiction of our essential nature, a lacking unity with the creative powers of life. See also Saiving, "Human Situation."

141. Tillich, *Systematic Theology*, 2:112.

142. Ibid., 2:113–14.

143. Tillich, *Courage to Be*, 188.

144. Tillich, *Systematic Theology*, 2:131; *Courage to Be*, 172.

145. Tillich, *Systematic Theology*, 2:144.

146. Ibid., 2:196–97.

makes faith possible and makes one justified.[147] It is a power beyond us that heals existential conflicts and sin, understood as estrangement from oneself, others, and the ground of being. It answers our ultimate concern and the quest for the ground of being.[148]

Limitations of the Correlation Method

In order to evaluate the effectiveness of the method of correlation for feminist theology, we will place it alongside a discussion of Tillich's own method and the types of critique it has received. Tillich, more than feminist theologians, describes a method of correlation that stresses the reciprocal nature of theological sources; however, such an approach is applied inconsistently. Feminist theologians seem to have adopted Tillich's flawed approach to some extent, thus leading to similar limitations in their method.

Autonomy vs. Reciprocity

The method of correlation involves two movements: (1) distinguishing the meaning of the tradition's symbols from current experience, and (2) bringing these together in such a way that they mutually condition each other.[149] The main metaphors Tillich uses to describe a correlative relationship are question-answer and form-content.[150] We have briefly considered the question-answer model above, but in addition to this model, correlation is sometimes explained in terms of form and content, characterized by the slogan: culture is the form of religion and religion is the content of culture.[151] With Jesus as the Christ operating as the criterion, that which makes Christian theology Christian, form and content are suited to a church theology that correlates cultural forms and religious content.[152] The question for us is: "Is it possible to conceive, let alone establish, a relationship between christianity and culture in

---

147. Ibid., 2:206.

148. Macquarrie, *Twentieth-Century Religious Thought*, 370.

149. Ormerod, "Quarrels with the Method," 708.

150. Clayton, *Concept of Correlation*, 17.

151. Ibid., 223.

152. Ibid., 225.

which there is a genuine and thorough-going reciprocity that threatens the autonomy neither of religion nor of culture?"[153] Tillich scholar John Clayton argues that neither model meets this challenge of reciprocity or autonomy.[154] Whereas the question-answer model stresses reciprocity between the discussion partners, the form-content model, which is intent on preserving the unique character of the Christian message, diminishes the reciprocity. Religious substance is immune from cultural critique and vice versa. Conversely, the form-content model distinguishes the Christian content from the cultural form of the message, while the question-answer model, with its stress on reciprocity and dialogue, fails to maintain the Christian-ness of Christianity.[155] Thus, the reciprocity of the correlation method is illusory. There is no mutual interaction on the same level between question and answer. Likewise, form does not mutually affect form, nor content mutually affect content.[156]

Moreover, there is a concern with Tillich separating the form and content of the Christian message. The questions are to control the form, not the content, but can this actually occur? For instance, in Christology it is paradoxical that the Logos became flesh. Such a paradox is not determined by human questions, in fact, quite the opposite is true. Because Tillich holds Jesus as the Christ to be the foundation of Christian tradition, and this foundation is rooted in the Bible as the source of the original revelatory event, it is apparent that scripture carries a certain weight that the human situation does not. Tillich has not allowed the human question to change the answer or its form.

Another critic, David Tracy, also finds Tillich's method of correlation lacking. Tracy understands Tillich's method as correlating questions from one source and answers from another, arguing that if the situation is to be taken seriously, its own answers should be considered. A commitment to two sources for theology implies the need of cor-

153. Ibid., 42. Clayton considers this the necessary question for any mediation theology along the lines of Schleiermacher. By reciprocity Clayton means a sense of mutual influence or mutual dependence (45).

154. Clayton, *Concept of Correlation*, 159.

155. Ibid., 226.

156. Schüssler Fiorenza, "Crisis of Hermeneutics," 130 n. 40. Fiorenza states that "Tillich's de facto use of the method of correlation does not always coincide with his definition. In addition, the notion of correlation in terms of question and answer differs from the correlation between form and content."

relating principal questions and answers from each source. According to Tracy, Tillich does not actually correlate, but juxtaposes questions from the situation with answers from the message.[157] Meanings discovered as adequate to human experience must be compared to meanings disclosed as appropriate to the Christian tradition. This is part of the task of critical correlation.[158] However, what we see in Tillich is that the questions implicit in the situation are to be formulated by philosophical analysis independent of theological controls. Answers are given *to* human existence yet are shaped according to the form of the question.[159] Therefore, it seems that as regards the human situation, philosophy is able to influence theological reflection, but theology does not affect philosophical analysis. For Tillich, rather than philosophy and theology existing in correlation as mutually interdependent and transformative, philosophy appears to gain the primacy. The expression of the self-understanding of an age of people, placed in correlation with the Christian gospel, seems to come first in Tillich's method of correlation.[160] Nevertheless, Tillich insists the method of correlation does not begin anywhere, but is circular. Although Tillich argues that the point of unity may be in the human person's essential being, existentially the system begins with the human person.[161]

The inconsistencies of Tillich's system are beginning to surface. He requires both reciprocity and autonomy in correlation, but seems to do justice to neither. Similarly, in the feminist use of the method of correlation the autonomy of one half of the correlation, human experience, is given a particular independence that the text is not, and therefore, a genuine reciprocity does not occur.[162] Schüssler Fiorenza reclaims

---

157. Tracy, *Blessed Rage for Order*, 46. Tracy supports a view of theology that investigates the sources for theology (human experience and Christian texts). The first is investigated by a hermeneutical phenomenology of the religious dimension and the second by a historical, hermeneutical investigation of Christian texts. The results are correlated to determine the differences, similarities and truth value of each (53).

158. Ibid., 79. Georgia Masters Keightly notes that Tracy's combining of human experience and Christian tradition is a task most feminist theologians agree with, but urges these feminists to approach these sources with much more care and critique than they have to date (Keightly, "Challenge of Feminist Christology," 52).

159. Welch, "Paul Tillich," 253.

160. Clayton, *Concept of Correlation*, 67.

161. McKelway, *Systematic Theology of Paul Tillich*, 48.

162. With the possible exception of Russell, who attempts to give equal weight to both sources; see above.

the authority of scripture not on its own merit or witness to the self-revelation of God, but through women's experience. Experience conditions how one deals with the text, but it is unclear how the text informs an understanding of experience. Likewise, related to Tracy's critique of Tillich, feminist theologians are reluctant to correlate the questions and answers from each source. Because the Christian Bible and tradition have been influenced by patriarchy, human experience is already a negative factor in that side of the correlation, that is, feminist theologians feel justified in using women's experience as they do since there is no theology that has not been affected by experience. Nevertheless, the feminist understanding of women's experience appears more connected to philosophy than theology in that the analysis of the human situation is not directly touched by theological reflection. We have seen that the feminist understanding of women's experience is given a priority and autonomy that is not given to the biblical text. However, the two sources, message and situation, are not as disparate as correlation insinuates.[163] Furthermore, Tillich's system, along with feminist liberation theology, does not seem to allow revelation to be culturally transformative, lacking the development of the means by which the New Being transforms existence. Such a perspective neglects the fact that the present situation is partly constituted by this revelation.[164] Any analysis of the present situation would be incomplete without theological input.[165] In both cases, we must ask if there has been an actual correlation. Moreover, are the questions based on an accurate interpretation of the human situation and is the answer of God's self-manifestation in Jesus Christ actually heard?[166]

Jesus as Symbol

Clearly, the principle of correlation requires symbolism. Whenever the finite is correlated to the infinite in such a way that it participates in the infinite, everything points to the ground of being and is able to

---

163. Ormerod, "Quarrels with the Method," 711–12.

164. Ibid., 718.

165. Ibid., 715. A similar critique is lodged by Thomas, "Method and Structure," 103.

166. McKelway, *Systematic Theology of Paul Tillich*, 70.

be a symbol of the ultimate, capable of being a medium of revelation.[167] According to Tillich, "every symbol opens up a level of reality for which non-symbolic speaking is inadequate."[168] The method of correlation analyzes the human situation then interprets revelation in symbols adequate to that situation.[169] This leads to a view of theology as an explication of symbols used in the Christian message because religious symbols are the characteristic form of the content of the Christian message.[170] Tillich does not consider metaphorical language about God to be a downfall, but rather, claims that a symbolic way of speaking reveals the depth of meaning in theological language.[171] Religious symbols do not merely open up a new level of reality, one alongside others, but the fundamental level of reality, "the ultimate power of being."[172] According to him, symbols as the source of theology must have a criterion or norm for interpretation, and the norm for the present period is "New Being in Jesus as the Christ as our ultimate concern."[173]

For Tillich the biblical picture of Jesus as the Christ replaces historical inquiry as the foundation of Christian faith. He claims that our faith cannot guarantee the historical reality of Jesus, but it can guarantee the fact to which Jesus refers, that is, the power of New Being actual in a historical person.[174] His is similar to an aesthetic approach where the picture of Jesus as the Christ is perceived as a work of art.[175] The content of the picture is not what communicates meaning; likewise, the picture of Jesus provides a medium of religious meaning rather than the

---

167. Mondin, *Principle of Analogy*, 133.

168. Tillich, *Theology of Culture*, 56.

169. McKelway, *Systematic Theology of Paul Tillich*, 60.

170. Kelsey, *Fabric of Paul Tillich's Theology*, 3.

171. Heron, *Century of Protestant Theology*, 140.

172. Tillich, *Theology of Culture*, 59.

173. Kelsey, *Fabric of Paul Tillich's Theology*, 5–6. Tillich states that the symbol of the cross of Christ is the criterion for all other symbols (see Tillich, *Theology of Culture*, 67).

174. Clayton, *Concept of Correlation*, 230–31; Heron, *Century of Protestant Theology*, 143. Heron judges Tillich as doing less justice to the history of Jesus than either Schleiermacher or Ritschl. Tillich would disagree, claiming that Christianity is based on an event given in history, not derived from experience as Schleiermacher stated (Tillich, *Systematic Theology*, 1: 51).

175. Kelsey, *Fabric of Paul Tillich's Theology*, 8.

specific content of this meaning.[176] In order to avoid the errors revealed by historical-critical method, Tillich attempts to maintain the authority of scripture instead by conceiving it as a "verbal icon," but such a view leads one to understand scripture as not making any claims, just like an aesthetic object.[177] Christologically, Jesus is seen as a symbol, a manifestation to us of the New Being.[178] Tillich perceives the man Jesus as a transient medium for an eternal principle that points to a God who we only know to be the ground of being.[179] Such a view is at odds with a christological purpose for theology, for talk of Jesus as the Christ ends up being highly general, not forming any proposals about Jesus as the Christ or the biblical picture.[180] Revelation gives the answer of Jesus as the Christ, the bearer of New Being, but it is unclear that claims about New Being are objective claims about Jesus or an expression of something he exemplifies or symbolizes.[181]

This reading of the tradition from the standpoint of Jesus as the Christ is the foundation for Tillich and reflects an approach that seems to remove Jesus from the whole of the Christian tradition in such a way that he becomes a timeless principle.[182] Ruether's Christology is quite similar. Like Tillich, she operates with a core biblical principle as the norm for her theology: the prophetic-liberating tradition of biblical faith.[183] In her system Jesus is understood as resymbolizing

176. Clayton, *Concept of Correlation*, 234.

177. Kelsey, *Fabric of Paul Tillich's Theology*, 196.

178. Heron, *Century of Protestant Theology*, 141. Because Tillich considers religious symbols to have a lifespan—that is, symbols may live, die, or cease to exist when the situation in which they were born changes or ceases to exist—one wonders about the status of the symbol of Jesus (see Tillich, *Theology of Culture*, 58). Although he goes on to argue that the symbol of the cross expresses a superior truth, there seems to be the possibility that the cross could cease to be a meaningful symbol if the church's situation changes in a particular way (ibid., 67).

179. McKelway, *Systematic Theology of Paul Tillich*, 100.

180. Kelsey, *Fabric of Paul Tillich's Theology*, 194.

181. Heron, *Century of Protestant Theology*, 139.

182. Clayton, *Concept of Correlation*, 96. Clayton's own approach, a remedy to Tillich's method, utilizes Wittgenstein's concept of "family resemblance." Rather than basing Christian theology on the unchanging content of Jesus as the Christ, incorporating family resemblances in Christology could account for the complexity of Christian theology, while at the same time being sufficient for maintaining Christian theology (237).

183. Ruether, *Sexism and God-Talk*, 24.

the messianic prophet as a servant rather than king.[184] She describes him as an exemplary prophet and the paradigm of liberated humanity. This perspective is characteristic of a symbolic emphasis in Ruether's Christology that leads to a diminishment of the historical Jesus, and to a stress on Christ's identity as redemptive humanity, continued in the life of the Christian community. Such idealism is akin to what we find in Tillich's view of Jesus Christ. However, although Ruether uses symbolism to understand Jesus, she warns of the danger Christian symbols provide for feminism. She argues that since christological symbols have been used to enforce male dominance, we must see Jesus' model of redemptive humanity as partial and fragmentary, disclosing in one person, time, culture, and gender something of the fullness feminists seek. Other models, symbols, must be drawn from many times and cultures, including from women's experience.[185] Both Tillich and Ruether incorporate an understanding of symbolism in their theological systems, and particularly in their Christology, whereby the subject of theology becomes religious symbols, not God, and what is authoritative is found *in* scripture, but is not identified *with* scripture.[186]

The Risk of Natural Theology

Like Schleiermacher and those after him who attempted to bring together religion and culture, Tillich's own efforts make him open to accusations of natural theology, even though he tried to replace a natural theology independent of revelation with what could be called a "supernatural theology."[187] While he denies a natural theology, he understands human beings to have some natural ability to apprehend the divine, thus allowing reception of revelation. In fact, he would find the concept of revelation inexplicable if there was not an innate human ability to

184. Ibid., 121.

185. Ibid., 114.

186. Kelsey, *Fabric of Paul Tillich's Theology*, 4. Kelsey also notes that theology ought not be concerned with symbols that express a person's religious experience, but with the original revelatory event. He wonders if Tillich lies subject to a Feuerbachian critique if he does not adequately distinguish between religious experience and revelation, between giving and receiving (39).

187. Heron, *Century of Protestant Theology*, 139.

ask for and know revelation.[188] Still, God is understood to be the one
who first gives the answers, out of which humans ask the questions.
Although Tillich speaks of revelation, his position seems somewhat
ambiguous. He identifies Jesus as the Christ as the original revelatory
correlation. All other revelation is dependent revelation, hinging on this
original event. And yet, despite any development of an understanding
of revelation, allowing a natural capacity in humans that can ask for
revelation sounds too much like natural theology. Furthermore, he has
an epistemological sense of correlation, between the subject and object,
revelation and its reception, in which the mind's ability to know and
grasp revelation is like a natural theology with little distance between
giver and recipient.[189] Indeed, Tillich may function with an *a priori* of
the precedence of God's revelation, but it is not explicit.[190] His doctrine
of revelation implies a natural, ontological relation between humanity
and God that differs from a natural theology only in degree.[191] Moreover,
in keeping with natural theology, Tillich's method of correlation does
not adequately preserve God's transcendence. In his scheme, God and
human beings are interdependent, thus denying the infinite distance
between the two.[192]

   In fact, it could be argued that Tillich's theology does not draw
on revelation much at all, but upon a concept of God as being-itself.[193]
Tillich appears to gain his doctrine of God more from an analysis of being than from revelation. If the existential question determines the form
of the theological answer then the form of the question is affected by the
prior theological commitment of the theologian.[194] Since the criteria required for correlation are unclear, each theologian uses her or his own,
often uncritical, "commonsense" criteria that appear arbitrary from the
methodological viewpoint.[195] In the case of feminist liberation theology,

---

188. McKelway, *Systematic Theology of Paul Tillich*, 96–97. Tillich repudiates natural
theology in its pantheistic forms, which he understands as identifying God too closely
with the finite and where God ceases to be the transcendent ground of finite being.

189. Clayton, *Concept of Correlation*, 80–81.

190. McKelway, *Systematic Theology of Paul Tillich*, 102.

191. Ibid., 33.

192. Mondin, *Principle of Analogy*, 132.

193. Heron, *Century of Protestant Theology*, 143.

194. McKelway, *Systematic Theology of Paul Tillich*, 141.

195. Ormerod, "Quarrels with the Method," 712.

the criterion for correlation generally is a view of the "full humanity of women" and yet, the means of arriving at this criterion are not explicated. On the contrary, in liberation theology, the basic criterion related to the situation of the poor is rooted in God's revelation through the Bible. The commitment to the poor is grounded in the God of our faith, not in any direct experience we may have or in human compassion. It is rooted in the unmerited love of God.[196] Feminists seem to have a "commonsense" view of human equality that is grounded upon self-evident truths (not unlike the American Declaration of Independence).

Part of any natural theology is an emphasis upon the human being, upon anthropology. There is an aspect of Tillich's method of correlation, also found in feminist theology, which makes theology contingent upon the current human situation, thus giving more merit to the anthropological than the theological. The pluralistic and contextual nature of the method of correlation is seen in an approach that does not mean to apply theological principles to Christian dogma indefinitely.[197] Tillich understood his efforts at correlation to be specific for his own period, relating current culture to religion. Feminist and liberation theologians claim a "standpoint dependent" position, which acknowledges that every theology is a construction of particular persons and faith communities who confess faith in God in languages, metaphors, and thought patterns appropriate to their own context.[198] According to feminist liberation theology, if God is the guiding reality then truth is based upon the extent to which the current idea of God takes account of reality and integrates this present experience. The idea of God must keep pace with developing reality. If present experience pulls people on, then God may fade from memory.[199] For Schüssler Fiorenza, the authority of theological discourse about Jesus Christ is not derived from "revelatory," "feminist," or "spiritual" experiences. Rather it must be "proven 'right' again and again" within the ongoing struggles for justice and positioned within the tradition of women-church.[200]

196. Gutiérrez, *Theology of Liberation*, xxvii.

197. There is an irony in that correlation seems context-specific in application, yet there is an effort to preserve some universal, "timeless" foundation such as "Jesus as the Christ."

198. Russell, *Household of Freedom*, 30.

199. Johnson, *She Who Is*, 15.

200. Schüssler Fiorenza, *Jesus* 127–28.

Conclusion: Who Is the First Speaker?

We appear to have two voices in the method of correlation—religion and culture, text and experience. The question seems to be, who gets the first word? In other words, what is given priority in a theological method utilizing a correlative approach? The theologies we have been considering in this chapter have different answers to this question. Liberation theologians, Paul Tillich, and feminist liberation theologians each employ aspects of correlation in their theological method. All three have a desire to link the human, finite world, the world of existence, to that of the divine. Rightly incorporating elements of an apologetic theology, each seeks to justify the Christian faith in light of human experience. This is an important challenge for theology. Yet, how are these approaches distinct?

To some extent liberation theology attempts to maintain God as the first speaker while also giving human experience equal, if not simultaneous, voice. Liberation theology desires to begin theological discourse in reflection on what God says about the situation.[201] By developing the hermeneutical circle, liberation theology attempts to avoid a sense of Enlightenment foundationalism with its unshakable foundation, and although the circle does have a starting place, the experience of oppression, it is understood dialectically as beginning with God and God's word to us. Liberation theology grounds its understanding of oppression in the Word of God, allowing God and scripture to shape and transform human existence.

In Tillich, we seem to have an effort at making God the first speaker, yet in the scope of his system Tillich fails to give God the first word. Tillich seeks the common denominator between the Word of God and

---

201. C. Boff, "Methodology," 15. It should be noted that one could argue that liberation theology does not actually give God the first word, but rather utilizes a human understanding of Marxist political theory and applies it to theology, thereby giving the human side of the correlation the priority. William Dyrness notes, however, that the Marxist influence on liberation theology should not be overemphasized. There was gathering social unrest and yearning for liberation long before Marxism as an ideological framework had influence. "It is certainly true that Marxists exploited this dissatisfaction, but it is false to say they created it" (Dyrness, *Learning about Theology*, 78–79). For further comments on the relationship of Marxism to liberation theology, see also Segundo, *Liberation of Theology*, 35 n. 10. The purpose here is not to explore this debate, but to outline liberation theology's own perspective on theological method and how it relates to the method of Tillich and feminist liberation theology.

the human word in order to make them understandable to each other. This common denominator is "being."[202] In fact, Tillich does not want a first speaker at all, rather he understands the method of correlation to be circular, a mutual relationship of two sources. If this is Tillich's intent (we have argued that in actuality the correlation lacks the desired mutuality and reciprocity), then he fails to preserve the transcendence of God. If God and humanity can speak to one another as equals, then why does humanity need God in the first place? If we can understand revelation inherently, then why ask for it at all?

Finally, feminist theologians, particularly Ruether and Schüssler Fiorenza, clearly reject God as the first speaker. Rather, it is women who speak first and last, having the final say on what counts as revelation. Schüssler Fiorenza asks a telling question: "Must . . . a feminist critical hermeneutical key be derived from or at least correlated with the Bible so that scripture remains the normative foundation of feminist biblical faith and community?"[203] It could be argued that if one wants to have a "feminist *biblical* faith and community" the Bible must be normative and authoritative in some significant way.

If one understands God and human beings to be radically different, the method of correlation as described by Tillich will prove unsatisfactory, although any mediating theology will require some form of correlation. A more sufficient account of how the divine and human relate is needed; an account that allows God to have the first and last word, while upholding the value of human experience, particularly the experience of women, for the construction of a beneficial feminist theology.

---

202. McKelway, *Systematic Theology of Paul Tillich*, 262–63.

203. Schüssler Fiorenza, "Politics of Otherness," 314.

PART TWO

Women's Experience and Feminist Theologies of Atonement

The Role of Women's Experience in Feminist Theologies of Atonement

Introduction: Women's Experience in Context

UP TO THIS POINT OUR DISCUSSION OF THE ROLE OF EXPERIENCE IN feminist theology has been somewhat theoretical, without considering the use of the category in actual practice. Therefore, we now turn to the role of experience used within the development of a specific Christian doctrine in feminist theology—soteriology. The insights we have gained in feminist understandings of women's experience thus far will be helpful as we examine the role of such experience in feminist theologies of atonement. By placing the discussion of women's experience within a particular theological context, we can better understand the role of experience in feminist theology. We will examine three major feminist positions: (1) the critique of classical understandings of atonement as "divine child abuse" represented in the work of Rita Nakashima Brock and Joanne Carlson Brown; (2) the re-imaging of atonement symbols as the "birthing of God" in Mary Grey's approach; and (3) the paradigm of liberated humanity in Christ developed by Rosemary Radford Ruether.

Divine Child Abuse

An important feminist position that is critical of traditional views considers the death of an innocent son, at either the hands or by permission of the father, to be an example of child abuse that perpetuates systems

of abuse within the Christian tradition. One feminist accurately sum-
marizes this general critique as follows:

> An angry male god wills and accepts the death of his only son
> as a substitute for the death of the ones who deserved god's an-
> ger. In the words of some critics this understanding parades di-
> vine child abuse as salvific and then lauds the child who suffers
> "without even raising a voice" as the hope of the world. This
> conviction moreover communicates the message that suffering
> is redemptive.[1]

The main feminists who offer this type of critique are Rita Nakashima
Brock, Joanne Carlson Brown, and Rebecca Parker.

Rita Nakashima Brock

Brock begins from a perspective that wants to redefine love. She argues
that the highest form of love has been considered to be self-sacrifice,
when it should be intimacy; an intimacy grounded in a feminist view of
love as the power of all human life.[2] Important to Brock's approach is an
understanding of relationship; we are constituted by our relationships
and are intimately connected. This ontological relational existence is our
life source, our original grace, yet this inherent connectedness causes us
to be vulnerable and it is this vulnerability that is the source of the damage that leads to sin. In other words, Brock argues that because we are
at the core relational, connected beings, our vulnerability to brokenness
lies in the separation and disconnectedness we experience and that the
damage of this disconnectedness is what leads to sin. Furthermore, she
maintains that this sin does not require punishment, but healing.[3] There
is a fundamental power within us that heals the brokenness, makes us
whole, and liberates us, something Brock describes as "feminist Eros"
or "erotic power."[4] This divine erotic power is embodied in all beings,
incarnate as life-giving power, and what Brock calls the "Heart of the
Universe."[5] This erotic power also is the energy that produces "creative

1. Van Wijk-Bos, "Shadow of a Mighty Rock," 5.
2. Brock, *Journeys by Heart*, xii.
3. Ibid., 7.
4. Ibid., 25.
5. Ibid., 46.

synthesis," that which is necessary to interpret experience, a concept based on arguments from process thinkers Alfred North Whitehead and Charles Hartshorne who emphasize experience and action as the key to human awareness. Such experience is influenced by its data but never wholly determined by it. Therefore, creative synthesis is needed to interpret the experience.[6] These concepts are the background to Brock's understanding of atonement.

Before offering her own interpretation of atonement, Brock identifies four traditional views she believes project a wrong view of authority: (1) the enemies of God are reconciled to each other through Jesus' death; (2) humanity under the bondage of sin requires the ransom of Jesus' death; (3) sin causes humanity to be at a deficit so Jesus' debt pays its debt; and (4) Jesus is a pure sacrifice that cleanses humanity of sin.[7] Generally speaking, Brock understands traditional atonement doctrine as follows: There is a notion of original sin whereby the human race is dependent upon the father to restore us. As a result of original sin, the father determines that the punishment of one perfect child will allow him to forgive the other children. In the doctrine's more benign forms, the father does not actually punish the son, but allows the son to suffer evil, while the father is in passive anguish as the son is killed. Someone else's suffering has atoned for the children's flaws, becoming the sacrifice that is the way to new life. Trinitarian formulas of this understanding absolve the father because he actually takes on the consequences for sin himself.[8] According to Brock, what is missing from this basic scheme is interdependence and mutuality, because although atonement doctrine emphasizes God's grace and forgiveness for all, it is still contingent upon the suffering of one perfect child.[9] Brock draws analogies between society's culture of child abuse and what happens in the Christian tradition, understanding such doctrines of salvation to reflect images of the neglect of children or, even worse, child abuse, "making it acceptable as divine behavior—cosmic child abuse, as it were."[10] Although a belief

6. Ibid., 49.

7. Ibid., 55.

8. Ibid., 55. See also Brock, "And a Little Child," 52.

9. Brock, *Journeys by Heart*, 56.

10. Ibid. This analogy also relates to how the church creates scapegoats (i.e., women, pagans, Jews, etc.), which is not unlike how an abused child, who has an ideal image of the parent, develops a rage due to repeated association of hurt with love, and projects

in forgiveness can lead to self-acceptance and forgiveness of others, traditional theology has perpetuated patriarchal family structures by its emphasis on the power of the father to exact punishment on guilty children.[11] Therefore, for Brock, "the shadow of the punitive father must always lurk behind atonement."[12]

Because Brock's central concerns with traditional atonement doctrine center upon the issue of authority, she wants to distance herself from any Christology that contains what she describes as a unilateral understanding of power. Instead, the passion narrative reveals Jesus as the symbol of woundedness, his death a revelatory moment that points us toward vulnerability. In his death Jesus is bound up with the vulnerable who actually accompany him to his death, as he is too wounded to suffer alone. In this alternative interpretation of the death and resurrection, life surfaces through connection.[13] Rather than focusing on Jesus, Brock centers Christology in relationship and community as the "whole-making, healing center of Christianity." Avoiding identification of Christ with a heroic individual, Brock focuses salvation on Christa/Community.[14] "To understand the meaning of Christ, we must be willing to acknowledge the Child in ourselves and in each other and we must acknowledge our interdependence. In those moments of acknowledgment the tomb of death becomes a womb of life."[15] The Child is a divine image that we all carry within us, and the divine spirit is the Child incarnate in us, revealing the need to stay connected to the original grace.

Despite her rejection of classical Christian theologies of atonement, Brock desires to remain within the Christian tradition since it has been liberative for some women in spite of its patriarchal influences.[16]

these feelings of rage onto others (56–57). Mary Daly identifies a similar problem in maintaining the view of Jesus as scapegoat whereby the imitation of such a sacrificial lifestyle leads some to feel guilty over their inability to imitate Jesus, thus making the "Other" to be the imitator and hence, the scapegoat (Daly, *Beyond God the Father*, 75–76).

11. Brock, *Journeys by Heart*, 57. Brock notes that similar critiques have been well articulated in Christian liberation theologies.

12. Brock, "And a Little Child," 53.

13. Ibid., 58.

14. Brock, *Journeys by Heart*, 52, 113 n. 2.

15. Brock, "And a Little Child," 59.

16. Brock, *Journeys by Heart*, xv. Because of Brock's challenge to the divinity of

She finds inspiration for a Christology of erotic power in the Christian scriptures, particularly in the Markan miracle stories, especially those about exorcisms and healings of brokenheartedness.[17]

Joanne Carlson Brown and Rebecca Parker

Joanne Carlson Brown is another feminist theologian who attacks traditional atonement theologies primarily on the issue of divine child abuse. Brown identifies two major problems with traditional atonement doctrine: (1) it communicates that suffering is redemptive and that it is good to sacrifice ourselves; and (2) it supports a view of Jesus as being obedient to the Father.[18] "Divine child abuse is paraded as salvific and the child who suffers 'without even raising a voice' is lauded as the hope of the world. Those whose lives have been deeply shaped by the Christian tradition feel that self-sacrifice and obedience are not only virtues but the definition of a faith identity."[19] Brown, writing with Rebecca Parker, acknowledges that the Christian tradition has formulated the doctrine of atonement in different terms, yet maintains that it has not challenged its central problem, that is, Jesus' suffering and death and God the Father's responsibility for that suffering and death.[20] Moreover, Brown and Parker see that there are many different interpretations of how we are saved by the death of Jesus, but consider no classical theory of atonement to question the necessity of Jesus' suffering, in addition to the fact that every theory of atonement commends suffering to the

---

Christ, Jacquelyn Grant identifies Brock as falling somewhere between a rejectionist and liberationist feminist position (Grant, *White Women's Christ*, 181).

17. Brock, *Journeys by Heart*, 67. She looks closely at stories of demon possessions and the healings of the hemorrhaging woman and Jairus' daughter. Brock also develops an interpretation of the Passion, related to her understanding of erotic power. She does consider the resurrection, believing that there were witnesses to the resurrection even if these only imagined the event in some sense. If these witnesses had some kind of experience in which they found that they saw or believed in the resurrection, then there is adequate basis for Brock to include it as part of her analysis of erotic power.

18. Brown, "Divine Child Abuse?" 24. In contrast, Mary VandenBerg contends that "at least one instance of suffering, the suffering of Christ, is redemptive" (VandenBerg, "Redemptive Suffering," 394).

19. Brown and Parker, "For God So Loved?" 2.

20. Ibid., 4.

disciple.[21] They examine particular atonement traditions: (1) *Christus victor*, (2) satisfaction or Anselmian, and (3) moral influence.

CHRISTUS VICTOR

Brown and Parker understand this theory as claiming that suffering is a prelude to triumph and that suffering itself is an illusion. Jesus' death represents the apparent triumph of evil, but his resurrection reveals that God is the greater power whose purpose will prevail. In this approach, redemption is liberation from evil forces.[22] Furthermore, a believer who is influenced by this view will be persuaded to endure suffering as a prelude to new life. God is pictured as working through suffering and the believer may look upon pain as a gift in which God provides guidance and purpose. Brown and Parker understand this theology to have devastating effects on human life because they believe that victimization never leads to triumph, but rather, to the "destruction of the human spirit through the death of a person's sense of power, worth, dignity, or creativity," as well as to actual death. "By denying the reality of suffering and death, the *Christus victor* theory of the atonement defames all those who suffer and trivializes tragedy."[23]

SATISFACTION/ANSELMIAN

In this view, sin leads humanity to owe so great a debt to God that it is unable to pay and that only by the death of God's own Son could God receive satisfaction. According to Brown and Parker, Anselm saw God's desire for justice and God's desire to love as in conflict, therefore understanding that wrongs were to be punished rather than righted.[24] Because God has been so offended by human sin, God cannot be reconciled to the world, consequently, the Son submits to a sacrificial death out of overwhelming love for God and the world. Anselm's medieval forensic categories reflect his social context of coercion and terror and seem to sanction the suffering of a victim. This sanctioning of suffering has been the legacy of the satisfaction theory of atonement. If suffering

21. Ibid.
22. Ibid., 5.
23. Ibid., 7.
24. Ibid.

is sanctioned as an experience that frees others, the faithful disciple, suffering in the place of others, will endure in the conviction that her pain will free another she loves. Brown and Parker see such a view as encouraging women to be more concerned about those who abuse them than about themselves.[25] "The image of God the father demanding and carrying out the suffering and death of his own son has sustained a culture of abuse and led to the abandonment of victims of abuse and oppression."[26]

A less important, but related critique of the satisfaction theory is its deep roots in biblical images of sacrifice, and how these images are evoked in the liturgies, hymns, and piety of the church. Brown and Parker identify four major themes related to the biblical view of the power of blood sacrifice: (1) blood protects, (2) blood intercedes, (3) blood establishes covenant, and (4) blood makes atonement.[27] Brown and Parker suggest that religious imagery of the atonement is founded upon the robbery and subsequent defamation/degradation of women's experience (of menstruation and birth, both involving blood) and such imagery is replaced by Jesus' blood, which implies he is the true mother who gives new birth and life through his flesh.[28]

Moral Influence

Brown and Parker understand this view as beginning with Abelard's questioning of the satisfaction theory. Abelard understood the barrier to reconciliation between humanity and God not to be in God but in human beings. We need to be persuaded faithfully to believe in God's overwhelming mercy and Jesus' willingness to die for us is evidence of that love. God held our souls in such high esteem that we should recognize our loved condition and in gratitude commit ourselves to obedience like Jesus'.[29] Such a view is founded on the belief that an in-

---

25. Ibid., 8.

26. Ibid., 9.

27. Ibid.

28. Ibid., 10.

29. Ibid., 11. The authors identify Martin Luther King Jr.'s view as similar to the "moral influence" theory in that unjust suffering has the power to move the hearts of perpetrators of violence. Brown and Parker have difficulties with such a view because it seems to ask people to suffer for the sake of helping evildoers see their evil ways (20).

nocent, suffering victim for whose suffering we are in some way responsible has the power to confront us with our guilt and move us to a new decision. This belief has subtle connections to how victims of violence can be viewed and how, in fact, we have victimized certain groups (e.g., races, classes, women) throughout human history for our moral edification, using their suffering to move the powerful to repentance and responsibility. "Holding over people's heads the threat that if they do not behave someone will die requires occasional fulfillment of the threat."[30] Brown and Parker consider such a threat much more than merely moral persuasion.

These views of atonement as interpreted by Brown and Parker lead them to reject any form of Christianity that includes atonement: "We must do away with the atonement, this idea of a blood sin upon the whole human race which can be washed away only by the blood of the lamb."[31] Brown contends that women should only remain within the Christian tradition as long as it condemns suffering. There should be no glorification of suffering. On this point Brown and Parker are in agreement with Carter Heyward who also rejects any view of suffering as salvific.[32] However, they see it as a failure that Heyward does not identify the traditional doctrine of the atonement as the primary source for the oppressiveness of Christianity.[33] Rather, Heyward sees Jesus' death as an unnecessary, violent evil done to him by humans and tries to redeem the doctrine by re-imaging Jesus as demonstrating that salvation consists in an immediate, intimate love relationship with God. For her, redemption is a passionate knowledge of God.[34] In contrast, Brown considers that those women who remain in the church are as victimized as any battered women, comparing their staying in the church to the same foolish reasons battered wives stay with their abusive husbands.[35] There is no original sin from which we need saving, but rather, we need to be liberated from the oppression of patriarchy. Despite their harsh critique, Brown and Parker maintain that Christianity can be at the heart of such

30. Ibid., 13.

31. Brown, "Divine Child Abuse?" 28; and Brown and Parker, "For God So Loved?" 26.

32. Heyward, "Suffering, Redemption, and Christ," 384.

33. Brown and Parker, "For God So Loved?" 26.

34. Heyward, "Suffering, Redemption, and Christ," 385.

35. Brown, "Divine Child Abuse?" 25.

justice if we reject the foundations of abuse and adopt new interpretations of salvation. They present Jesus as one who lived a life in opposition to unjust, oppressive cultures and who was unjustly put to death by humans who chose to reject his way of life. This travesty of suffering is not redeemed by the resurrection and is not an acceptable sacrifice for the sins of the whole world. To know God is to do justice, therefore God does not need to be appeased and does not demand sacrifice. For Brown and Parker, "no one was saved by the death of Jesus."[36]

Mary Grey and the "Birthing of God"

Mary Grey has devoted an entire book to the subject of atonement from a feminist perspective; therefore, we will consider the atonement theology she develops in her book *Redeeming the Dream*. Grey understands redemption as "right relation" and explores whether right relation or "mutuality-in-relating" can function as the *how* of Christian redemption.[37] She agrees with many feminist theologians that the sufferings of Jesus on the cross have led women to be viewed as victims and the scapegoats of society, and asks if there can be alternative symbols from those of "satisfaction," "sacrifice," "victim," and "expiation" to explain the how of atonement.[38]

Before presenting her understanding of redemption, Grey surveys three general views of atonement. First, Grey identifies what she terms the Patristic model of atonement, in which she finds four basic motifs: (1) the atonement is the example, teaching, and new direction given by Christ; (2) in Christ all human actions and achievements are summed up so we can share and be drawn into his actions; (3) atonement is not achieved by pressure of divine power but by victory through a genuine struggle; and (4) atonement is about the divinization of humanity, community with God, forgiveness of sins and true life.[39] Second, she describes the Latin or Western view. It is this form of atonement doc-

---

36. Brown and Parker, "For God So Loved?" 27.

37. Grey, *Redeeming the Dream*, 110.

38. Ibid., 118. Regardless of the positive strands of the tradition, Grey considers the classical imagery to be damaging to women (119). Nevertheless, she cannot accept what she considers a "cruel distortion of the Christian cross" in the work of Mary Daly, Joanne Carlson Brown, and Rebecca Parker (16).

39. Grey, *Redeeming the Dream*, 110–11.

trine that is most frequently found in popular belief and worship and is most often the version to which feminists react in a hostile manner. The Latin version, attributed to Anselm of Canterbury, considers the idea of satisfaction as integral. Grey desires to rescue this view from its negative interpretations, which often focus on satisfaction in regard to an offended deity who demands compensation. Grey prefers to interpret the satisfaction as demanded by the world, not God, because the world is what has been defaced by sin, not the personal honor of God. Such an understanding links the individual in a sacramental way to Christ's objective salvific work. Grey considers her approach as both subjective and objective, making Christ the representative, not the scapegoat.[40] Third, Grey identifies three modern ways of construing atonement. First, a view that understands Christ as revelation, teaching, and an ethical ideal, not simply as a moral influence, but as the ideal of true humanity. In this approach it is not so much the person of Christ, but the event that is redemptive, the ideal more than the bearer of the ideal is important. Grey notes Immanuel Kant as an example of this form. Second is a view of speculative idealism in which atonement is seen in terms of the developing consciousness of the unity of God and the human subject. Grey cites F. C. Baur as an example of this approach. Third is a view stemming from Schleiermacher where Jesus is a human prototype with an actual causal function. In this account the believer's own God-consciousness is linked with the mediation of Christ.[41]

Grey believes women's experience has not been brought to bear on atonement theories and that it has been problematic for women to identify with Christ's suffering on the cross. Even if this identification is based on a misinterpretation of the Latin view of atonement, it has led to a dual role for women: "as Lord he was to be submitted to; as victim he was to be identified with."[42] Grey identifies other problems with traditional atonement theories as well. There is mention of bondage to sin, but it says little of sexism as a form of such bondage, making talk of victory meaningless. The classical view contains a notion of obedience, which is a dangerous concept for women who, locked in submissive roles, do not question the integrity of the authority that

40. Ibid., 112–14. According to Grey, the penal or forensic view of atonement is a distortion of satisfaction presented here (195 n. 24).

41. Ibid., 116–17.

42. Ibid., 122.

demands obedience. The classical atonement model is also abhorrent to some because it relies on victory through violent death. Jesus' death becomes the focus of the content of redemption.[43] Grey claims that a feminist interpretation of atonement can find value hidden beneath the classical views, wherein Jesus is punished not as a result of the wrath of God against a guilty world, but as the culmination of his dynamic mutuality in relation.[44]

Grey understands atonement as fundamentally at-one-ment; a drive for unity. "*At-one-ment* itself is a metaphor which evokes the goal of mutuality and the process of achieving it."[45] Grey considers psychotherapy as part of the at-one-ment process, providing a model in which the redemptive process is found in the relationship between the client and therapist, where the therapist empathically accepts the client. For Grey, this model is an analogy to the cross whereby God felt sin's destructiveness, endured it and received humanity into relationship. In this approach sin is not equated with guilt but with a bondage from which one must be liberated. Grey asserts that a feminist emphasis on this view would focus on the need for judgment upon the sinful structures that break down mutuality.[46] Although such an account achieves much in redeeming the image of God from punitive and vengeful features and touches the level of lived experience in its affective dimension, Grey admits that an emphasis on mutuality and the dynamics of personal relationships alone does not address those structures of society and church that prohibit the full becoming of women. Therefore, a more radical "re-imaging" of atonement symbols is required.[47] The symbol she proposes in this re-imaging enterprise is that of the "birthing of God." Grey understands birthing as providing a contrast to the passivity that perpetuates living as a victim. She argues for an interpretation of atonement that unifies creation and redemption.[48] If "creation is about giving birth,

43. Ibid., 123–24.

44. Ibid., 125.

45. Ibid., 126.

46. Ibid., 131–32.

47. Ibid., 134.

48. Ruether describes Grey's as a "creation-based model of 'right relation'" (Ruether, *Women and Redemption,* 199). God is the creating and redeeming energy of right relation.

then so is redemption, transformation and, ultimately, at-one-ment. It is also the symbol which unites divine and human activity."[49]

For Grey, giving birth is a powerful image that displays "the creation of new forms of mutuality through *life-giving* processes, not through death and destruction."[50] Why, she asks, should violence and death symbolism be so influential in the church when the Judeo-Christian tradition contains maternal imagery, which has so much saving potential?

> What I am arguing is that as Christianity has now had two thousand years of death symbolism, it is at least *possible* that the slaughter perpetrated in the name of Christendom is related to its symbols of death, blood-guilt and sacrifice, and that an *alternative* way of encapsulating the redemptive events might stimulate more compassionate lifestyles.[51]

Therefore, according to Grey, it is right to reclaim the creative image of birthing as a link between women's experience and redemption. It is an image rich with transformative possibilities when it is interpreted as atonement in which submission to pain is necessary in order for a new world to be born. It provides an alternative way to experience conflict and even death.[52] In death there is a "disintegration" or letting go as well as an experience of separation and stillness. Grey recognizes similar experiences in the birthing process where there is a "letting go" of pain and struggle for the creation of a new being, a separation between mothers and children, and a stillness of "waiting" for newness of life, ideas, opportunities.[53] Grey emphasizes a dynamic process while minimizing the role of the historical Jesus. Her view seeks to establish a pattern for a relational understanding of atonement as one where we are all caught up in a process of redemption with God. This was Jesus' pattern and is salvific for us because it is the basic pattern of the world. However, Grey means to say more than that Jesus' life was purely exemplary. "A feminist theology of interconnectedness makes it possible to hold together the relational being of God with human activity as

49. Grey, *Redeeming the Dream*, 139.

50. Ruether, *Women and Redemption*, 199, 143. She quotes Sara Maitland who compares the Passion to giving birth—it is a mysterious and bloody, hard labor that brings joy and new life afterwards (ibid., 141; see Maitland, "Ways of Relating," 124–33).

51. Grey, *Redeeming the Dream*, 139.

52. Ibid., 146–47.

53. Ibid., 148–50.

co-creating, co-redeeming, together with the world's own inner healing resources," which leads to the static image of Jesus as perfect man giving way to the image of the "Body of Christ."[54] Grey maintains the cross as the symbol which keeps alive the memory of redemptive, relational power "at the heart of existence, enfleshed by the whole cross event."[55] In addition, the cross is a symbol of at-one-ment that calls us to take responsibility to be co-sufferers, co-redeemers and co-creators.[56]

The Paradigm of Liberated Humanity in Rosemary Radford Ruether

Ruether claims that traditional Christian theology has portrayed Christ as the model for redeemed humanity, what we have lost through sin and can recover through redemption. Such christological symbols have been used to enforce male dominance and are, therefore, problematic for feminist theology. Consequently, Ruether seeks to determine whether the person of Jesus of Nazareth can be a positive model of redemptive humanity for feminist theology.[57] The central question for Ruether, as discussed briefly in a previous chapter, is whether the limitations of Christ as a male person must lead to the conclusion that he cannot represent redemptive humanity for women. Will women need to "emancipate themselves from Jesus as redeemer and seek a new redemptive disclosure of God" in female form?[58] Ruether's starting point will not be the accumulated doctrine about Christ, but rather his message and praxis as presented in the Synoptic Gospels, where she considers Jesus' criticism of religious and social hierarchy as remarkably parallel to feminist criticism.[59]

Unlike the preceding feminist theologians, Ruether does not develop extended critique of specific atonement theologies; however, she does outline what she considers to be the patriarchalization of Christology, which she understands as taking place over five centuries

54. Ibid., 151.

55. Ibid.

56. Ibid., 152.

57. Ruether, *Sexism and God-Talk*, 114.

58. Ibid., 135.

59. Ibid.

during which the early Christian church was transformed from a mar-
ginal sect within first-century Judaism into the imperial religion of the
Christian Roman Empire.[60] Related to these changes in Christology are
changes in redeemer imagery, the history of which Ruether traces in a
chapter of her book *Womanguides*, beginning with ancient pagan myths
up through Jesus Christ whom she understands not as a powerful king
but as a servant who suffered on behalf of the poor. Those suffering
persons who acknowledge the lordship of Christ, "the resurrected
Crucified," are enabled to become inwardly emancipated.[61] She considers this understanding as a type of kenosis Christology, which became
linked to a philosophical cosmology where Christ is not only the new
liberating being but the original *Logos* or Word of God, a concept related
to earlier female symbolism of Sophia or Wisdom. This Logos-Wisdom
is the power by which the world is created, guided, ruled. It is important
to Ruether to avoid a split between creation and redemption, which she
considers to be the primary danger of any view that leads one to see
the *Logos* as the foundation of the powers of the world, thus sacralizing
existing corrupt systems, declaring them the "order of nature."[62] She asserts that this identification of Christ as *Logos* took place in the fourth
century with the establishment of the Christian church as the imperial
religion under Constantine and provided the "sacred canopy" over the
existing political and social hierarchy, thereby making Christology the
"apex" of a system of control.[63] Therefore, Ruether's own Christology is
an attempt to understand Christ outside the influence of political hierarchy, in light of a messianic prophetic tradition.

Fundamentally for Ruether, Jesus renews the prophetic vision by
proclaiming a reversal of the system of religious status, where the Word
of God does not validate the existing social and religious hierarchy
but speaks on behalf of the marginalized. This reversal of social order
aims at a new reality in which dominance is overcome as a principle
of social relations. Ruether argues that we see this vision in practice
in what Jesus says: he uses the familiar *Abba* for God, he speaks of the
Messiah as servant rather than king, and he says we are to call no man

60. For Ruether's discussion of the patriarchalization of Christology see *Sexism and God-Talk*, 122–26.

61. Ruether, *Womanguides*, 108.

62. Ibid., 109.

63. Ruether, *Sexism and God-Talk*, 125.

"Father." Relation to God liberates us from social hierarchies. The role of women is also part of the vindication of the lowly and oppressed: the conversation between Jesus and a Samaritan woman at the well, the challenge from the Syro-Phoenician woman who sees redemption for Gentiles, the significance of widows as the most destitute of the poor, the healing of the woman with the flow of blood, the place of prostitutes as the furthest from righteousness.[64] These women are portrayed as the oppressed of the oppressed and hence are seen by Jesus, in light of the reversal of the social order, "as the last who will be first in the Kingdom of God."[65] Rather than seeing women in the Gospels as exemplifying the "essence" of femininity or woman, Ruether understands them to be those who have no honor in the system of religious righteousness, since, she believes, the Gospels are directed at sociological realities in which maleness and femaleness in part make up the definition of social status. Jesus is the liberator who calls for the dissolution of these status relationships.

Yet, it is not his maleness that is of significance here, but the fact that he renounces this system of domination and "seeks to embody in his person the new humanity of service and mutual empowerment."[66] Theologically speaking, the maleness of Jesus has no significance, but it does have social significance. "Jesus as the Christ, the representative of liberated humanity and the liberating Word of God, manifests the *kenosis of patriarchy*, the announcement of the new humanity through a lifestyle that discards hierarchical caste privilege and speaks on behalf of the lowly."[67] Despite this relationship between the redeeming Christ and redeemed women, Ruether asserts that one should not consider them as ultimate theological gender symbols. "Christ is not necessarily male, nor is the redeemed community only women, but a new humanity, female and male."[68] The relationship between the redeemer and the redeemed is dynamic, not static, wherein those who have been liberated can become paradigmatic, liberating persons for others. This is

---

64. Ibid., 136.

65. Ibid., 137.

66. Ibid.

67. Ibid. Elizabeth Johnson is in agreement with Ruether on this point (see Johnson, "Redeeming the Name," 127).

68. Ruether, *Sexism and God-Talk*, 138.

how Ruether views Jesus of Nazareth—as a paradigm.[69] The fullness of redeemed humanity is partially disclosed under the conditions of history through encounters with persons whose authenticity discloses the meaning of liberated personhood. By holding on to the memory of our experiences with such persons, we recognize authenticity in ourselves and others. In Ruether's Christology, Christ is to be understood as a paradigm of liberated humanity, where Jesus saves us by modeling authentic, liberated humanity, rescuing us from sinful distorted relationality and challenging us to save others. All who would live with this sense of liberation, who live as brothers and sisters, are offered redemption.[70]

Because the redeemer manifests the gracious, liberating face of God and our own true human potential, an exclusively male Christ may alienate women from their humanity. It seems that Ruether does not want the only face of a redeeming God and our authentic humanity to be the face of Jesus. The Christ-image should be ever projected on the horizon of history leading us to our unrealized potential.[71] In other words, the Christian community continues Christ's identity. It is redemptive humanity going ahead of us, "calling us to yet incompleted dimensions of human liberation."[72] A liberating encounter with God is an encounter with our authentic self "resurrected" from our alienated self and experienced in and through relationships, healing the brokenness in our relations with our bodies, others, and nature.[73]

Womanist and Asian Feminist Views on Atonement

Critique of traditional atonement theology also comes from womanist and Asian feminist theology and is worth considering briefly. Given their historic experience of surrogacy, womanist theologian Delores Williams argues that black women need to construct a Christian under-

69. Ibid., 114. She refers to McFague, *Metaphorical Theology*, ch. 4.

70. Snyder, *Christology of Ruether*, 101.

71. Ruether, *Womanguides*, 112. Ruether's position is in some contrast to Letty Russell who maintains the lordship of Christ in dialectical tension with the servanthood of Christ. Ruether raises the possibility that Jesus may not be uniquely Lord. For a comparison of Ruether's and Russell's developments of Christology see Grant, *White Women's Christs*, ch. 4.

72. Ruether, *Sexism and God-Talk*, 138.

73. Ibid., 71.

standing of redemption that is more meaningful for them. She claims the Synoptic Gospels provide such resources, by suggesting that "the spirit of God in Jesus came to show humans *life*—to show redemption through a perfect *ministerial* vision of righting relations between body (individual and community), mind (of humans and of tradition) and spirit."[74] God's gift through Jesus was an invitation to humanity to participate in such a vision, and the response to such an invitation was the "horrible deed" the cross represents where humanity tried to kill the vision of life-in-relation which Jesus brought. However, his death was not the last word because the resurrection meant the flourishing of God's spirit and the victory of the *ministerial* vision over the evil that tried to kill it. "Thus, to respond meaningfully to black women's historic experience of surrogacy oppression, the womanist theologian must show that redemption of humans can have nothing to do with any kind of surrogate or substitute role Jesus was reputed to have played in a bloody act that supposedly gained victory over sin and/or evil."[75] Williams considers it an affront to the intelligence of black women to support a view of Jesus' death on the cross whereby he took human sin upon himself and therefore saved humanity. For Williams, it seems more intelligent and more scriptural to understand that redemption had to do with God, through Jesus, giving humankind a *ministerial* vision as a resource for ethical thought and practice through which to build positive, productive lives.[76] Williams understands Jesus to have conquered sin, not in death but in life. Through his ministry of teaching, healing, and casting out demons, Jesus showed humanity a vision of righting relations. "Humankind is, then, redeemed through Jesus' *ministerial* vision of life and not through his death. There is nothing divine in the blood of the cross. God does not intend black women's surrogacy experience."[77]

74. Williams, *Sisters in the Wilderness*, 164–65.

75. Ibid., 165. Carter Heyward agrees with Williams and rejects any blood sacrifice imagery in atonement (Heyward, *Saving Jesus*, 178).

76. Williams, *Sisters in the Wilderness*, 165.

77. Ibid., 167. Williams is critical of other black liberation theologians (e.g., James Deotis Roberts) whose view of atonement is unsettling for womanists in the way images of redemption are associated with the cross, thus supporting a structure of domination (surrogacy) in black women's lives (168–69). For a similar womanist perspective, see Douglas, *Black Christ*. Like Williams, Douglas stresses images of life rather than death. According to her, Jesus' ministry informs womanist theology's emphasis on Christ's presence in the movement for black life. This understanding of Christ appears to be

Like Williams, womanist theologian Jacquelyn Grant begins with black women's experience and understands the significance of suffering within that experience. Because Williams interprets black women's experience primarily in terms of surrogacy, she must reject any view of redemption that implies substitution. Grant, on the other hand, though she may agree with Williams in broad terms, develops no such concept and can therefore find more value in the role of Jesus, including his suffering. According to Grant, black women of the past identified with Jesus because they believed Jesus identified with them. His suffering was not that of a mere human, but of God incarnate, and became a source of empowerment for the weak, including black women.[78] Calling Jesus the Black Christ, Grant asserts that there is an implied universality that made Jesus identify with others: the poor, the woman, the stranger. Jesus identifies with the "little people," black women, he affirms the basic humanity of the least, and he inspires active hope in the struggle for resurrected, liberated existence.[79] This Black Christ, his life and ministry, crucifixion and resurrection, is found in the experiences of black women.[80]

As we have touched upon in earlier chapters, Asian feminist theology is not quick to dismiss Jesus' suffering as valuable for women. Admittedly, the subject of suffering is ambiguous for Asian women because it can either be seen as the seed of liberation or the impetus for oppression of women. However, because Asian women's experience is filled with suffering and obedience, it is only natural for them to identify with Jesus, whose own experience enables Asian women to find meaning in their own suffering.[81] Filipino Lydia Lascano argues that Filipino women understand Jesus neither as a masochist who enjoys suffering nor as a father's boy who does blindly what he is told to do. On the contrary, Jesus is understood as a compassionate man who identified

---

able to be imaged by black men and women who are acting to establish life and wholeness for the black community (ibid., 110).

78. Grant, *White Women's Christ*, 212–14.

79. Ibid., 217. This universality minimizes the significance of Jesus' maleness. His salvation was for all (219). Due to the focus of this thesis we have chosen not to pursue a discussion of the Black Christ in black and womanist theologies, a concept developed by James Cone. For a womanist discussion see Douglas, *Black Christ*.

80. Grant, *White Women's Christ*, 220.

81. Chung, *Struggle to Be*, 54.

himself with the oppressed: "This image of Jesus' suffering gives Asian women the wisdom to differentiate between the suffering imposed by an oppressor and the suffering that is the consequence of one's stand for justice and human dignity."[82] Jesus is the suffering servant who undergoes passive suffering along with powerless Asian women, accompanying them in their struggle for liberation. He is the prophetic Messiah creating a new humanity for oppressed Asian women.[83] Likewise, Asian feminist theologian Chung Hyun Kyung considers the role of Jesus to be important for Asian feminist theology in a way it is not for white feminists. She understands women's experience of self to lead to knowledge of God. Pain and suffering are the "epistemological starting point for Asian women." It is an epistemology of the broken body longing for healing and wholeness.[84] As Asian women suffer they meet God who discloses to them their value as creatures made in the divine image. "To know the self is to know God for Christian Asian women."[85]

White feminist Elizabeth Johnson defends the need to maintain an understanding of the suffering of Christ in theology. Feminists can go too far in countering the omnipotence of God by emphasizing God's powerlessness and weakness in Jesus on the cross. This type of suffering for love is dangerous to women's humanity.[86] However, she wonders if this means that we should not speak of God's suffering at all. Sensitivity to the tremendous suffering of people outside the First World should lead us to use new categories besides "power-over and victimization to speak about pain."[87] Johnson sees the symbol of a suffering God as signaling the mystery of God's solidarity with those who suffer, showing that divine compassion transforms suffering and reorders human beings toward compassionate solidarity themselves.[88] The cross event is a reflection of God's solidarity with the suffering and lost, encouraging

82. Ibid., 57.

83. Ibid.

84. Ibid., 39. Sally Alsford has noted that neglecting sacrificial imagery in atonement theology may result in the dismissal of that element of women's (and oppressed groups) experience and lead to a limitation in our atonement theology (Alsford, "Sin and Atonement," 164).

85. Chung, *Struggle to Be*, 52.

86. Johnson, *She Who Is*, 253.

87. Ibid., 254.

88. Ibid., 267–68.

powerful human love that overcomes disaster and violence.[89] In contrast, Elisabeth Schüssler Fiorenza is concerned about any emphasis on suffering because she maintains that by willingly suffering violence one always serves kyriarchal interests, even if such suffering is understood as redemptive.[90] She is aware that such a position separates her from much of mainstream theology as well as from Latin American, African, and Asian feminist liberation theologies that stress suffering and death as part of the struggle for justice and liberation.[91]

Conclusion: Experience in Feminist Atonement Theology

We have considered the main critique and core elements of feminist atonement theology, but will now examine how an understanding of women's experience affects a feminist theology of atonement. Some feminists address this question more explicitly than others. According to Jacquelyn Grant, "[f]eminist theologians, as liberation theologians, utilize the particular experience of women to determine the questions asked regarding the significance of Jesus."[92] For instance, Grant sees Ruether's alternative imagery for Christ as possible because women's experience is her primary source for doing theology. Women's experience of oppression under social, political, and religious hierarchies is the factor that determines, at least in part, Ruether's understanding of Jesus' death on the cross as *kenosis of patriarchy*. Similarly, white feminist Elisabeth Schüssler Fiorenza understands feminist critical assessments of the theology of the cross as generated by the experi-

89. Johnson, "Redeeming the Name," 124. See also Kathryn Tanner, "Incarnational, Cross, and Sacrifice," 47. Tanner argues that Jesus' true solidarity comes in his incarnation rather than in his death; however, she does not want to dismiss the cross altogether and acknowledges that there is something saving about the cross, although there is "nothing saving about suffering, death or victimhood, in and of themselves."

90. Schüssler Fiorenza, *Jesus*, 14. We recall that by kyriarchy she means the rule of the emperor/master/lord/father/husband over his subordinates. This is not to imply that all men dominate and exploit all women without difference to culture of economic status. Whereas patriarchy implies an opposition between male and female, Schüssler Fiorenza seeks to develop an understanding of domination and oppression that goes beyond this.

91. Schüssler Fiorenza, *Jesus*, 102.

92. Grant, *White Women's Christ*, 10.

ence, in particular, of violence against women and the oppression of women in general.[93] Feminist discussion of the theology of the cross explicitly claims women's experience and authority for assessing and rearticulating mainstream theological meaning, thus forcing one to ask *who* are the agents of such meaning-making processes.[94] For Schüssler Fiorenza, theological discourse about Jesus does not derive its authority from "revelatory," "feminist," "spiritual" experience, rather it is articulated and proven right through continuing practices of struggle for survival, justice, and well-being—in other words, as a political vindication for the world.[95]

However, as a womanist, Grant wonders if a source such as experience is helpful because white feminists may have failed to understand the particularity of non-white women's experience.[96] If white women's experience determines theological doctrine, it is problematic for non-white women because Christian doctrine will lack a full understanding of women's experience. Womanist Kelly Brown Douglas says womanists do Christology in the sense that they attempt to discern from the perspective of *black women* what it means for Jesus to be the Christ.[97] Likewise, Delores Williams states that for womanists, talk about Jesus in relation to atonement theory must be "guided more by *black Christian women's* voices, faith and experience than by anything that was decided centuries ago at Chalcedon."[98] However, to ensure the relevance of theological doctrine, will we be forced to have each particular set of women writing theology for their own group? Will white feminists, womanists, and Asian feminists, for instance, each have a different understanding of atonement that suits the experience of each set of women? It is not our intention to devalue the contribution of non-white feminists by questioning their insistence that particular women's experience must inform christological and soteriological doctrines. Rather, we are identifying the tendency in feminist theology, white and non-white, to use a particular understanding of women's experience not merely to inform,

93. Schüssler Fiorenza, *Jesus*, 120.

94. Ibid., 121.

95. Ibid., 127–28.

96. Grant, *White Women's Christ*, 145.

97. Douglas, *Black Christ*, 111 (italics added).

98. Williams, *Sisters in the Wilderness*, 203 (italics added). See also Douglas, *Black Christ*, 111.

but rather to determine the content of various Christian doctrines, in this case, the doctrine of the atonement. However, should there not be a distinction between what is meaningful to a particular context and what is considered normative for theology?

The work of the feminists presented in this chapter demonstrates that what could be considered a proper abhorrence of women's experience of oppression may lead to the exclusion of those elements of the biblical narrative and the Christian tradition of atonement that contain aspects of violence and oppression, aspects that would resonate with the distressing experience of many women. The exclusion of the violence and suffering of Jesus' death from atonement theology leads to an emphasis on Jesus' life rather than his death and resurrection. In this way, an understanding of women's experience has a bearing on how one interprets atonement. Because women's experience has so often been one of oppression, including physical abuse and domination, any interpretation of the cross that seems to contain a form of oppression must be rejected because it will perpetuate the negative experiences of women, or else affirm others' efforts at domination. Therefore, the three major critiques covered in this chapter emphasize the life and ministry of Jesus as the source of redemption (Mary Grey's position possibly allows more space for the pain of Jesus' death), an approach which seems to lead to an individualism whereby liberation comes out of one's choice to live a life modeled on Jesus' life. It lacks a cosmic dimension and reflects a failure to understand the magnitude of human sin, which, in the light of the severity of women's experience of oppression, seems contradictory to the feminist hope for transformation of patriarchal society.

Let us return to feminist standpoint epistemology, which seeks to expose the world that men have constructed as partial and perverse. One might say that feminist theology considers the theology of atonement, which up to now has been written almost exclusively by men, as providing a partial and perverse view of redemption. However, regarding this study, it seems that a feminist standpoint approach is in danger of constructing a "partial and perverse" version of the theological landscape in respect to atonement. Before we pursue an extended critique of feminist interpretations of atonement, let us first examine the traditional doctrines themselves, permitting us to return to the feminist views with a better understanding of whether the feminist theologians have gotten their critique right and how the category of experience affects their interpretations.

5

The Subjective Element of Feminist Atonement Theologies

Introduction: Traditional Atonement Theology and the Feminist Critique

THE PREVIOUS CHAPTER EXAMINES SOME OF THE MAJOR FEMINIST views on atonement, which we will now consider specifically in relationship to the traditional theories they critique. This critique is typically done in general terms, often without extended attention to particular theologians. As we can see, the feminist rejection of traditional atonement is lodged against three major positions: a satisfaction theory developed by Anselm, the *Christus victor* model expounded by Gustaf Aulén, and a moral influence position often attributed to Abelard. We will briefly examine these three, keeping in mind that, for the purpose of this thesis, each will be considered in a broad sense, relying on basic points of theological agreement, rather than dealing with variant interpretations that continue to be the subject of scholarly debate. A general understanding of each perspective will be quite sufficient to address the basic feminist critique, comparing and contrasting the feminist theologies of atonement presented in the previous chapter with the more traditional views at the root of feminist objections to atonement. Through our consideration of the feminist views on atonement in relation to the traditional understandings they criticize, it is our aim to expose the weaknesses of the feminist theologies of atonement and how an understanding of women's experience contributes to such weaknesses.

Three Traditional Models of Atonement

Anselmian/Satisfaction

To some extent, most feminist critique of atonement is directed at the predominant Western understanding characterized by the theology of Anselm, hence we will devote more of our attention to his position than to the other two. In particular, those feminists who allege that atonement doctrine portrays "divine child abuse" find the Anselmian formula to consist of the punishment of one perfect child at the hands (or by permission) of the father in order to atone for human sin. This child serves as a substitute or sacrifice for the other children and is the only means of satisfaction that God the Father could receive. Such a theory appears to place God's love and justice at odds with each other and consequently, the Son's love for God and the world is submitted in sacrificial death to appease the divine justice. However, does this common feminist characterization of the satisfaction theory of atonement fall short of adequately considering Anselm? Before attempting to address that question, let us first summarize Anselm's position.

Cur Deus Homo

In *Cur Deus Homo* Anselm seeks to explain the reason God was made a man and how, by his death, he gave life to the world. His presentation comes in the form of a dialogue between Boso acting as questioner and Anselm acting as respondent. In spite of feminist claims to the contrary, Anselm was not ignorant of the difficulties in explaining the cross. For instance, in Book I Boso asks how it could be proved just or reasonable that God would so treat (or permit to be treated) the man he calls "beloved Son." Would not God be worthy of condemnation for condemning the innocent?[1] Anselm replies that the Father did not compel the Son to die nor permit him to be killed unwillingly. Jesus Christ bore his death by his own free will in order that he might save the human race (I.viii[2]).

---

1. This is the very nature of the question we see Rita Nakashima Brock, Joanne Carlson Brown and Rebecca Parker asking. In fact, Brown and Parker state that no classical theory has questioned the necessity of Jesus' suffering at all (Brown and Parker, "For God So Loved?" 4). See St. Anselm *Cur Deus Homo* I.viii. Further citations from this source will be included in the text.

2.

Even so, Boso still finds it difficult to understand that God would require the blood of the innocent so that he might spare the guilty (I.x). According to Anselm, the proper response to this dilemma lies in one's position regarding sin, meaning for him that the gravity of sin requires this particular action from God. All owe a debt to God, that is, all owe to God a life of obedience. Sin is the dishonor brought on God when one does not give to God what is due. Furthermore, it is not enough to repay what was abstracted, but one must return more than was taken, hence the satisfaction owed to God (I.xi).[3] "It is therefore necessary that either the honour abstracted shall be restored, or punishment shall follow; otherwise, God were either unjust to Himself, or were powerless for either, which it is a shame even to imagine" (I.xiii).

A satisfaction is required, one that can only be made by God, but one that only a human being should make, therefore Anselm determines that the satisfaction should be made by one who is both God and human (II.vi). Because Christ did not dishonor God, but rather lived a life of obedience, he owed no satisfaction. Yet, since he died as an innocent, his death is a merit which is assigned to those for whom Christ became incarnate and died. His death is an example of dying for righteousness' sake and it is only because human beings share in his merits that we are imitators of him (II.xix). Anselm understands the Triune God as active in atonement and as determining the road to salvation, not because he is bound to a law outside himself, but by his own freedom (I.xii). In other words, God must be consistent within himself.

Four basic themes emerge in Anselm's view: (1) the voluntary nature of Christ's death, (2) the value of Christ's death, (3) the application of merits, and (4) Christ's death as an example to others.[4] Anselm expends a good deal of effort trying to convince Boso in Book I that although God requires obedience of human beings, Jesus still submits to his death out of his own free will. Anselm wants to say both, that God wills the death of Christ (in order to save humanity) and that Christ's obedience is free (I.ix).[5] Whatever God's plan for the salvation

3. It should be kept in mind that Anselm does not mean that human beings can somehow take something away from God or in some sense diminish God's character.

4. McIntyre, *St. Anselm and His Critics*, 154.

5. Ibid., 160. Feminist theologians have difficulty with either side of the issue. They criticize a view of God in atonement whereby God requires Christ's death as the means to save humanity (primarily from God's wrath). At the same time, they dislike the no-

of humankind, there remains the voluntary nature of Christ's death; the Father did not compel him to die. No necessity of God's preceded Christ's free will, because he had the power to lay down his own life (II.xviii). Jesus Christ freely made recompense for those who could not, that is, he offered God the honor which was due to him as well as his own life, the life of a sinless and innocent man. This offering by Christ became the merit for sinners. Jesus' death is what might be called vicarious or representative satisfaction.[6] Often considered strictly an objective view of atonement, Anselm's theory does have a subjective element whereby he understands Christ's death as an example for redeemed humanity (II.xix).[7] Anselm scholar John McIntyre offers a helpful summary of human salvation as deduced by Anselm:

> The Son, by reason of His free Death which He offered to God as a gift, must needs be recompensed by God for this great deed. But since all that is the Father's is His also, and since, too, He has committed no sins which God might forgive in return for this gift and thus cancel the debt to God created by them, the question arises of how God can make recompense for the Death of Christ. The answer given by St. Anselm is that God makes over the reward to those for whose salvation the Son became man, and to whom He held up the example of persisting in righteousness even unto death. When the transaction is completed, the sinful men are forgiven the debts they owe, for they are given that which by reason of their sins they lacked. Concerning the achievement of participation in such grace and the manner in which he is to live by it, Holy Scriptures everywhere provide instruction.[8]

ANSELM'S THEORY: THE MAIN POINTS OF FEMINIST CRITIQUE

We have provided a brief summary of Anselm's *Cur Deus Homo,* the primary account of the satisfaction theory of atonement predominant in Western Christianity (and the recipient of most feminist criticism). Despite the fact that the most accurate interpretation of *Cur Deus*

tion of Christ's free obedience as it leads to the violent suffering and death of an innocent person. Either way, feminists determine that traditional atonement theology is bad for women.

6. Ibid., 172.
7. Ibid., 186.
8. Ibid., 180.

Homo continues to be a source of scholarly debate, we are still able to
rely on several consistent theological conclusions in order to respond
to the feminist critique. First, a primary focus of critique is the point
that Anselm's theory focuses on punishment rather than healing or salvation.[9] However, many consider the emphasis of Anselm's theory not
to be on punishment, but rather on merit, that is, the cross is not penal
but meritorious. God in Christ offered what others could not offer.[10]
Jesus was obedient to God, but this does not mean that God coerced
Jesus into accepting death on the cross. Jesus submitted to death as a
result of his obedience.[11] Anselm does not regard Christ's death as penal
substitution, but that the value of Christ's death arises from his very
person, as well as his sinlessness, and becomes a merit that is transferred
to sinners. This is how vicariousness works.[12] Penalty is secondary and
demonstrates Anselm's concern to account for the enormity of human
sin.[13] Feminists often read punishment into Anselm when in fact he
shows that God intervened in order to avoid punishment.[14]

Even so, the feminist concern regarding punishment has some
validity in that Anselm's theory does appear to allow for an element
of punishment since he seems to argue that, due to the moral order-
ing of the universe, God is not free to forgive without punishment. For
Anselm, it would be inconsistent with God's nature and character to
treat righteousness and wickedness the same (I.xii).[15] Anselm's theory
places much weight on the action of Jesus toward the Father, appearing
to equate salvation with remission of penalty.[16] Harnack finds Anselm's
biggest flaw to be what he calls a "mythological" conception of God as
the "private man who is incensed at the injury done to His honour and

9. Brock, *Journeys by Heart*, 7. This point is related to the concern about innocent suffering also voiced in other feminists, including Brown and Parker.

10. Hart, "Anselm of Canterbury," 319. See also McIntyre, *St. Anselm*, 195; Harnack, *History of Dogma*, 6:68. Harnack is one of Anselm's biggest critics, yet he recognizes that Anselm's is not a theory of penal substitution and that punishment is actually averted in Anselm's theory.

11. Hart, "Anselm of Canterbury," 320.

12. McIntyre, *St. Anselm*, 87, 182.

13. Ibid., 196.

14. Megill-Cobbler, "Feminist Rethinking of Punishment," 16.

15. McIntyre, *St. Anselm*, 99.

16. Gunton, *Actuality of Atonement*, 93.

does not forego His wrath till He has received an at least adequately great equivalent."[17] Feminist theologian Margo Houts also acknowledges a similar weakness in Anselm because he tends to be concerned with the remission of penalty of sin (justification) rather than release from power of sin (sanctification). However, distinct from the typical feminist critique, Houts recognizes the element of punishment but considers the Reformers, not Anselm, to be insistent on that aspect.[18]

A second area of critique is related to the claim that Anselm's thought is influenced by certain types of analogies related to his historical and cultural context, resulting in a view of atonement tainted by a particular place and time. Some see the mark of feudal imagery where the servant dishonors a good master.[19] Likewise, Aulén saw Tertullian's concepts of satisfaction and merit as applied to the system of penance as even more influential on Anselm than Germanic law.[20] The early Latin Fathers were lawyers and predisposed to express relations with God in legal terms.[21] Although theologians acknowledge the influence of feudal society and juridical concepts, there is concern that such a view eclipses the real meaning of Anselm's theory. Colin Gunton argues that such imagery should be appreciated rather than dismissed. According to him, the feudal ruler had a duty to uphold order and justice within society, without which it would collapse, a concept that helps one to see that God operates analogously, as the upholder of universal justice.[22] Gunton admits that there are juridical influences on the Anselmic metaphor, but that Anselm is most concerned about the relation between the creature and Creator, not a concept of abstract justice.[23] The under-

17. Harnack, History of Dogma, 6:76.

18. Houts, "Atonement and Abuse," 30.

19. Hopkins, Companion to St. Anselm, 197.

20. Aulén, Christus Victor, 81–82. McIntyre considers Aulén wrong on this point, noting that Anselm recognized that penitential practices do not of themselves remove debt, although he allows that sinful human beings require spiritual disciplines, though not for forgiveness (McIntyre, St. Anselm, 177).

21. Gunton, Actuality of Atonement, 85–87. Gunton agrees with Harnack on this point, although things may not have been as stark as Harnack put it. Still, there was a tendency to conceive of relations to God in terms of legal obligations.

22. Gunton, Actuality of Atonement, 89.

23. Ibid., 91. Here Gunton is in agreement with Balthasar. Balthasar believes Anselm's theory is not overly juridical; he did not see a juridic transaction at the heart of atonement (Olsen, "Hans Urs von Balthasar," 56).

lying correspondence between feudal honor and vassal service never eclipses the exemplary nature of Christ's death—God's mercy toward humanity is manifested in atonement.[24] Although Anselm interprets the efficacy of Christ's death in terms of a monastic penitential system, the examples of a feudal system and monastic penitence should not be understood as depicting atonement in a purely calculating way. God seeks to lift humanity out of sin, not just repair his own honor.[25] Any analysis of *Cur Deus Homo* that sees it as inference from Teutonic law or medieval penance systems misses the deeper significance that is set in the *aseitas* of God.[26] McIntyre identifies the concept of *aseitas* as of supreme importance to Anselm, in other words, the grounds for God's actions and criterion for revelation are found in God himself.[27] It is not that God is personally offended by human transgression, but that the order and beauty of the universe is at stake (I.xv).[28] God is unwilling to let his creatures destroy themselves. Salvation is an act of the Triune God.[29] Anselm's purpose is to show how atonement follows from the very nature of God and not a rationality external to God.[30] In the debate about the influence of cultural analogies upon Anselm, "[s]o much hangs on a sensitive appreciation of what are the possibilities and limits of the legal metaphor."[31]

Finally, feminists appear to conflict most strongly with the objective aspect of atonement characterized by Anselm, accusing Christian soteriology of justifying the victimization of women. To put it another way, feminist theologians ask if the Christian understanding of the cross, particularly the Anselmian/satisfaction theory influential in Reformed doctrine, promotes abuse. A few reactions to these challenges have surfaced in recent years. In a response to Joanne Carlson Brown, Margo Houts disagrees with Brown's assessment that atonement theology in all its forms is irredeemably oppressive. For Houts, theology is no longer Christian if it does not retain the assertion that humanity needs

24. Hopkins, *Companion to St. Anselm*, 198.

25. Ibid., 211.

26. McIntyre, *St. Anselm*, 185.

27. Ibid.

28. Gunton, *Actuality of Atonement*, 90.

29. Ibid., 91–92.

30. McIntyre, *St. Anselm*, 203.

31. Gunton, *Actuality of Atonement*, 101.

a savior and that Jesus is in some sense this savior. She acknowledges that atonement theology has operated with an abusive edge, but rightly understood, it can be a resource for countering patriarchal oppression.[32] Likewise, Richard Mouw is prepared to concede that some Reformed understandings of the cross have encouraged abusive practices, however, it does not follow that Reformed views about the atonement promote abuse.[33] Saying that atonement theology is often used abusively is different from saying it is always and necessarily abusive.[34]

Within the feminist critique there is a tendency to assume that penal imagery is the dominant metaphor for the tradition, as well as to caricature traditional understandings of atonement.[35] There is a lack of Trinitarian understanding of God in much feminist atonement theology which leads to seeing the atonement as a transaction between divine personalities. Therefore, "[w]e can expect imagery to run rampant when the controls which Trinitarian doctrine places on atonement imagery are removed."[36] Houts considers Brown to be critical of all forms of suffering, charging God with sadism because God is responsible in some way for Jesus' suffering and death. "But what Brown fails to acknowledge is that the allegation of sadism comes into view only when Jesus is severed from the Godhead and made an object of divine action against him."[37] Furthermore, abusive practices may occur in spite of what a theologically shaped culture may teach. Regarding Calvinism in particular, Mouw's sense is that popular Calvinism is more shaped by a picture of God as a distant, male authority figure than by the cross, when, in fact, atonement doctrine serves as an antidote to this distorted view.[38] Mouw is convinced that a proper understanding of atonement provides spiritual and moral resources for combating

32 Houts, "Atonement and Abuse," 29. See also Van Dyk, "Do Theories of Atonement Foster Abuse?" 21. Van Dyk does agree with parts of the feminist critique, noting that Christian pastors have counseled battered women to "bear their cross."

33. Mouw, response to Van Wijk-Bos, 2–3.

34. Van Dyk, "Do Theories of Atonement Foster Abuse?" 24.

35. Megill-Cobbler, "Feminist Rethinking of Punishment," 16; Houts, "Atonement and Abuse," 29.

36. Houts, "Atonement and Abuse," 30. Van Dyk agrees that the feminist critique lacks adequate understanding of the Trinity (Van Dyk, "Do Theories of Atonement Foster Abuse?" 24).

37. Houts, "Atonement and Abuse," 31.

38. Mouw, response to Van Wijk-Bos, 3.

abusive behaviors.[39] Due to the diversity of biblical images (borrowed from the altar, battlefield, courtroom, marketplace, family, and Hebrew concept of corporate community), every theory will have strengths and weaknesses. "The apostolic community, however, allowed all images to stand in complementary relationship rather than reducing them to a single theory."[40] Therefore, it seems possible that Christian theology, when liberated from certain distorting errors, does no legitimate abuse to women.[41]

Perhaps much feminist critique of atonement has failed to address the complexity of the situation: how a culture of abuse develops from atonement imagery and how the church sustains abusive relationships. The connection between penal imagery as a significant atonement metaphor and actual abusive relationships within the church must be more thoroughly examined if it is to be the centerpiece of critique. Certainly there is some validity to feminist claims, as acknowledged by those mentioned above, however, there is more to be considered.[42] Furthermore, as some womanists, Asian feminists, and white feminists (e.g., Jacquelyn Grant, Chung Hyun Kyung, Elizabeth Johnson) have noted, there is a need to maintain an understanding of the suffering of Christ in theology. It is valuable for women to identify with the suffering of Jesus as they undergo their own pain and suffering. Although it may be a fine line for feminists to walk, speaking of suffering shows sensitivity to and solidarity with those who suffer, particularly those outside the first world.

One can see the complex nature of debate surrounding Anselm's *Cur Deus Homo* and note the inadequate treatment of the debate within

39. Ibid., 4–6. Although Mouw does not consider that a Reformed view can relinquish the sense that Christ did suffer the divine wrath against sin in some important sense, he wonders if this view actually promotes violence and abuse. The Reformed tradition's teaching on violence came out of a desire to place moral limits on the use of violence, insisting that violence is permissible only if certain moral guidelines are intact (this is in the context of "just-war" theories). In addition, the once-for-all character of the atoning work of Christ is an important emphasis in the Reformed tradition. In contrast, Mennonite theologian J. Denny Weaver blames the excesses of penal atonement on the Reformers more than on Anselm (Weaver, *Nonviolent Atonement*, 192).

40. Houts, "Atonement and Abuse," 30.

41. Van Dyk, "Do Theories of Atonement Foster Abuse?" 21.

42. Heim, "Saved by What Shouldn't Happen," 220. Heim's essay outlines the complexities in viewing the cross sacrificially, stating that sacrifice is a diagnosis not a prescription.

feminist critique. The dismissal of certain elements of Anselm's theory without due consideration of the theory itself, let alone of how the theory has been understood within the Reformed tradition historically, reveals a tendency in feminist theologies of atonement to generalize traditional views without properly engaging them. But let us explore the other main views under their attack before continuing.

Redemption in Peter Abelard

Although the critique against Abelard is less pervasive than that against Anselm, some feminist theologians reject the notion that innocent suffering has the power to persuade us to believe in God's mercy and move us to a loving response (e.g., Brown and Parker). However, Abelard is often attributed with a "subjective" understanding of atonement that might be considered more closely akin to current feminist interpretations.[43] While perhaps finding fault with the exemplarist aspects of Abelard's position, it seems that some feminists still might find him a positive resource since they often accuse traditional atonement theories of lacking a subjective element, for example, accusing Anselm of being overly objective and failing to include an element of salvation that relates to the human experience. Let us consider Abelard to see exactly what he and feminist theologians might have in common.

Like Anselm, Abelard was against the Augustinian view that the devil had rights over humanity; that Christ's death was a ransom paid to the devil.[44] Despite this minor agreement, the two are most often contrasted as representatives of the opposing objective (Anselm) and

---

43. Gunton distinguishes between a subjective and an exemplarist view. The former sees the central feature of Christ's life and death as its effect upon the believer while the latter stresses the objective basis of atonement doctrine, that is, the life of Jesus and love of God are examples to believers rather than a substitutionary transaction (Gunton, *Actuality of Atonement*, 157). Alister McGrath argues against Hastings Rashdall's conclusion that Abelard is exemplarist. McGrath considers Abelard to uphold Christ as an example to be imitated, but not that this imitation means redemption, rather it is because believers are redeemed that they wish to imitate Christ (McGrath, "Moral Theory," 206). When referring to Abelard as exemplarist, we mean it in the sense that McGrath describes.

44. Abelard, "Exposition of Romans," 281. See also Luscombe, *School of Peter Abelard*, 137. Please note that for consistency we have used the spelling "Abelard" vs. "Abailard."

subjective (Abelard) views of atonement.[45] Abelard's view is that the love of God is the means and motive for redemption.[46] He understood Christ's death not as a debt paid either to God or to the devil,[47] but considered reconciliation to be something spiritual. Christ's death draws us away from love of self and wins for us approval in God's sight.[48] His view of atonement is related to his understanding of sin as something that affects our relationship with God, rather than as an injury to God's majesty.[49] Our repentance springs from our love for God[50] for which the cross is the incentive and example, showing us how we should live.[51] Sin is characterized as personal responsibility[52] and redemption is effected by Christ's life and death as spiritual transformation of sinners.[53] In the words of Peter Abelard from his "Exposition of the Epistle to the Romans,"

> Now it seems to us that we have been justified by the blood of Christ and reconciled to God in this way: through this unique act of grace manifested to us—in that his Son has taken upon himself our nature and persevered therein in teaching us by word and example even unto death—he has more fully bound us to himself by love; with the result that our hearts should be enkindled by such a gift of divine grace, and true charity should not now shrink from enduring anything for him.[54]

Hastings Rashdall describes Abelard's understanding of Christ's death as the voluntary death of the innocent Son that moves the sinner to gratitude and answering love, including the consciousness of sin.[55] Abelard emphasizes a subjective view of atonement, portraying

45. Aulén, *Christus Victor*, 2.

46. Fiddes, *Past Event and Present Salvation*, 143.

47. Sikes, *Peter Abailard*, 207.

48. Ibid., 211.

49. Ibid., 183–84.

50. Ibid., 194.

51. Ibid., 207–8.

52. Weingart, *Logic of Divine Love*, 44.

53. Ibid., 210.

54. Abelard, "Exposition of Romans," 283.

55. Rashdall, *Idea of Atonement*, 358. Rashdall interprets Abelard as explicitly explaining the efficacy of Christ's death by its subjective influence. Abelard's inclusion of sin as part of the subjective response is in contrast to modern subjective theories that emphasize the love aspect but fail to draw attention to repentance and personal sin.

Christ's life and passion as an example of love, however, were one to reject Abelard on this basis it may be from reading him too narrowly.[56] It can be argued that Abelard developed his argument a bit one-sidedly, but did not deliberately reject objective elements of atonement.[57] He says that through the price of Christ's blood God has made way for our redemption.[58] Abelard denies Christ's work as substitution, yet never presents it as merely an inducement for human beings to effect their own salvation. God in Christ does for humankind what it cannot do for itself. Abelard's approach is faithful to biblical sources and New Testament metaphors.[59] McGrath agrees with Weingart's assessment that Abelard's is a thoroughly theocentric understanding of salvation whereby atonement is an act of divine love.[60] He argues that Abelard understands Christ to be our example in that because we are redeemed we wish to imitate him:[61] "Wherefore, our redemption through Christ's suffering is that deeper affection in us which not only frees us from slavery to sin, but also wins for us the true liberty of sons of God, so that we do all things out of love rather than fear."[62] Abelard's theory is subjective and exemplarist in that Christ's life and death have an effect upon the believer and that Jesus' love is an example for the believer. However, it is not exemplarist in that merely by Christ's example somehow we receive redemption. For Abelard salvation is achieved by God alone, not by the human ability to follow Christ's example.[63]

Despite the differences in scholarly interpretations of just how exemplarist or subjective is Abelard's understanding of redemption, it seems feminist theologians would find his concern to relate the experience of redemption to the human situation an element of atonement

56. Luscombe, *School of Peter Abelard*, 137.

57. Ibid., 138.

58. Abailard, "Exposition of Romans," 283.

59. Weingart, *Logic of Divine Love*, 159.

60. McGrath, "Moral Theory," 208; Weingart, *Logic of Divine Love*, 131.

61. Ibid., 209.

62. Abelard, "Exposition of Romans," 284.

63. McGrath, "Moral Theory," 200. Both McGrath and Weingart reject critics' accusation of Abelard's theory being exemplarist. McGrath condemns Rashdall's assessment of Abelard. Rashdall apparently finds inspiration for his own perspective from Abelard, however, McGrath sees Rashdall's theory as amounting to nothing more than salvation by merit—something quite distinct from Abelard.

theology they could endorse. Since the focus of many feminist theologies of atonement is away from the understanding of some divine transaction toward the lived experience of women, Abelard's emphasis could be considered useful. However, it appears that he maintains some key aspects of traditional atonement theology that feminists reject, for instance, his affirmation of the significance of Jesus' death as necessary to a theory of redemption. Therefore, feminist theologians are led to oppose him because they refuse to accept an understanding of atonement that finds value in the suffering of the individual, regardless how meaningful it is to the human experience. Despite the subjective focus of his conception of redemption, which could have been a point of agreement, the role of Christ's suffering in atonement remains the focus of feminist critique regarding Abelard because he appears to relate to a more objectivist tradition.[64]

Victory over Death in Gustaf Aulén

The third main area of feminist critique is directed at the understanding of the cross as representing Christ's victory over death, most famously presented in the work of Gustaf Aulén. The concern with this view is that suffering and death are seen to result in triumph and considered a prelude to glory, a view feminists argue encourages believers to endure suffering. In Aulén's classic text, *Christus Victor*, he presents Anselm and Abelard as representing the standard contrast between objective and subjective views, describing the objective view as showing atonement to be the continuous act of God while the subjective shows God's act to be discontinuous, that is, carried out by a human being.[65] In contrast to both these views, Aulén identifies what he calls the "classic" view, based on early church fathers (he names Irenaeus first and foremost, then Origen, Athanasius, Basil the Great, Gregory of Nyssa, Gregory of Nazianzus, Augustine, Gregory the Great), as more accurate to the

---

64. Abelard is subjectivist (and exemplarist) in the sense that Christ is objectively an example to be followed by a subjective response. Exemplarism as demonstrated by the feminist views is not merely subjective, but the nature of the objective event is no longer, as on the traditional account, something that objectively changes the human standing before God.

65. Aulén, *Christus Victor*, 5.

biblical text. [66] The central theme of this position is the concept of the atonement as a divine conflict and victory (*Christus victor*) where Christ fights against the evil powers of the world and through this struggle reconciles the world to God.[67] The conflict and subsequent victory constitutes atonement because the victory over evil powers brings to pass a new relation of reconciliation between God and the world.[68] Aulén understands the classic view to have been neglected in the atonement theologies of the eighteenth and nineteenth centuries and considers his book to be a historical analysis rather than an actual presentation of the classic idea. However, it is apparent that Aulén considers the classic view to be a return to genuine Christian faith.[69]

Most feminist theologians are in agreement that any atonement formula that emphasizes the victory-over-death motif, such as that found in Aulén's position, is unacceptable for women. They are rightfully concerned with how such a stance may lead some women (at the behest of their pastors) to undergo extended pain and suffering, particularly as victims of an abusive spouse, with the goal of obtaining some kind of glory in their suffering. Unfortunately, in these situations, the model of victory over death is removed from its context of redemption and placed upon women as a way to approach all undeserved suffering. Distinct from the pastoral problems, it might be beneficial for feminist theologians to consider exploring how the *Christus victor* model is distinct, within the context of Jesus' life and his work of redemption, from the daily struggles of battered women. The problem may not turn out to be the *Christus victor* model in particular, but how it has been applied in the Christian church.

Women's Experience and Sin in Feminist Atonement Theology

In Part One of this book we have been trying to understand how women's experience plays a role in feminist theology, and now in Part Two we consider how the category of women's experience affects feminist the-

66. Ibid., 46.
67. Ibid., 4.
68. Ibid., 5.
69. Ibid., 159.

ologies of atonement. Because of the theological relationship between sin and redemption, we cannot determine the role of women's experience in atonement theology without considering how experience has informed an understanding of sin. We may gain clues to understanding the relationship of experience to atonement theology by examining experience in relation to concepts of sin.

Sin Understood as Estrangement

As we have already discussed, a significant feminist perspective on sin developed by feminists, such as Valerie Saiving and Judith Plaskow, links sin to experience; and yet, except for its relation to patriarchy, feminist theologies of atonement neglect the subject of sin.[70] Reformed theologian Leanne Van Dyk considers the subject of sin to be crucial to theology. She sees a great deal of evidence that there is a deep longing for salvation prevalent in society (e.g., the burgeoning co-dependency literature, proliferation of 12-step programs, phenomenon of drug and alcohol addiction, and alarming rate of depression and suicide among teenagers). It seems that feminists want to begin their theology of atonement with human experience, yet do not consider adequately these significant experiences of need. In other words, by not discussing signs of longing for salvation, the subjects of sin, estrangement, and redemption are not addressed.[71]

Understandably, the notion of sin has presented serious problems for women in the Christian church over the centuries, beginning with an association of sin with Eve and women, with nature as inferior to spirit. Further, Saiving and Plaskow identified the predominant definition of sin as one developed exclusively in terms of pride, thus failing to portray accurately many women's experience of sin. Because of the negative relationship between women and sin in Christian theology, many feminists choose to focus on subjects with more constructive potential for women. This may be one explanation for the lack of feminist discussion of sin and one reason that feminist atonement theology does not take account of sin more thoroughly. Nevertheless, feminist theolo-

70. Alsford, "Sin and Atonement," 160. Alsford recognizes that our theologies of atonement and sin must be related to lived experience. Salvation must have a genuine relationship to this experience.

71. Van Dyk, "Vision and Imagination," 6.

gies of atonement do communicate some general understandings of sin as it relates to the need for redemption.

Broadly speaking, the feminists discussed in the previous chapter understand sin as somehow related to relationality; that is, there is a disconnectedness with others and with oneself. We find this particularly in Brock, Grey, and Ruether. Such brokenness, it is argued, does not need punishment but healing. Hence, wholeness becomes the norm by which these feminist theologies of atonement are governed.[72] The purpose of atonement is to restore mutuality in relationships and help women find their authentic selves, no longer alienated from themselves, the creation, and others. Such an understanding is not unlike what we find in Paul Tillich's view of sin and atonement. Tillich also interprets salvation as "healing," which corresponds to his identification of existence as primarily a state of estrangement. "In this sense, healing means reuniting that which is estranged, giving a centre to what is split, overcoming the split between God and man, man and his world, man and himself. Out of this interpretation of salvation, the concept of the New Being has grown."[73]

Tillich describes the doctrine of atonement as "the effect of the New Being in Jesus as the Christ on those who are grasped by it in their state of estrangement." He attempts to include both an objective and subjective element, that is, the manifestation of the New Being which has an atoning effect, and that which happens to humanity under the atoning effect.[74] The divine act involves overcoming estrangement as a matter of human guilt. This guilt is removed as a factor separating humanity from God. However, this divine act is effective only if humanity accepts the removal of guilt and the offer of divine reconciliation.[75] It is right that salvation should have a genuine relationship to human

72. Megill-Cobbler, "Women and the Cross," 153. See also Ruether, *Women and Redemption*, 8. She describes redemption in the modern feminist context as being about the reclaiming of an original goodness, not being reconciled to God.

73. Tillich, *Systematic Theology*, 2:192. Rita Nakashima Brock views sin as brokenness and socially produced, therefore, salvation is healing. See Young, "Diversity in Feminist Christology," 83; and also Fiddes, *Past Event*, 7. Throughout the various atonement theologies and historical imagery for the human predicament, Fiddes finds the constants of estrangement, loss of potential, and rebellion. These constants, with the exception of rebellion, fit with the general perspective of contemporary feminists.

74. Tillich, *Systematic Theology*, 2:196–97.

75. Ibid., 2:197.

experience; however, a desire to connect salvation to experience may lead to a theory of atonement that is overly subjective.[76]

Sin and a Subjective View of Atonement

An understanding of redemption connected to an understanding of sin that is characterized primarily in existential terms can lead to an atonement theology that appears to be more subjective than objective, explaining atonement as something that occurs in human existence rather than between God and humanity or in cosmic terms. Abelard, whose view on atonement was the first to be labeled "subjective," may have been led down that path due to his dislike of what came to be known as penal substitution, as well as for his conception of sin which focused more on the intent of the individual than on dishonoring the majesty of God, as in Anselm's view. Abelard was concerned with the internal motives of the individual and intended his understanding of atonement to address this, stressing that by God's redemption we experience an internal change of heart, so to speak.[77] However, let us not consider Abelard as the only example of a potentially subjective view of atonement. Another major theologian who might better fit this charge is Schleiermacher, who we might add is also helpful due to his relation to feminist theology and theologies of experience.[78] Aulén found it natural to compare the two, seeing Abelard as emphasizing Christ as a great teacher and example who arouses responsive love, and Schleiermacher as revealing the greatest weakness of the subjective view whereby the atoning work of God is dependent upon the ethical effects in the individual.[79] In other

---

76. Any knowledge of Christ must show how it brings "saving benefits" to the human situation. See Baillie, *God was in Christ*, 159; and also Fiddes, *Past Event and Present Salvation*, whose purpose in this book is to trace the historical understanding of the human predicament and atonement, therefore integrating the subjective and objective views.

77. Sikes, *Peter Abailard*, 189–90.

78. See chapter 2 above. Although both Abelard and Schleiermacher are from a subjectivist tradition, Schleiermacher is clearly basing his position on an experiential account of faith, whereas Abelard is still relating to a more objectivist tradition. What both dislike (and for similar reasons) is penal substitution.

79. Aulén, *Christus Victor*, 96, 139.

words, the emphasis in atonement becomes "that which is done in men and by men."[80]

Schleiermacher's Understanding of Redemption

Schleiermacher understands the Redeemer's redemptive activity to consist in the assumption of believers into the power of his God-consciousness. This understanding fits with Schleiermacher's conception of sin as that which arrests the God-consciousness within us; hence, redemption is that which empowers or grows our God-consciousness.[81] The redemptive activity precedes anything we might do on our own.[82] We are assumed into the fellowship, activity, and life of the Redeemer, which is a divine creative activity. On our part, we have a receptive activity in ascending to his influence that is "only the continuation of the creative divine activity out of which the Person of Christ arose."[83]

Schleiermacher understands two aspects of Christ's redeeming work: a reconciling aspect, which is the forgiveness of sins, and a communication of blessedness in fellowship with Christ.[84] Christ's total obedience to the divine will brings about our assumption into fellowship with him and in that fellowship we are moved, that is, "His motive principle becomes ours also."[85] The traditional aspects of Christ's work of atonement are summed up for Schleiermacher under the heading "passive obedience," meaning that in order for Christ to assume us into the fellowship of his life, it was necessary that he first enter into our fellowship. His suffering in this fellowship was on behalf of those for whom he stood in fellowship, that is, the whole human race. Out of his sympathy with human guilt and liability to punishment, arose Christ's victory over sin, overcoming its connection with evil as well. Therefore, "we may say that through the suffering of Christ punishment is abolished, because in the fellowship of His blessed life even the evil which is in process of disappearing is no longer at least regarded as

80. Ibid., 141.
81. Schleiermacher, *Christian Faith*, 425.
82. Ibid.
83. Ibid., 427.
84. Ibid., 434.
85. Ibid., 456–57.

punishment."[86] According to Schleiermacher, this understanding is the real meaning of the traditional statements that Christ's willing surrender to suffering and death satisfied the divine justice and set us free from the punishment of sin.[87] Although Schleiermacher ascribes no reconciling value to Christ's physical sufferings, he does understand the conviction of Christ's holiness and blessedness to arise primarily when we "lose ourselves in the thought of His suffering."[88] Schleiermacher understands Christ's work to contain an element of satisfaction and an element of vicariousness, however, he resists the term "vicarious satisfaction," instead preferring

> satisfying representative: in the sense, first, that in virtue of His ideal dignity He so represents, in His redemptive activity the perfecting of human nature, that in virtue of our having become one with Him God sees and regards the totality of believers only in Him; and, second, that His sympathy with sin, which was strong enough to stimulate a redemptive activity sufficient for the assumption of all men into His vital fellowship, and the absolute power of which is most perfectly exhibited in His free surrender of Himself to death, perpetually serves to make complete and perfect our imperfect consciousness of sin.[89]

From such a perspective, Schleiermacher's understanding of redemption does not appear to be entirely subjective. He does seem to try and retain God as the original actor in the process; however, redemption is actually *known* only by the subjective experience of the believer.[90] Schleiermacher's exposition of God's redeeming activity is based "entirely on the inner experience of the believer," the purpose being merely to elucidate that experience with the hope that doubters will be brought to the same experience the believer has had.[91] The weakness of subjective theories is a failure to treat sin seriously enough and it is this very weakness that we find in Schleiermacher's subjective view of reconciliation. Schleiermacher produces a strongly subjective interpre-

86. Ibid., 457–58.

87. Ibid., 458.

88. Ibid., 437, 9.

89. Ibid., 461–62.

90. Barth, *Theology of Schleiermacher*, 196. Barth notes that redemption in Schleiermacher's thought is only a state of consciousness.

91. Schleiermacher, *Christian Faith*, 428.

tation of atonement where meaning is realized more in the experience of the Christian, in her own consciousness, than in any reference to a historical incarnation and the cross.[92]

Tillich's Understanding of Redemption

Now let us return to Tillich's understanding of redemption to see if we find in it a helpful contrast to Schleiermacher's subjective view. Tillich is in agreement with Abelard that the impression of Christ's self-surrendering love on the cross awakens love in human beings, but that such a perspective is not sufficient to take away the anxiety about guilt feelings. Therefore, in an effort to maintain an objective and subjective aspect of atonement, Tillich claims the message of divine love must also include divine justice or else become weak and sentimental. Human beings need a good conscience and that comes from maintaining both love and justice.[93]

He outlines six principles of atonement: (1) the atoning process is created by God alone; (2) there is no conflict between God's reconciling love and retributive justice; (3) the removal of guilt is not an act of overlooking the reality and depth of existential estrangement; (4) God's atoning activity is understood as his participation in existential estrangement and its self-destructive consequences; (5) in the cross the divine participation in existential estrangement becomes manifest; (6) through participation in the New Being, we participate in the manifestation of the atoning act of God.[94] Based on these principles it appears that Tillich does preserve some significant aspects of the objective view. He stresses that atonement is purely God's action, which combines both God's love and justice. It also takes sin seriously. At the same time, there is the subjective element, a subjective reception; in other words, accepting that one is accepted. Because Tillich's understanding of human sin is so closely related to humanity's existential situation, the atoning activity of God is primarily summed up in God's participation in existential estrangement, albeit manifest on the cross. Defining sin in terms of human experience keeps Tillich's theory leaning toward a more subjec-

---

92. Gunton, *Actuality of Atonement*, 15.

93. Tillich, *Systematic Theology*, 2:199.

94. Ibid., 2:200–203.

tive than objective understanding.[95] Still unclear is the significance of Jesus' death and resurrection. The main point of Tillich's model seems to be Jesus' participation in existential estrangement, which leads to a rather individualistic understanding of atonement. In other words, because Christ has participated in our existential estrangement and was not overwhelmed by it, we can now participate in the New Being ourselves.

The similarities between these more subjective understandings of atonement demonstrated by Schleiermacher and Tillich, and the feminist views of the preceding chapter, are becoming apparent. The emphasis upon experience, whether one's inner experience of redemption (Schleiermacher) or the existential predicament as the content of human sin (Tillich), establishes the force of one's notion of redemption. Likewise, when sin is considered within feminist theology, it is discussed in terms of women's experience, particularly in terms of oppression and abuse. This in turn determines what is achieved in a theory of salvation, that is, liberation, healing, and atonement.

In a doctoral dissertation on feminist views of atonement, Thelma Megill-Cobbler disputes feminist rejections of classical atonement, arguing that feminist and Christian doctrine must be shaped by tradition. Furthermore, because much of women's experience (the predominant category informing feminist atonement theologies) is defined primarily in terms of white women's experience, feminists must consider that some women have been oppressors themselves and therefore need an understanding of liberation that maintains important objective elements. Yet, it is the objective views of atonement that feminists most strongly oppose. Colin Gunton rightly notes that both the Old and New Testaments show God and Jesus as examples for human beings to follow, therefore the subjective implications of atonement cannot be ignored by any objective theory.[96] However, the feminist views above have an inadequate understanding of the subjective side of atonement due in part to their neglect of the objective aspect of Christ's saving work.

---

95. The weakness in Tillich's effort to maintain a balance between objective and subjective aspects of atonement seems to parallel the weakness of his correlation method in which he attempted to give equal weight to the sources for theology. Although religion and culture are to be the correlative sources in his theological method, the role of human experience seems to take precedence.

96. Gunton, *Actuality of Atonement*, 157.

The Objective Aspect of Atonement

The subjective emphasis of feminist theologies of atonement is a result of the role of women's experience, a category that not only provides feminist theology with an understanding of sin but also with a definition of salvation. Salvation is understood in terms that address the oppression women experience under patriarchy (i.e., liberation, justice, healing). To some extent feminist theology has gotten it right: women (and men) need healing from their experience of patriarchy. Human beings are estranged from themselves, one another, and the world, and atonement brings a change in these relationships. Theology characterizes the human predicament as estrangement, loss of potential, and rebellion, a characterization that feminist theologians would support (excluding traditional understandings of rebellion).[97] Feminists want to live redeemed lives, and yet it seems that ultimately they will fail to do so if their lives are based upon the predominant theories of atonement provided by feminist theology since these do not account for an objective element of atonement. How are we capable of being "redeemed humanity" without being redeemed people?

Such a question returns us to the concept of sin. The fall produces an estrangement the extent of which feminist theologians seem unaware. There exists a fractured framework of the self, others, and God whereby relationships are distorted. "The sense of who one is in relation to and with God—which gives shape and form to everything about one, within oneself and in relationship to others—is out of reach."[98] Feminist views acknowledge fractured relations, but fail to identify the source. Feminist theologies of atonement are grounded upon particular views of sin and redemption that are defined by the category of women's experience and not determined by an understanding of our relationship to God; therefore, feminist atonement models lack an objective element and contain the various flaws discussed in this thesis. Furthermore, feminist theologies of atonement stress the need for changed lives, oriented toward mutuality in relationships and striving for justice, yet ignore forgiveness as an experience that leads toward an ethically changed attitude toward others, ourselves, and our world.[99] Without an experience of forgiveness

97. Fiddes, *Past Event*, 7.

98. Solberg, *Compelling Knowledge*, 74–75.

99. Mackintosh, *Christian Experience of Forgiveness*, 152.

there is not opportunity for change. Forgiveness is not an element of feminist views on atonement because the sin women experience is understood primarily as a result of patriarchy and not a broken relationship with God. Forgiveness is effective only through an alteration of the conditions that created the offence.[100] However, if there is no offence, then there is no forgiveness.

In the atonement models put forth by feminist theologians there is not a changed relationship with God, and the subjective experience is limited to a human understanding of broken relationships. Experience is conceived from a human point of view rather than informed, at least in part, by God's role in our relationships. Sin, understood from the perspective of our broken relationship with God, is a social phenomenon which then affects all levels of relationship.[101] Alienation from God is antecedent to alienation from our selves and our neighbor.[102] Feminist theologians perceptively reveal the pervasiveness of fractured relationships within humanity and the world, but do not accurately account for the reason why.[103] It is as if feminists have rightly identified the major symptoms of a disease while failing to diagnose it. They recognize the pain of a headache resulting from a brain tumor without perceiving the source and utilizing the proper medicine to eliminate the tumor. By defining sin from outside the point of view of relationship to God, where it must be defined, feminist theologies of atonement are diminished and lose any element of objective atonement.[104] Feminist versions of redemption include significant categories such as healing, liberation, and reconciliation, but fail to acknowledge that "reconciliation with God . . . is the necessary condition for reconciliation between people and peace with the environment."[105] Human sin reveals the distinction between what we are and what we ought to be and requires that we look openly at our moral obligations and our incapacity to meet them.[106]

---

100. Gunton, *Christian Faith*, 76.

101. Jüngel, *Justification*, 129; Gunton, *Christian Faith*, 61.

102. Mackintosh, *Christian Experience of Forgiveness*, 53.

103. Rosemary Radford Ruether understands humankind to have lost an element of original goodness. See note 70 above. Many feminists, as presented in this thesis, blame patriarchy and hierarchical social structures for the disunity in human relationships.

104. Jüngel, *Justification*, 93.

105. Gunton, *Christian Faith*, 72.

106. Mackintosh, *Christian Experience of Forgiveness*, 52.

When the human condition is understood primarily in terms of our relationship to God rather than by an interpretation of our experience, justification becomes a key element in any concept of atonement. Justification is not a word used by feminist theologians as it is too closely associated with the views of atonement they criticize. However, it is a concept that incorporates the qualities of redemption developed in feminist models of atonement because ultimately justification is about restored relationships. Eberhard Jüngel describes it as an eschatological interruption that heals, making possible unbreakable fellowship with God.[107] The fundamental act of salvation is to create communion with God and with others.[108] The notion of restored relationships goes back to the divine covenant given to Abraham in the Old Testament.[109] Salvation begins there when God makes a covenant with Abraham (I will be your God, and you will be my people). Karl Barth understands atonement as Jesus Christ who maintains, accomplishes, and fulfills the divine covenant.[110] The fulfillment of covenant has the character of reconciliation because it "speaks of the confirmation and restoration of a fellowship which did exist but had been threatened with disruption and dissolution." Because humanity has not always kept the covenant as God has, the act of reconciliation by Christ heals the breach that the broken covenant created.[111] Humanity has been justified by Christ as a covenant partner with God; atonement is God's fulfillment, on our behalf, of the broken covenant.[112]

Human beings are sinners, not only through the individual acts we commit, but also through the state in which we live, that is, we live in enmity toward God. In covenantal terms, this means that we have not kept our part of the covenant. Rather than letting ourselves be defined as God's people, we crave divinity, desiring to define ourselves, to have our identity outside our relationship with God.[113] "Sinners want to con-

107. Jüngel, *Justification*, 80–81. He states that the highest good of human beings is *"being together in fellowship* with God," (138).

108. Mackintosh, *Christian Experience of Forgiveness*, 23.

109. Gunton, *Christian Faith*, 65.

110. Barth, *Church Dogmatics*, 4/1:34.

111. Ibid., 4/1:89.

112. Ibid., 4/1:109, 138.

113. Clague, "BISFT Interview with Dr. Daphne Hampson," 51. In this interview with the Britain and Ireland School of Feminist Theology, Hampson states: "I have got

tradict God. But they don't want what goes with this: self-contradiction. Sinners want to live like God. But they don't want what goes with this: dying." The Bible sees this contradiction as the *punishment* brought upon sinners which is the logical consequence of our sin.[114] The cross creates redeemed forms of experience by virtue of changing our relationship to God. Sin as enmity toward God has consequences for how we experience the world, particularly other people. God in Christ bears, judges, and overcomes this enmity, leading humanity toward the possibility of an experience of forgiveness. We now live as forgiven and righteous people who are able to experience life with God and others, free and empowered to love others and be in fellowship. This "ethically changed" life is possible, not merely by trying to imitate Jesus through our own efforts, but through the Holy Spirit who generates God's love within us.[115] The primary aim of pardon is not to "affect character but to rectify our personal relationship to God."[116] Through the action of the Holy Spirit we experience at-one-ment and are restored to relationship with God and others.

A Trinitarian perspective must inform any view of atonement in order to avoid the very aspects of objective atonement models that feminist theologians criticize as well as to incorporate the subjective aspect they stress. In other words, there is no substance or efficacy in atonement unless in Jesus God is present, and there is no subjective effect unless the Holy Spirit is the means by which we experience justification and forgiveness and are empowered to live in the love of God.[117] Jüngel puts it this way:

> The God who justifies is the triune God who in the person of the Son of God became man, died for us and for our justification was raised from the dead. The Christian church believes in and confesses Jesus Christ as true God and true man. A key issue in the doctrine of justification is the identification of the

---

to see myself, in my relation to others, as at the centre of my world and not be a slave to anything . . . outside myself." These telling words are indicative of an attitude within feminist theology, Christian and post-Christian, often related to the problematic concept of authority.

114. Jüngel, *Justification*, 133.

115. Fiddes, *Past Event*, 153.

116. Mackintosh, *Christian Experience of Forgiveness*, 260.

117. Ibid., 208.

> Son of God with Jesus the man. The death of Jesus can only have
> any meaning for justifying sinners if *God himself* is also present
> in the death of this *man*. If Jesus' death on the cross were to be
> considered *only* as the end (whatever that may mean) of the life
> of a human being, then the cross of Christ would have no sav-
> ing effect, no power to justify sinners and no meaning for our
> salvation.[118]

Atonement depends upon the historical moment of Christ's death, though we must be careful not to lock it into that one place in time and space. "In this sense the cross stands at the centre of life and is relevant to all patterns of experience."[119] In complete identification with humankind, God in Jesus experienced the consequences of human sin (i.e., alienation, estrangement) in order to justify us and restore us to relationship with God.[120] Within the New Testament, the conception of *how* the reconciliation between humanity and God occurs is not developed through one uniform model of salvation; however, in whatever way the cross is conceived, "God's merciful attitude toward sinners is never regarded as the *result* of the process, but as its cause and source."[121] God is the initiator of our redemption (in Christ God was reconciling the world) and therefore, atonement grows out of God's deep love for humankind. The subjective and objective elements are necessary and interrelated: "Justification confronts us as objective for it is the act or pronouncement of God ... If it is an act of God then it is also an experience of human beings."[122]

Conclusion: Do Feminist Accounts of Atonement Provide Real Redemption?

Regardless of the necessity of atonement's objective aspects, we recognize the importance of a subjective theory of atonement that is faithful to the biblical witness and testifies to God and Jesus as examples for believers to follow. There is also the need for salvation to be understood, not simply as a past historical event, but experienced in our present

118. Jüngel, *Justification*, 149.

119. Fiddes, *Past Event*, 4.

120. Ibid., 91.

121. Baillie, *God Was in Christ*, 188.

122. Mackintosh, *Christian Experience of Forgiveness*, 153.

lives of faith. This does not mean that one gains salvation by following an example. Imitating Christ as an example is part of living as a redeemed person, not a means to redemption. The feminist theologies of atonement presented above do not account for the relationship between subjective views of atonement and redemption. If an important aspect of redemption is the subjective element experienced in the lives of people, how is it that this experience translates into redemption? Does experience equal salvation?

The feminist theories of the preceding chapter, although different in emphasis, have similar themes regarding the concept of salvation. In these views, Jesus is often understood as a paradigm or model and the cross is symbolic. Brock's interpretation of Jesus' death and resurrection leads to an understanding of salvation in the community where we find the image of the divine Child providing guidance to remain connected to an original sense of grace and erotic power. Brown and Parker reject atonement altogether and focus on Jesus as one who lived a life in opposition to injustice and oppression, leading him to be put to death in opposition to those who rejected his way of life. Mary Grey, more than the others, finds a place for pain and suffering in atonement as well as makes an effort to retain a subjective and objective aspect to her position. She identifies Jesus as establishing a pattern for a relational process of redemption that is salvific for us as the basic pattern of the world. She argues that this is not purely exemplary, but that there is the possibility of relationality between God and human activity as co-creators and co-redeemers. The cross is the symbol of this redemptive, relational power. Rosemary Radford Ruether portrays Christ as the model for redeemed humanity, claiming Jesus' prophetic vision announcing a reversal of existing social and religious hierarchy. Jesus saves us by modeling authentic, liberated humanity, and the memory of such persons leads us to recognize authenticity in ourselves and others. Christ is a paradigm of liberated humanity continued in the Christian community. Womanist Delores Williams also describes Jesus in similar terms as providing a ministerial vision as a resource for ethical thought and practice from which to build our lives. Each of these perspectives develops an understanding of Jesus and his part in human salvation in terms of example, that is, Jesus is a paradigm or model of how we should live as liberated people in opposition to oppressive structures.

These feminist views stress Jesus' life to the neglect or exclusion of his death and resurrection, arguing that what is important is how Jesus lived, how he healed people, cast out demons, and spoke out against the oppressors of his society. This is what must be claimed by humanity. To speak of his death is to glorify suffering, pain, and violence. Yet how can we speak of Jesus' life without speaking of his death? His very way of life led to his death. The cross, though unique in intensity of meaning, is inseparable from his life. Jesus conceived of his death as "inaugurating a new relation between God and man."[123] Feminist theologians appear to realize the fact that if one speaks against the dominant forces of culture and church one may be persecuted, even to death; however, they fail to explain the relationship between such a life and the possible death it risks. If women are to live according to the vision of Jesus, then what are they to do when it results in suffering and pain? A theology of atonement based on the life of Jesus must account for his life, death, and resurrection, for these are part of a whole. They cannot be separated, whereby we pick and choose which parts of Jesus' life we find inspirational or worthy of imitation without considering the whole of his life.

Feminist theologies of atonement transfer Jesus' theological significance from his death to his life and, in doing so, disallow Jesus from exemplifying suffering unto death, that which the Bible teaches is the undoing of sin and patriarchy, "namely, Jesus' victory over the powers through his death and resurrection, and not simply through his life."[124] The feminist critique of atonement does not take sin seriously and seems to claim that we can overcome the problems of the world simply by choosing to live authentically and courageously, drawing inspiration from Jesus and others who have lived as he. However, such a view simply does not reckon with the "pervasive, enslaving, and systemic nature of evil."[125] In other words,

> to ignore the fact that Jesus is shown in Scripture as bearing the consequences, according the will of God, of our breaches of universal justice—to forget that he was bruised for our iniquities—is again, to trivialise evil and to deny the need for an

123. Ibid., 197.
124. Houts, "Atonement and Abuse," 31.
125. Ibid.

atonement, a restoration of relationships which pays due attention to the way things are with the world.[126]

Theology must address the central themes of the Christian gospel including, sin, estrangement, and the promise of salvation and healing.[127]
The death and resurrection of Jesus are crucial to any genuine reconciliation, and feminists fail to differentiate Jesus' life or death from that
of other martyrs.[128] Ruether is unambiguous in her position that Jesus'
life and death are not unique, but like the presented paradigm, are continued in the liberated humanity, which is the Christian community.
Tillich agrees: "the Christ is not an isolated event which happened 'once
upon a time'; he is the power of the New Being preparing his decisive
manifestation in Jesus as the Christ in all preceding history and actu-
alising himself as the Christ in all subsequent history."[129] Here arises
the challenge that post-Christian feminist Daphne Hampson makes:
if Jesus is not unique, then how is a Christian position to be upheld?[130]
If Jesus exemplifies liberated humanity, ministerial vision, or reversal
of social hierarchy, and his identity is carried on in a community that
maintains similar ideals, then exactly how is it that Jesus is unique? How
is he distinct from all others who have lived exemplary lives consist-
ing of similar values? Further, if there is no atonement, if atonement is
completely rejected, then how is a theology Christian?

We have seen that a weighting of experience may lead to a model
of the atonement that is overly subjective, lacking a deep understanding of the seriousness of human sin and the need for redemption. A
subjective view offers an important dimension to atonement theology;
however, an objective element seems necessary if it is to provide genuine salvation, for it is difficult to see how following an example brings
true healing, liberation, and transformation. It appears that the objective understanding of atonement we are looking for will be found, not
in experience, but in revelation. By using an understanding of women's
experience as the primary source for atonement theology, feminists fail
to consider adequately other important sources for Christian theology,

126. Gunton, *Actuality of Atonement*, 165.

127. Van Dyk, "Vision and Imagination," 5.

128. Gunton, *Actuality of Atonement*, 158–59.

129. Tillich, *Systematic Theology*, 2:207–8.

130. Hampson, *Theology and Feminism*, 50.

specifically, the Bible and tradition. It is to that which we now turn as we examine the relationship between experience and revelation in feminist theology.

6

Trading Authorities: Experience and Revelation in Feminist Theologies of Atonement

Introduction: Feminist Atonement Theology's Lack of an Objective Element

IN THE LAST CHAPTER WE DISCOVERED THAT THE FEMINIST THEOLOGIcal foundation of women's experience leads to a particular tendency in feminist theologies of atonement, that is, the feminist models for redemption become overly subjective, lacking the objective element characteristic of many traditional atonement theologies. The words "objective" and "subjective" used to describe the atonement are just that—terms that in and of themselves are relatively unimportant. However, for the sake of our discussion about the specific nature of feminist atonement theologies, these terms are helpful designations and contribute to the possibility of identifying more specifically the shortcomings of the feminist perspective. *Objective* atonement generally implies that salvation is located in a past event outside contemporary experience, more precisely, located in the life, death, and resurrection of Jesus Christ as the divine source of atoning effect. A *subjective* understanding places the process of atonement in the present human experience, leading to a participation in the life of Christ and confidence in the Father's love.[1] It was also noted in the previous chapter that an atonement theology should encompass both elements, objective and subjective, and because the feminist versions fail to account sufficiently for the objective aspect, feminist theologies of atonement are prone to certain weaknesses.

1. Van Dyk, *Desire of Divine Love*, 90–91. See also Fiddes, *Past Event*, 26.

Most likely, the feminists mentioned in preceding chapters would not perceive the lack of an objective element in atonement theology as a defect, in fact, there seems to be a direct attempt to bypass an objective understanding of atonement and focus entirely on the subjective because that is the aspect that matters most to women. If the objective aspect of atonement is rooted in the concept of the violent death of an innocent son made as a sacrifice to a divine Father, then surely feminists have no misgivings with the charge that their interpretation of atonement is overly subjective. However, there are important issues at stake that must be addressed further. Due to the subjective emphasis of feminist versions of atonement, we are left with models of salvation fundamentally defined by Jesus' example. Such an account of human salvation exposes three basic deficiencies: it ignores its dependence on other models, overestimates human ability to follow Jesus' example, and fails to show how imitating Jesus is redemptive. Therefore, it seems that in order to regain an objective element of atonement, we need to look beyond women's experience toward the biblical witness to God's revelation, and yet, for all intents and purposes, feminist theology has replaced revelation with the category of women's experience, a rejection of revelation that appears related to the problem of authority.

The Pitfalls of a Purely Subjective Model of Atonement

Feminist versions of atonement outlined above provide an understanding of Jesus and his part in human salvation primarily in terms of "example." In other words, Jesus is understood as a paradigm or model of how we should live as liberated people in opposition to oppressive structures. The emphasis upon Jesus as an example is directly related to the subjective focus of feminist atonement theologies, resulting in various weaknesses in the feminist position. Here an observation by John McIntyre is helpful in identifying three significant drawbacks to such an approach:

> There are three difficulties about 'example' being a first order model for the description of the death of Christ. One is that the death of Christ is only an example if we first define what its nature in itself is, so that what is to be imitated then becomes clear. That definition will involve one or other of the models . . . so that the example model is dependent on one of the others, and insuf-

ficient in itself. The second difficulty in taking example as a first order model is that it presupposes that mankind has the moral and spiritual ability to imitate the example of Jesus Christ. But the absence of such ability in mankind is the very circumstance which made atonement a necessity in the first place. And thirdly, an example as such is not necessarily redemptive.[2]

The "Example" Model and the Role of Scripture

The first difficulty McIntyre identifies with the example model as the primary way to describe the death of Jesus is related to how such a definition is dependent upon other models of Jesus' death. The example model on its own is insufficient. Feminist theologies of atonement emphasize the exemplary nature of Jesus' life as an important part of their concept of redemption, yet do not explain the relationship of such a model to other models. If our understanding of Jesus' life and death is primarily gained from the representation of his life and death in the biblical witness, which provides multiple models for atonement, it would appear that scripture is the most significant resource for learning about atonement. How do feminists utilize scripture generally, and specifically, in their atonement theologies?

Feminist Theology's Use of Scripture

As we have discovered, feminist theologians like Joanne Carlson Brown and Rebecca Parker do not use scripture as a source for theological reflection about atonement at all, while others such as Mary Grey and Rosemary Radford Ruether make an effort to recover particular biblical elements in their atonement theologies. For instance, Grey finds birth imagery helpful in her account of redemption because the Judeo-Christian tradition does contain maternal images. She sees scripture as providing birth images that display mutuality through life-giving process, not through death and resurrection. In a way, she gains permission to de-emphasize the death imagery by her use of scriptural other

---

2. McIntyre, *Shape of Soteriology*, 49. Although McIntyre speaks of Christ's *death* as an example in contrast to the feminist emphasis upon Jesus' life, his argument still applies to feminist models.

imagery for redemption and new life.[3] Ruether interprets the prophetic liberating tradition evident in the Old Testament and in the narratives of Jesus in the Synoptic Gospels as a resource for understanding redemption within a Christian context. These feminist theologians could be considered "reformers" in that they consider it possible to find sources within the Christian paradigm for models that are liberating to women.[4] To some degree, one could argue that Schüssler Fiorenza also has a similar approach in that her feminist hermeneutics, because it involves an interplay between experience and the experiences of the early Christian church, keeps her rooted within the Christian tradition.[5] Alternatively, it could be claimed that, in fact, Schüssler Fiorenza engages a reconstruction of women's experience in the early Christian church more than the biblical texts themselves. Her hermeneutic involves an interplay that is more between experience and a historical reconstruction. Still, this reconstruction is in part dependent upon selective biblical texts, which connects her to the Christian tradition to a certain extent.[6] In contrast, Letty Russell has been seen to represent a feminist approach that more explicitly retains the Bible as a significant source for theology.

Despite the differences regarding the use of scripture for feminist theology, most Christian feminist theologians seem convinced that the biblical texts must be engaged at some level in theological reflection. In response to post-Christian Daphne Hampson, Ruether claims that Christian feminists are able to see "countervailing trends in the Scriptures and Christian tradition which are grounds for fundamental change in . . . patriarchal patterns."[7] Likewise, because Schüssler Fiorenza values the historical experience of women within biblical religion, she designates a place for scripture within her feminist hermeneutics.[8] Although the work of Ruether and Schüssler Fiorenza does reflect a Christian feminist attempt to incorporate the Bible into theological method, as

3. Grey, *Redeeming the Dream*, 143.

4. McFague, *Metaphorical Theology*, 167. McFague identifies herself as a "reformer" as well and argues that the root metaphor of Christianity is human liberation, from which she can then construct a Christian feminist theology.

5. Pears, "Women's Experience," 20.

6. Abraham, *Canon and Criterion*, 447. Abraham finds Schüssler Fiorenza more revisionary of scripture than Ruether. Francis Martin agrees; see *Feminist Question*, 216.

7. Ruether, "Is Feminism the End?" 393.

8. Schüssler Fiorenza, *Bread Not Stone*, xiii.

regards feminist atonement theologies, the use of scripture is minimal and we continue to find women's experience having the final say about what is included in theological doctrine. In each of the feminist theologians highlighted (Brock, Brown, Parker, Grey, and Ruether) the biblical imagery for atonement and redemption is all but ignored. One should acknowledge the influence of the historical context upon atonement metaphors, but, for instance, a contemporary stress on healing as salvific does not rule out other metaphors. Atonement theology should employ a wide range of biblical, traditional, innovative metaphors to express salvation.[9] The biblical text need not be the sole source for atonement theology, rather the witness of scripture should be a critically appropriated source for atonement theology along with other elements such as the sociopolitical context, the sacrificial metaphor, and eschatological hope.[10] If Christian feminists have argued that the biblical text and tradition do have a place in feminist theology, then the variety of atonement metaphors in the Bible should be considered in more detail as part of feminist theologies of atonement. The analysis within this thesis of three prominent feminist views on atonement reveals a serious neglect (beyond a broad critique) of several biblical models:

- Ransom: Mark 10:45; Acts 20:28; Rom 4:25, 5:9; 2 Cor 5:21; Eph 1:7; 1 Tim 2:6; Titus 2:14; Heb 9:12; 1 Pet 1:18; Rev 1:5

- Release: Lev 25:47-55; Luke 4:18-19; John 8:34, 12:31; Rom 8:35f; 1 Cor 15:24f; Eph 2:15; Col 2:15; Heb 9:15; 1 John 3:8

- Transformation: John 5:24; Rom 6:2,6, 7:4, 9, 10:4; 1 Cor 5:7, 10:16; Eph 2:6; Phil 3:21; 2 Tim 1:10; 1 John 5:11

- Atonement/reconciliation: Matt 26:28, 27:51; Rom 3:24f, 5:18; 1 Cor 11:25; Eph 2:18, 3:12; 1 Thess 1:10; Heb 10:19f; 1 John 2:2[11]

9. Van Dyk, "Vision and Imagination," 11. Van Dyk agrees with Fiddes' analysis of the change in emphasis on particular atonement metaphors based upon the specific historical context, recognizing that the image of "healing" is likely more predominant in the contemporary context.

10. Megill-Cobbler, "Women and the Cross," 410.

11. This selection of verses represents some general understandings of atonement within the biblical text (the categorization of which should be somewhat flexible, since some passages could work equally well under one type of metaphor as under another). Of course, the entire sacrificial system of the Old Testament would also need to be considered as a significant atonement metaphor.

Considering the great extent to which the Bible provides various metaphors for understanding atonement, it is unfortunate that Christian feminist theologians who retain a role for scripture in theology have not considered these biblical passages in any detail in their atonement theologies. A basic critique of traditional models is offered, but is directed more toward the tradition's interpretation and use of these rather than the witness of the biblical texts themselves.[12] In particular, the predominant atonement imagery of sacrifice in the Bible is regrettably neglected in most feminist perspectives on atonement. True, a primary emphasis upon such imagery can be harmful to many women; however, the omission of any talk of sacrificial, self-giving imagery may result in a limitation of the scope of atonement and lead to an element of women's experience being excluded from a theology of atonement.[13] Feminist theologies of atonement emphasize Jesus' vision of human liberation expressed in his words and actions. His life is a model for all who struggle against oppression, and yet any consideration of the biblical witness to his life reveals the significant relationship between Jesus' life and mission and his death and resurrection. It seems that a genuine "example" model of atonement could not ignore other biblical models, for in order to understand truly what we are imitating, an awareness of other models is required.[14]

In order to be a Christian feminist theologian, it is reasonable to believe that one must remain tied to the Christian tradition. The Bible is the primary witness to the events of Jesus' life, death, and resurrection, all of which play a critical part in developing atonement theology. As a member of the Christian community, it seems that one has a relation-

12. Bradley, *Power of Sacrifice*, 14–15. Bradley notes the importance of the feminist critique, which signals the need to get rid of a propitiatory theory of sacrifice that portrays God as angry and vengeful.

13. Alsford, "Sin and Atonement," 162–64. See also Bradley, *Power of Sacrifice*, 13. Bradley identifies a similar problem with the neglect of sacrificial imagery. Although he acknowledges that he tends to agree with feminists in most contexts, he would consider that sacrifice would have strong resonance with their concerns.

14. Megill-Cobbler considers that Brock's approach rules out *imitatio Christi* as redemptive, which would rule out the exemplarist or "subjective" dimension of atonement ("Women and the Cross," 382). However, we would argue that an example model is still valid for describing Brock's approach. Brock uses the Child as a divine image within each of us, which reveals the need to stay connected. The Child is an inspiration to live out mutuality and interdependence. This seems to be a description of redemption that remains within the exemplarist position.

ship to the normative text of that tradition and cannot simply do away with it while remaining a member of that community. Granted, most of the Christian feminists would assert that they are not doing away with the biblical text, but we would argue that they are undermining it in such a way that it no longer functions for them as it is meant to within the Christian community, that is, as a source and norm for theology and ethics.

Human Inability to Imitate Christ's Example

The second difficulty with the example model of atonement outlined by McIntyre is that it fails to account for humanity's inability to imitate the example of Jesus Christ. The problem of human sin has made atonement necessary, yet often an example model does not adequately deal with human sin. We touched upon feminist understandings of sin in the previous chapter, but now we want to address further how the feminist theologians' view of sin reveals the dilemma McIntyre identifies, that is, most feminist understandings of sin and the subjective understanding of atonement to which they lead do not sufficiently take into account the depth of human (including women's) sin and how this ultimately makes redemption by following an example no redemption at all.

Sin and Redemption in Feminist Theology

Feminist theologians are not opposed to discussing the concept of sin, but we have noted their reluctance to describe it in more traditional terms such as the fall or rebellion against God. They speak of alienation, not so much between God and humanity, but between human beings in their relationships to themselves, others and creation. This relational understanding of sin appears to be most prevalent in feminist theology and, in part, the determining factor of atonement theologies that emphasize the subjective element. There appears to be an avoidance of speaking about women's sin except as a result of patriarchy, although admittedly, this is not always a mistake.

A concept of the fall that makes women scapegoats for the advent of evil and uses this to "punish" women through historical subordination must be rejected. Because of the church's negative teaching in this

direction Ruether maintains that a new meaning of the fall can be discovered. The fall provides the theological insights that "humanity has
become radically alienated from its true relationship to itself, to nature,
and to God."[15] Ruether contends that feminism presumes a radical concept of sin, claiming that the basic expression of human community in
the relationship of men and women has been distorted into an oppressive relationship that victimizes one half of the human race, turning the
other half into tyrants. This primary alienation and distortion of human
relationality is reflected in dimensions of alienation: from one's self,
one's body, from the other who is different, from "nonhuman" nature,
and from God. In this sense, feminism understands sin not as simply
individual but referring also to a fallen state of humanity. Feminism's
claim to judgment means it cannot avoid the capacity of humanity for
sin.[16] Nevertheless, though Ruether acknowledges that women have
benefited from historical oppression along race and class lines as well
as have collaborated with sexism in violence toward other women, the
primary form of oppression originates with male oppression because
males have been the primary benefactors of sexism and have perpetuated it.[17] Ruether maintains that recognizing sin as sexism does not
mean that males are by nature more evil or capable of sin. Although as
human persons both males and females have the capacity to do evil, historically, women have not had the same *opportunities* to do so as men.[18]
The racist, classist, self-hating, and manipulative behavior of women is
part of an "overall system of distorted humanity in which ruling-class
males are the apex."[19]

In contrast to Ruether, most feminists avoid speaking of the fall
and/or original sin at all. Rita Nakashima Brock rejects the concept of
original sin, claiming that feminists see sin as socially and historically
produced, which requires personal responsibility to stop oppression and
suffering.[20] Joanne Carlson Brown is more explicit: "We do not need to

15. Ruether, *Sexism and God-Talk*, 37. See also West, *Deadly Innocence*, 69. West
identifies a similar view in post-Christian feminist Daphne Hampson who refers to the
possibility of female sin as a "break in connectedness."

16. Ruether, *Sexism and God-Talk*, 161.

17. Ibid., 165.

18. Ibid., 180.

19. Ibid., 181.

20. Brock, *Journeys by Heart*, 7.

be saved by Jesus' death from some original sin. We need to be liberated from this abusive patriarchy."[21]

Despite the lack of traditional concepts of sin, feminists do maintain some notion of sin and, therefore, a need for liberation. What does this liberation look like? We began to catch a glimpse of it in the previous chapter: Jesus (not necessarily the death of Jesus) is a paradigm of humanity living in opposition to oppression. Ruether argues that "revelatory" and transformative experiences allow humanity to liberate itself from the "sinful distortion of existence" to become a new redemptive community that announces a transformative mission against sinful society.[22] Grey would also see redemptive, relational power in Jesus and Brock interprets Jesus as leading to the image of the divine Child, which is within us, guiding us toward connection with erotic power. We find a similar model in Sallie McFague's metaphorical theology in which the "root-metaphor" of Christianity is Jesus of Nazareth as the exemplar of a certain kind of relationship.[23] Her model of God as Friend emphasizes sacrifice, support, solidarity with others and the world. God's saving activity is as a friend who suffers with us as we work with God to bring about a better existence.[24] Womanist Delores Williams' position is not unlike McFague's since she rejects an understanding of atonement that sees it as a victory over sin and evil and understands redemption in terms of a vision that God gives humanity in order to provide ethical guidance for a more productive, positive quality of life.[25] Although other feminists may be reluctant to include the concept of suffering found in McFague, generally speaking, her position would be in agreement with the preceding views, that is, they each seem to understand atonement as a new way of life for humanity. Jesus' life provides a vision that guides us toward a better existence.

---

21. Brown, "Divine Child Abuse?" 28.

22. Ruether, *Sexism and God-Talk*, 38.

23. McFague, *Metaphorical Theology*, 111. McFague considers atonement theory as a good example of the metaphorical theology she is trying to do because it allows for multiple models (117).

24. McFague, *Metaphorical Theology*, 186.

25. Williams, *Sisters in the Wilderness*, 165.

The Reality of Sin and the Hope of Redemption

The subjective emphasis upon concepts of redemption in feminist theology places it in a tradition of "example" models of atonement. What is perhaps most striking in such feminist positions is a failure to adequately address the reality of sin, an issue raised by some white feminists and particularly by feminists of color. If sin is understood primarily in terms of patriarchy, it seems to imply that women are somehow "innocent" of the oppressive sins of the world, which are perpetrated by men. However, we know from historical evidence that women have been oppressors as well as oppressed. Susan Thistlethwaite is one of the first white feminists to identify this fact, noting that even if sin is understood by feminists as disconnectedness (rather than primarily as patriarchy), this may apply to white women some of the time, but not to all women, including black women. This is one area where women's experience reveals that sin is not experienced by all women the same.[26] Such a position takes us back to the first chapter of the thesis where we noted that womanists were quick to recognize that the category of women's experience used by white feminists was in danger of oppressing women of color just as patriarchy had historically oppressed women.

Feminist theology's failure to address adequately the subject of women's sin leads to the flaws we are finding in feminist atonement theology. For instance, a recent doctoral dissertation concludes that the oppression of minority women by white women (racism) reveals the importance of an objective dimension of feminist atonement theology.[27] Likewise, we observe a similar conclusion in Angela West's book *Deadly Innocence*, which examines the matter within the context of contemporary British feminism, claiming that "white feminism has given insufficient attention to the Fall as a symbol of the depth of human intolerance for difference."[28] West refers to Claudia Koonz's analysis of women's roles in Nazi Germany as an example that women are not always purely and simply innocent victims.[29] She maintains that "women are indeed capable of sin, and although the nature of women's sins is conditioned by the nature of their particular social and historical experience, they

26. Thistlethwaite, *Sex, Race and God*, 87.

27. Megill-Cobbler, "Women and the Cross," 412.

28. West, *Deadly Innocence*, 47.

29. Ibid., 35. West cites Koonz, *Mothers in the Fatherland*, 1987.

are not fundamentally different from what feminists would recognize and identify as men's sins."[30] West determines that feminism shares with post-Enlightenment thought the view that somehow the conversion of our minds and affirmation of our intrinsic goodness can free us from the implications of sin.[31]

McIntyre's third point concerning the failings of subjective atonement models has been surfacing throughout the discussion above, that is, an example model of atonement is not necessarily redemptive. This is a lesson surely history has taught us. Much theology this century has been written out of the realization that such an Enlightenment perspective fails to deliver on its promises, and yet contemporary feminism appears to be committing the same fault, believing that human beings solely are able to transform the negative and oppressive structures of our world. Moreover, if the category of experience is to be taken seriously, it seems that women's experience reveals a lack of transformative power, a dilemma that feminist theologies of atonement do not adequately address. The liberation presented in an example model of atonement that feminist theology currently provides, consistently falls short of delivering the transformation it promises and inspires, due to an overly subjective understanding of atonement resulting from an insufficient doctrine of human sin. The theological inadequacies of the feminist debate over the nature of women's sin in effect undercut the intentions of feminist scholarship to heal the wounds inflicted by sexism.[32] As long as sin is understood either strictly in terms of patriarchy or in relational disconnectedness, and redemption in the Christian context is found by following Jesus as a paradigm for liberated humanity, we will continue to struggle on our own to live as liberated people with no genuine hope of ultimate transformation. Sin is radical rebellion, and genuine reconciliation can only come from the side of the divine, beginning and ending with Jesus Christ.[33] Within the general feminist paradigm of salvation, redemption is equated with an end to patriarchy

30. West, *Deadly Innocence*, 36.

31. Ibid., 205.

32. Greene-McCreight, "Gender, Sin and Grace," 415. Greene-McCreight offers Barth's harmartiology in *Church Dogmatics* as a possible way forward because he understands sin beyond the boundaries of pride alone. She does note, however, that Barth does not always promote healthy models for male and female relationships.

33. Greene-McCreight, "Gender, Sin and Grace," 431–32.

and the solution to ending patriarchy is to follow (some form) of Jesus' example. However, when we fail to follow the model presented by Jesus, where is redemption then to be found? In the face of our own failure to live as liberated people, working against oppressive structures, what are we to do?

It seems that if we consider our experience honestly, we will find resources for challenging a purely subjective view of atonement. However, is experience the only place to seek such insights? Is an emphasis upon experience in atonement theology essentially building atonement upon an anthropology constructed independent of the biblical drama?[34] A feminist replacement of the doctrine of sin with an anthropology that lifts up the particular sin of patriarchy will lead to a tendency, given the soteriology that matches this vision, to "ignore the concepts of justification, forgiveness, reconciliation, assurance, new birth, faith, humility, and the quest for a sanctification of perfect love."[35] As Christian theologians, we have much to learn about sin from revelation. The Bible as witness to the reality of God shows us that sin is equalizing for all humanity, that the struggle is between Creator and creature, not male and female.[36] We are beginning to uncover the source of the feminist lack of objective atonement, bringing us to the Bible as it interacts with women's experience. Herein lies a core problem for most feminist theologies of atonement—the place of revelation.

Feminist Theology's Displacement of Revelation

Part of the feminist failure to take sin beyond the scope of subjective understandings, and hence atonement theology as well, is due to the role of revelation in feminist theology. Human experience can only teach so much about our alienation from God, others, and the world, but something further is needed to explain the source of this alienation and the way through it to restored relationships. The real truth about sin and redemption seems to lie not in our experience (at least not exclusively) but in the biblical text. For the purpose of this thesis the term "revelation" will be used in reference to knowledge of God gained from

34. Ibid., 422.

35. Abraham, *Canon and Criterion*, 462.

36. Greene-McCreight, "Gender, Sin and Grace," 427.

the Bible understood as the primary witness to God's self-revelation in Jesus Christ. Our focus here will be on how feminists understand revelation in this sense and how women's experience relates to revelation. We will return to feminists discussed earlier, particularly Elisabeth Schüssler Fiorenza and Rosemary Radford Ruether.

Elisabeth Schüssler Fiorenza

Let us consider Schüssler Fiorenza at some length since she exerts a considerable influence upon feminist theology in general.[37] Although she admits to contradicting other feminist theologians, and though many do not explicitly acknowledge her influence, it is reasonable to conclude that her views have shaped much of the feminist perspective on the role of scripture in feminist theology.

Schüssler Fiorenza opposes a hermeneutical approach that is too closely aligned with a biblical historical model because such an understanding of the canon as a collection of different, even contradictory, writings underlines the "context and conditions of revelation" and engenders the need for formulating criteria for the theological evaluation of diverse biblical teachings. According to her, this theological search becomes a search for a canon within a canon and characterizes the neo-orthodox model found in much of Protestantism.[38] Thus, Schüssler Fiorenza finds liberation theology and feminist theologians like Letty Russell and Rosemary Radford Ruether guilty of aligning themselves too quickly with a neo-orthodox approach whereby they enlist the Bible on the side of the oppressed. Furthermore, she finds fault with feminists such as Russell, for whom the patriarchal imagery and language is identified as an element of the form, but not the content of biblical message.[39] Schüssler Fiorenza identifies Ruether's problem as a lack of critique of the biblical and prophetic traditions.[40] In contrast, Schüssler Fiorenza wants feminist biblical theology to confront the "patriarchal stamp" of

37. Hays, *Moral Vision*, 267. Hays identifies Schüssler Fiorenza as the "standard-bearer" of feminist hermeneutics.

38. Schüssler Fiorenza, *In Memory of Her*, 14.

39. Ibid., 15.

40. Ibid., 17.

the Bible rather than using a feminist perspective to "rehabilitate the authority of the Bible."[41]

According to Schüssler Fiorenza, biblical texts are androcentric and legitimate patriarchal oppression, and therefore cannot claim to be authoritative or revelatory of the Word of God. What is authoritative is "personally and politically reflected experience of oppression and liberation" of women.[42] However, this view of revelation as located in the community or *ekklēsia* of women in contrast to the Bible and/or tradition of the patriarchal church is not thoroughly explained.[43] Generally speaking, one understands ethical issues as driving her claims to authority: "[O]nly those traditions and texts that critically break through patriarchal culture and 'plausibility structures' have the theological authority of revelation."[44] Schüssler Fiorenza's position seems somewhat ambivalent because she basically undermines the authority of scripture, but rather than reject it entirely (e.g., Mary Daly) she aims to develop the means to retain parts of it as long as it meets her criterion. By remaining connected to scripture her position can claim a certain authority. In other words, it seems that she is aware that in order to have some authority as a Christian feminist, she cannot do away with scripture entirely. The irony of such a position is that she attacks a neo-orthodox approach for retaining scripture as authoritative, yet she too wants to utilize the biblical text in order to establish authority for her position.[45] For instance, she acknowledges egalitarian texts of the New Testament, which function as a source of theological critique of those texts that perpetrate women's secondary status in Christianity.[46] She also sees the biblical religion as part of women's heritage, asserting that "our heritage is our power."[47] However, although revelatory authority is lodged in fragments of the tradition (e.g., Gal 3:28), it is the present-day struggle of

41. Ibid., 21; speaking specifically against the work of Phyllis Trible.

42. Ibid., 32.

43. Martin, *Feminist Question*, 218.

44. Schüssler Fiorenza, *In Memory of Her*, 33.

45. Arguably, Schüssler Fiorenza would still see herself as distinct from "neo-orthodox" feminists because she would argue that, more than these feminists, she approaches the text through a hermeneutic of suspicion which is critical of the "patriarchal stamp" of the Bible.

46. Schüssler Fiorenza, *In Memory of Her*, 56.

47. Schüssler Fiorenza, *Bread Not Stone*, xii–xiii.

women for liberation that remains the locus of authority.[48] This stance is expressed in Schüssler Fiorenza's belief that a "feminist hermeneutics cannot trust or accept Bible and tradition simply as divine revelation. Rather it must critically evaluate them as patriarchal articulations."[49]

Therefore, Schüssler Fiorenza argues that feminist theology must challenge "biblical theological scholarship to develop a paradigm for biblical revelation that does not understand the New Testament as an archetype but as a prototype."[50] The model of prototype locates revelation not in texts but in Christian experience and community.[51] The notion of historical prototype means the text is open to its own critical transformation while allowing that the whole Bible can be reclaimed, "not as a normative immutable archetype, but as an experiential authority that can 'render God' although it is written in the 'language of men.'"[52] Schüssler Fiorenza understands an archetype to take historically limited experiences and texts and posit them as universals, becoming authoritative and normative for all times and cultures.[53] According to her model, "revelation is located in the experience of God's grace and presence among women struggling for liberation from patriarchal oppression and dehumanization" in the context of women-church as part of feminist critical hermeneutics.[54] Feminist interpretation places biblical texts under the authority of feminist experience insofar as it "maintains that revelation is ongoing and takes place 'for the sake of our salvation.'"[55]

> A feminist theological interpretation of the Bible that has as its canon the liberation of women from oppressive sexist structures, institutions, and internalized values must affirm, therefore, that

---

48. Hays, *Moral Vision*, 276. It seems unclear precisely how Schüssler Fiorenza's position differs from the "canon within a canon" approach she criticizes in feminists like Ruether. If Schüssler Fiorenza is utilizing parts of scripture to substantiate points of her position, then it appears that, practically speaking, some form of a canon within a canon is employed.

49. Schüssler Fiorenza, *Bread Not Stone*, x.

50. Schüssler Fiorenza, *In Memory of Her*, 33.

51. Ibid., 34.

52. Schüssler Fiorenza, *Bread Not Stone*, xvii.

53. Ibid., 10.

54. Ibid., xvii.

55. Ibid., 14.

only the nonsexist and nonpatriarchal traditions of the Bible and the nonoppressive traditions of biblical interpretation have the theological authority of revelation if the Bible is not to continue as a tool for the oppression of women.[56]

Jesus Christ and Atonement in Schüssler Fiorenza

Schüssler Fiorenza considers the role of Jesus and how this is understood within scripture and tradition. She understands the earliest Jesus traditions to eschew any understanding of the ministry and death of Jesus in cultic terms as atonement for sin, arguing that such an interpretation of Jesus' death as atonement for sins is much later than generally assumed in New Testament scholarship. This view does not express the Jesus movement's understanding and experience of God but is a later interpretation of the violent death of Jesus in cultic terms.[57] "The suffering and death of Jesus, like that of John and all the other prophets sent to Israel before him, are not required in order to atone for the sins of the people in the face of an absolute God, but are the result of violence against the envoys of Sophia who proclaim God's unlimited goodness and the equality and election of *all* her children in Israel."[58] "Jesus' execution, like John's, results from his mission and commitment as prophet and emissary of the Sophia-God who holds open a future for the poor and outcast and offers God's gracious goodness to *all* children of Israel without exception. The Sophia-God of Jesus does not need atonement or sacrifices. Jesus' death is not willed by God but is the result of his all-inclusive praxis as Sophia's prophet."[59] Furthermore, Schüssler Fiorenza understands the disciples of Jesus as standing in succession of Sophia-prophets, continuing what Jesus did, namely, "making the real-

56. Ibid., 60.

57. Schüssler Fiorenza, *In Memory of Her*, 130. She refers to H. Kessler, *Die theologishe Bedeutung des Todes Jesu*; and S. K. Williams, *Jesus' Death as Saving Event* as substantiating her point. She also refers to M. Hengel's *The Atonement* as a contrary opinion.

58. Schüssler Fiorenza, *In Memory of Her*, 135. By "Sophia" Schüssler Fiorenza draws on the earliest Jesus traditions, which perceive the God of gracious goodness as divine Sophia (wisdom). She identifies the Q community as stressing that the most eminent of Sophia's children are John and Jesus, noting that only Matthew identifies Sophia with Jesus.

59. Schüssler Fiorenza, *In Memory of Her*, 135.

ity of God's *basileia* and the all-inclusive goodness of the Sophia-God of Jesus experientially available."[60]

What we find in Schüssler Fiorenza's account of Jesus Christ and atonement is not dissimilar to the content of feminist theologies of atonement discussed above. There is an emphasis upon Jesus' life and mission to the oppressed, which excludes an interpretation of his death as a part of that mission as well as its necessity for understanding atonement. Both Francis Martin and Richard Hays, while acknowledging the value of feminist hermeneutics as providing a challenge to false interpretations of the Bible used to oppress women, see similar weaknesses in Schüssler Fiorenza's approach, namely, that she concentrates on the life of Jesus to the neglect of the cross and resurrection, which are surely the center of the New Testament and what give us the understanding of true liberation and oppression.[61] Such an approach might ultimately undermine the authority of the New Testament such that the liberating power of it would be lost.[62]

Rosemary Radford Ruether

Ruether illustrates the Western theological tradition by a hermeneutical circle of past and present experience: every "great religious idea begins in the revelatory experience." By *revelatory* she means a breakthrough experience beyond the ordinary fragmented consciousness that provides interpretive symbols, and since "consciousness is ultimately individual, we postulate that revelation always starts with an individual."[63] Regardless of how much the individual teacher is magnified, "the revelatory experience becomes socially meaningful only when translated into communal consciousness."[64] Ruether understands religious traditions as beginning with breakthrough experiences that shed revelatory light on contemporary events, which are then transformed into paradigms of ultimate meaning. Such experiences, like the exodus or resurrection,

---

60. Ibid., 136.

61. Martin, *Feminist Question*, 219–20; Hays, *Moral Vision*, 268, 281. Furthermore, Martin considers the terms prototype and archetype cast the Bible as merely a model rather than a means of communication.

62. Hays, *Moral Visiont*, 282.

63. Ruether, *Sexism and God-Talk*, 13.

64. Ibid.

are the "primary data of the religious tradition." However, these experiences do not interpret themselves.[65] A formative community appropriates revelatory experience and seeks to develop a historical community around its interpretation. According to Ruether, an authoritative body of writings becomes canonized as the correct interpretation of the original divine revelation and, in the process, the controlling group suppresses other branches of the community and their texts, declaring itself the privileged line of interpretation.[66] Yet, no matter how much a community seeks to secure access to divinely revealed truth, it cannot ignore the experience of the present community. The contemporary community is in a constant process of revision of the symbolic pattern in a way that reflects their experience. "Received ideas are tested by what 'feels right,' that is, illuminates the logic of the symbolic pattern in a way that speaks most satisfyingly to their own experience of redemption."[67] Reminiscent of Schleiermacher, Ruether reflects an idealist view of revelation based on religious experiences where there is a fundamental experience of the transcendent as an other, expressed in religious symbolism proper to various and conflicting historical communities. This experience is absorbed into the fundamental feminist experience, that is, oppression.[68] Therefore, "a religious tradition remains vital so long as its revelatory pattern can be reproduced generation after generation and continues to speak to individuals in the community and provide for them the redemptive meaning of individual and collective experience."[69] Ruether views the exodus-Passover pattern for Jews and the death-resurrection paradigm of personal conversion for Christians as one instance of how the "contemporary community appropriates the foundation paradigm as the continuing story of its own redemption in relation to God, self, and one another."[70]

For Ruether, "religious traditions fall into crisis when the received interpretations of the redemptive paradigms contradict experience in

65. Ruether, "Feminist Interpretation," 112.

66. Ruether, *Sexism and God-Talk*, 14.

67. Ibid., 15.

68. Martin, *Feminist Question*, 179.

69. Ruether, *Sexism and God-Talk*, 15–16.

70. Ibid., 16.

significant ways."[71] Such crises can lead to radical revision of the tradition (e.g., the Reformation, ideological criticism of Marxism). Ruether asks why we should even seek alternative traditions at all. Why not just go with contemporary experience? Her answer: the received patterns of authority create a need to find an authoritative base of revealed truth "in the beginning" as well as a need to justify the new by reference to recognized authority. "These needs reveal a still deeper need: to situate oneself meaningfully in history."[72] Ruether believes that by finding an alternative historical community and tradition that is more deeply rooted than those that have become corrupted one touches a deeper "bedrock of authentic Being upon which to ground the self," thus providing a secure place from which to lever criticism.[73] Ruether's approach does not seem entirely different from Schüssler Fiorenza's, especially in what is perceived to be the final result. Again we find a feminist effort to bind theology to some form of authority. Initially, feminist theologians appear as though they oppose all forms of authority, yet it is merely an authority from outside women's experience that is rejected. The question becomes not whether or not we have authority, but whose.[74]

While there are subtle differences between feminists on the subject of revelation, a common thread appears to be the firm conviction that women's experience can be revelatory of the divine. The core of the feminist critique against traditional language and categories of revelation is the consistent marginalization of women's experience from what the Christian church has named revelation.[75] However, while feminists claim revelation is located in experience, the meaning of this is unclear. Exactly which experiences are considered revelatory?[76] The feminist appeal to experience does not explain how such an appeal is construed,

71. Ibid., 16.

72. Ibid., 18.

73. Ibid.

74. Gunton, *Brief Theology of Revelation*, 38–39. This point is related to one made by Gunton who shows that the very nature of the world necessitates some form of revelation (the world has been created so as to be known). So the question is not whether revelation, but which.

75. Hilkert, "Experience and Tradition" 60.

76. Ibid., 77. If women's experience of the struggle for liberation is revelatory, it is unclear what are the content and criteria of such revelation. Does it exclude other types of women's experience, for instance, religious experiences that might be argued as mediatorial of God's word?

and likewise, how the moral principle of full humanity is derived from experience.[77] A new meaning of canon emerges: what is truly canonical in the feminist context is the scriptural material that liberates the oppressed.[78] "In the case of Ruether and Schüssler Fiorenza, the true canon becomes a criterion and is identified as an appeal to women's experience, which is simultaneously interpreted as the medium of divine grace, divine revelation, and divine wisdom."[79] The feminist hermeneutics of Ruether and Schüssler Fiorenza locate divine revelation not in the Bible or tradition but in women's oppression (*ekklēsia of women*).[80] Although Catholic feminist Sandra Schneiders considers herself in general agreement with Schüssler Fiorenza, she finds unsatisfactory an approach that excises biblical texts as oppressive or denies the Bible revelatory status; rather, she envisions a feminist approach that neutralizes the oppressive potential of the Bible while invoking its liberating power. For Schneiders, scripture as a whole is or is not the medium of divine self-disclosure.[81] Furthermore, she argues that there are theological, ecumenical, and spiritual motives for retaining the revelatory function of the Bible: theological because the Bible is the normative witness for the Christian community regarding Christian identity; ecumenical in that the common faith resource for all Christian communities is the Bible and to discard it as such may affect possibilities for unity; and spiritual since the Bible is the source of spiritual life.[82]

Conclusion: The Problem of Authority in Feminist Theology

The common feminist rejection of the Bible as revelation seems related to the problem of authority. The weakness in liberationist positions like those of Ruether and Schüssler Fiorenza is an almost partisan position on revelation that appears to "equate 'revelatory' with 'authoritative' in an almost simplistic way, then to reject as nonrevelatory whatever does

77. Abraham, *Canon and Criterion*, 442–43.

78. Ibid., 434.

79. Ibid., 462–63.

80. Martin, *Feminist Question*, 212–13.

81. Schneiders, "Bible and Feminismy," 49.

82. Ibid., 51.

not fit according to its own narrow criteria."[83] Why the refusal to accord revelatory status to the biblical text?

Revelation and Authority

Angela West rightly identifies the issue of authority as the central component of the feminist reluctance to consider the biblical witness. She challenges such a view, asking if tradition really must be viewed as stifling authoritarianism.[84] Perhaps the work of Letty Russell offers something of an alternative approach. Rather than placing an ethical criterion derived from women's experience in opposition to the biblical text, Russell gains an understanding of liberation from the Bible: "The actions of the communities are . . . tested by the Biblical witness to the meaning and purpose of human liberation as part of God's plan for all of the groaning creation."[85] Because she borrows from liberation theology the view of salvation as a social event, the meaning of sin takes on a different shape as well. "Sin as the opposite of liberation is seen as *oppression*, a situation in which there is no community, no room to live as a whole human being."[86] For Russell, the contemporary theme of salvation is *conscientization*, whereby human beings take responsibility for shaping their individual and social history. There is a process of self-awareness that helps individuals to learn their potential for changing the world.[87] Conscientization is related to dialogue and community building, and does not view liberation as a simple process of identifying a common enemy and reversing the roles.[88] Moreover, in the biblical context salvation in God's actions is seen as liberation. The challenge is to interpret this meaning so that it relates to the experience of free-

---

83. Osiek, "Feminist and the Bible," 104.

84. West, *Deadly Innocence*, 91–92.

85. Russell, *Human Liberation*, 50–51.

86. Ibid., 62.

87. Ibid., 66. This self-awareness is different from the feminist exemplarist versions of atonement we have been considering. Russell wants to let scripture have more of a say regarding the definition of liberation. Although she still sounds somewhat like other feminists we have been discussing because she speaks of human responsibility and changing the self, she remains distinct from the "subjective" models they promote because she appears to take sin more seriously.

88. Russell, *Human Liberation*, 67.

dom that happens today as conscientization among oppressed people.[89] Salvation as a new wholeness and liberation for human beings brings with it a sense of sin as a collective reality, taking into account the individual and social responsibility for sin.[90]

It seems that Russell is able to appeal to scripture as authoritative because she approaches the matter from a distinct perspective than many other feminist theologians who speak about authority (related to revelation). We have seen that feminist theology is a rather modern project, despite any efforts, directly or indirectly, to be otherwise, and its portrayal of the concept of revelation is no exception. The heart of the modern offence with revelation is the problem of authority, because it appears to violate human autonomy.[91] We encounter the problem of authority in Hampson's discussion of autonomy where language of the parent-child relationship is invoked.[92] Similar strategies can be seen in other feminist theologians. Regarding language for God, Ruether suggests that the parent model for the divine leads to a kind of permanent parent-child relationship to God where becoming autonomous and responsible for our own lives equals the gravest sin against God. "Patriarchal theology uses the parent image for God to prolong spiritual infantilism as virtue and to make autonomy and assertion of free will a sin."[93] In contrast, Ruether wants to start with language for the Divine as redeemer and liberator, the one who "fosters full personhood," speaking of God as the source of being.[94] McFague also considers harmful the image of human life as infantile, needing an all-powerful father, which is a focus of an objective account of God in traditional atonement models.[95] Carter Heyward rejects what she considers the dominant violent atonement tradition as producing a deity that reigns over children like a parent.[96] Autonomy is equated with being an adult and heteronomy

89. Ibid., 104.

90. Ibid., 111. Russell admits that some feminist theologians' reluctance to speak of sin is reasonable considering that sin often has been associated with women and sex (112).

91. Gunton, *Brief Theology of Revelation*, 31.

92. See chapter 2 above.

93. Ruether, *Sexism and God-Talk*, 69.

94. Ibid., 70.

95. McFague, *Metaphorical Theology*, 185.

96. Heyward, *Saving Jesus*, 160.

(which defines our relationship to the Christian God) is emblematic of being a child. The ethical stance of feminism demands that women no longer consider themselves like children, but as independent, autonomous adults.

Related to authority understood within a paradigm of parent/child relationships, Rita Nakashima Brock's contention against traditional atonement theology is what she sees as its protection of the authority and omnipotence of the father.[97] Associated with authority is a concept of power that feminists often understand as power *over*, resulting in a lack of power that leads to a humility and self-abnegation that should not be adopted by women. Brock accuses Christianity of being guilty of a wrong view on power: "Christianity is afflicted with a hierarchical view of power that undercuts its understanding of love in its fullest incarnation—that we are all part of one another and co-create each other at the depths of our being."[98] Brock notes the issue of power as central to the problems with traditional atonement theology, which she considers lacks interdependence and mutuality and encourages us to look to suffering and power outside us.[99] This is why Brock focuses her Christology away from Christ and onto the community. Salvation is found in mutuality in community rather than in a heroic individual.[100] Somewhat in contrast to Brock's approach, Mary Grey understands the Gospel stories of Jesus as providing us with a re-imaging of power in the man Jesus whose energy for justice making is not a passive self-martyrdom.[101] However, the content of redemption is a power-in-relation that can be interpreted as a "passionate divine energy for justice," a concept still related to the issues of mutuality raised by feminists who identify any authority as a problem for women.[102] Therefore, although Grey portrays Jesus as revealing a different kind of power, her version of redemption does not appear to be all that distinct from the likes of Brock who emphasizes mutuality.

97. Brock, "And a Little Child," 52.

98. Brock, *Journeys By Heart*, 49.

99. Ibid., 56.

100. Ibid., 52.

101. Grey, *Redeeming the Dream*, 105.

102. Ibid., 108.

An Alternative View of Authority

On the other hand, we find Russell willing to consider authority as relevant to women because she addresses it within a particularly Christian context. Russell refuses to give up the biblical basis of her theology since her paradigm of authority is the Word of God.[103] Russell also regards an appeal to the authority of the future as important to feminist theology. Women's experience has authority, but this experience is primarily of the old creation and patriarchal structures of church and society.[104] In a world patterned by patriarchal paradigms of reality, power and authority are often exercised through domination, however, this does not have to be the case. Authority can be exercised through empowerment when people are seeking to live out the gospel vision of shared community of service.[105] The Christian community considers an authoritative witness to God in Jesus Christ to include human experience as well as scripture and church tradition.[106] This pattern of criteria is not what is authoritative, but the "connection of that pattern with the divine self-revelation of God that gives it authority and limits its claims."[107] Authority built on this foundation is dependent on orthopraxy and orthodoxy. Certain teachings gain our assent when we see them leading toward the "actualization of Christ's ministry in both word and deed."[108] Russell conceives of a feminist/liberation theological paradigm of authority in community that appeals to experience in relation to other theological sources. Experiences of those struggling for full personhood deepen our vision of God's promise and become the lens through which we understand the gospel message. The "critically reflected experience" leads to new paradigms such as the shift from seeing authority in terms of partnership rather than domination.[109]

Russell claims that as Christians "we live under the authority of the Word of God, an authority that tells us quite a different story."[110]

103. Copeland, "Journeying," 34.

104. Russell, *Household of Freedom*, 18.

105. Ibid., 23.

106. Ibid.

107. Ibid., 24.

108. Ibid.

109. Ibid., 31–33.

110. Ibid., 44.

She considers herself a "house revolutionary" who does not want to demolish the house, but rebuild it using the "master's tools" in service to others. These new tools include critical analysis as well as tools for rebuilding and rediscovering our theology while continuing to survive in the old house.[111] Russell rejects Schüssler Fiorenza's opposition to women's reality and biblical texts as both possible loci of revelation. She sees Schüssler Fiorenza as calling for a single critical principle based on the concrete life experience of women and expressed in the political task of advocacy and liberating praxis.[112] Schüssler Fiorenza insists on the authority of women over the Bible, and this assertion is understood not simply in terms of the desire of feminism to advance the cause of women but also in terms of a critical theory that refuses to validate its claims by appeal to a "transcendent other." For Schüssler Fiorenza, if there are "biblical texts that support women's struggle against oppression, they do so because women claim them in this struggle, not because God (or any other transcendent, de-historicized ideal) says so."[113]

In addition to issues of autonomy and power, we here encounter another key point in the problem of authority within feminist theology: the subject of transcendence. Earlier we observed the emphasis upon immanence in Hampson's theism as it is related to the concept of authority. Hampson strongly resists any notion of authority that comes from outside the individual. Perhaps the Christian feminists under consideration do not state matters as plainly as Hampson, but if we look closely, we recognize similar language of autonomy/heteronomy, adulthood/childhood, and a fear of authority coming from outside the self, from an other who stands over and against us.[114] However, in exchanging women's experience for revelation, have not feminist theologians

---

111. Ibid., 64. These words stand in stark contrast to those of Audre Lorde who claimed that it would be impossible to rebuild the house with the "master's tools" (Lorde, "Master's Tools," 110–13).

112. Russell, *Household of Freedom*, 68.

113. Camp, "Feminist Theological Hermeneutics," 159. Camp agrees with much of Schüssler Fiorenza's approach, but still finds value in feminists such as Trible and Ruether who allow more authority for the biblical text (161). See also Hays, *Moral Vision*, 278. Hays claims Schüssler Fiorenza's discourse about God is in danger of losing the aspect of transcendence.

114. McFague, *Metaphorical Theology*, 187. McFague contrasts her approach with a transcendent view of God, saying that God is part of our being and also the source of life.

merely exchanged one authority for another? Their response to such a challenge would likely be to argue that this authority is from within women's own experience, not the patriarchal Christian Bible or tradition and, therefore, valid for feminist theology. Nevertheless, it seems that this trading of authorities will present the same problem with which feminists have struggled for so long, that is, grounding theological doctrine upon a universal authority or foundation derived from experience, be that male experience in the case of most traditional theology or women's experience in contemporary feminist theology.

And so, what are we left with? Concerning feminist atonement theology it appears that we are given no sense of genuine redemption or transformation of ourselves, our relationships to others and the world, and most importantly our relationship to God. With experience as the ultimate authority, it seems that each particular group of women may develop a version of redemption that suits their experience, but where is the hope of reconciliation between women, between women and men, between Creator and creature within such a paradigm? In general, a Christian theology of atonement should contain an awareness of the depth and extent of sin, an emphasis upon God's gracious initiative, and a relating of the objective and subjective aspects.[115] We have observed the pitfalls of a subjective view of atonement that is constructed to the exclusion of the objective element, yet there must be a way for women's experience to be a valid and significant theological source while maintaining the authority of God's revelation to us through scripture in order to develop an atonement theology that provides both aspects. In order to meet the ambitions set out by Christian feminist theology it seems that nothing less should be expected.

115. Van Dyk, "Vision and Imagination," 9.

7

Feminist Atonement Theology:
Where Do We Go From Here?

Introduction: Women's Experience
and Atonement Theology Reconsidered

ATONEMENT, REDEMPTION, REVELATION, AUTHORITY. THESE IMPOR-
tant topics bring us back to the core of this thesis, that is, women's experience. This category continues to grow in significance as feminist
theologians examine more closely the methodological roots of feminist
theology. Because feminists in large part see their role in terms of giving voice to those who have been voiceless, they consider the category
of women's experience in the construction of theological doctrine as
crucial, and therefore, one can hardly examine a central Christian doctrine such as atonement without investigating the notion of women's
experience.

In the early days of feminist theology, the category of women's
experience primarily provided a source of critique against traditional
male theology, which had ignored the specific circumstances of women
and yet intended theological doctrine to apply to men and women alike.
Feminist theologians noted that women's particular voice had been
excluded from the theological arena, thus recognizing that centuries
of theological reflection had failed to address the specific realities of
women. Feminist theologians like Valerie Saiving and Judith Plaskow
were among the first to realize how an important Christian doctrine
had been colored by a predominantly male perspective that does not
necessarily relate to the experience of women. Their work demonstrates
that the interpretation of the doctrine of sin by an influential twentieth-

century theologian like Reinhold Niebuhr fails to acknowledge the reality of women's experience; in other words, women do not experience sin as a sense of pride or self-exaltation, but rather as an underdevelopment or negation of the self. Regardless of whether one agrees with Saiving's or Plaskow's final conclusions, such work brings to the fore the fact that human experience, whether acknowledged or not, is a significant aspect of all theological reflection, therefore, feminist theologians are compelled to include women's experience in Christian theology. Moreover, feminist theology does not merely expose the role experience plays in theological reflection, but positions the category as a crucial part of theological method as well.

Related to the concerns that have been raised throughout this thesis, Angela West rightly identifies a problem within feminist theology that she terms "justification by gender."[1] According to West, somewhere along the way, feminist theology cleared women of any real sin except that due to their social and historical experience of living under patriarchy. Identifying the role of women's experience in feminist theology as partly responsible for the resulting failure to take women's sin more seriously, West challenges their position and directs feminist theologians to the Christian tradition to re-evaluate its rich resources for understanding and experiencing genuine liberation. In this thesis, we have similarly identified feminism's methodological roots in the problematic category of women's experience, which is both critical to all feminist theology as well as at the core of some of its weaknesses. We have attempted to untangle the category of women's experience in feminist theology: its meaning and content, use and function, and in particular, its effect on theologies of atonement. From here we can begin to grasp the value of the category of women's experience and also its drawbacks for atonement theology. Are these drawbacks related more to the category itself, its meaning, or to the way it functions in feminist theology? If such flaws contribute to an inadequate doctrine of atonement, what changes should be made in order to lead us toward a doctrine of reconciliation that provides us with an understanding of real redemption?

1. Speaking specifically of Daphne Hampson's position, West argues that Hampson has a creed of equality, but appears to maintain that women are superior morally. "There is something very arbitrary about grounding one's ethics in an implicit doctrine of the superior morality of women. It is tantamount to a faith in justification by gender" (West, "Justification By Gender," 107).

What Is Women's Experience?

One of the first concerns in utilizing women's experience as a category in feminist theology is the inherent problem of defining it. We attempt to gain a basic understanding of the category of women's experience in our first chapter where we identify several predominant ways in which women's experience is understood. Feminist theologians use the term *women's experience* in various ways, emphasizing different concepts: religious or spiritual experience, bodily experience, or sociopolitical experience to name a few. Religious experience is often related to a type of metaphysical understanding that consists of beliefs in a divine foundation of reality.[2] Bodily experience is readily accepted by feminists who recognize that all experience is embodied experience; however, there is a level of physical experience that is unique to women reflected in such specifically female experiences as menstruation, pregnancy, childbirth, lactation, and menopause. Probably the most significant understanding of women's experience is related to sociopolitical aspects, primarily, women's experience of oppression by men. This notion of women's experience is defined by women's struggle against patriarchy and is basically an aspect of all feminist theology either implicitly or explicitly. Hence, we find that one of the greatest difficulties with the category of women's experience is that it eludes precise definition, and furthermore, is often included in feminist theology without much explanation.

Recognizing the obvious obstacles in narrowing the content and meaning of women's experience, the question of how the category is used in feminist theology emerges, specifically, its function in feminist theologies of atonement. Despite its diverse meanings, women's experience is used in a consistent manner throughout feminist theology in the respect that women's experience is considered a source and norm for theological reflection. Most feminists understand the limitations of claiming women's experience as the only source, and therefore, identify other theological sources as well, for instance, pragmatic concerns, ecological insights, and Christian tradition. However, it appears that

2. There is a difference between religious experience and Christian faith. Many feminist theologians talk about religious experience within the context of Christianity, but it seems to be somewhat distinct from what it means to have Christian religious experience or Christian faith. The concept of Christian faith is more concrete than religious experience; more specific than "connecting with God."

women's experience also functions as the norm in feminist theology, determining which material would make an appropriate contribution to feminist theological discourse and which would not. This is seen most clearly in feminist hermeneutics, where biblical scholars such as Elisabeth Schüssler Fiorenza maintain that only the nonsexist and non-patriarchal traditions of the Bible and the nonoppressive traditions of biblical interpretation are theologically authoritative. Such an approach leads to a "canon within a canon," which considers only certain parts of scripture valid while rejecting others, thus calling into question the normative status of the Bible.[3] Women's experience as source and norm means that it provides the raw material for theological reflection as well as the criteria by which other sources are incorporated or excluded. Such a function of women's experience as norm arguably makes it a founda-tion for feminist theology in that the category of women's experience operates as the lens through which alternative sources are viewed.

This foundationalist tendency has not gone unnoticed by feminist theologians. Ironically, in its use of women's experience, feminist theol-ogy seeks to shake the foundations of traditional theology and yet it reveals its post-Enlightenment dependency upon authoritative founda-tions. In other words, within feminist theology, claims to experience are essentially claims to authority. One feminist theologian in particular, Sheila Greeve Davaney, has criticized what she sees as the implicit foun-dationalism of feminist theology, challenging the view that feminist interpretations of reality are somehow truer to reality in that they are closer to how things *really* are, and therefore, are epistemologically nor-mative. She argues that Rosemary Radford Ruether, for instance, aligns a notion of the full humanity of women with divine reality and that Schüssler Fiorenza claims the feminist viewpoint is more valid than

3. See Watson, *Text, Church and World*, 201. Watson highlights the limitations of historical critical approaches such as Schüssler Fiorenza's which expose the extent of the influence of patriarchy upon biblical texts but fail to deal with the complexity of these influences within a particular historical context. This leads to a selective approach toward scripture whereby some parts are usable and other are rejected. Watson consid-ers such a response to the texts as too easy, unable to take seriously the depth of the problem (one reason why he finds merit in the literary-feminist approach). Watson himself seeks to maintain a "critical-theological estimation of these texts as 'holy scrip-ture', which has led to an exploratory attempt to discover structurally significant stand-points within the texts from which critique of their own patriarchal ideology might proceed and from which, still more importantly, a constructive theological alternative to that ideology might be outlined" (ibid.).

other positions, basically making women's perspectives (historical and contemporary) normative. Ruether and Schüssler Fiorenza also make a connection between women's struggle for liberation and the divine in such a way as to claim authority: it is in liberation experience that God's liberating and revelatory presence is known.[4] Although Davaney's position has received some criticism from within feminist circles, many feminist theologians are in agreement and also recognize the foundationalist tendencies and the drawback of making women's experience the ultimate source and norm for theology.[5] Davaney maintains that the problems of foundationalism may be avoided by a historicist understanding that focuses on the contextual, concrete, and particular.[6] Considering herself to be reinterpreting feminist norms in a "historic pragmaticism," Davaney holds experience as somewhat normative, but not foundational in the way it often has been used in feminist theology.

In addition to critique like Davaney's, the category of women's experience has come under scrutiny from women of color who accuse white feminist theology of establishing a view of women's experience intended to be representative of all women. In other words, feminists of color argue that white feminist theology repeats the same offenses as previous male theology, which represented *male* experience as *human* experience. Womanist and Asian feminist theologians claim that white feminists have been sloppy in their descriptions of women's experience, drawing attention to the fact that most feminist theology is written from the perspective of white, North American or European women, disregarding the particular experiences of African-American and Asian women. The complex issues of race and class and how these are related to gender are not adequately considered by most white feminist theologians for whom racism becomes just another layer of the oppression which all women experience. Oppression is basically accepted as the

---

4. Davaney, "Limits of the Appeal," 35.

5. See Davaney and Chopp, eds., *Horizons in Feminist Theology*. The contributors to this volume reject gaining any normative criteria from the past and do not want the feminist norm of experience to be defined by essentialist tendencies. The focus of their critique of the category of experience is related to the formation of identity in an attempt to rethink subjectivity in light of the dissolution of feminists' historical appeal to women's experience.

6. Davaney, "Continuing the Story," 209.

fundamental experience of women, yet the meaning of oppression is not adequately defined, in particular, in light of race. The experience of oppression or sexism cannot be separated from racial or class identity, and merely claiming that black women, for instance, suffer racism in addition to the sexism which all women experience fails to consider the contexts within which women experience oppression and how the aspects of a woman's identity are woven together. Because history has shown women to be subjugated to men in a multitude of ways, feminists are correct to emphasize oppression as a significant aspect of women's experience, but a more comprehensive view of the category is needed. It should be noted that white feminists do attempt to avoid universalizing women's experience by recognizing the particularity of women's experience and the fact that women of color have different experiences of oppression than white women. However, in light of the critique, white feminists' efforts to develop a comprehensive view of women's experience have been insufficient. White women must both claim the truths of their lived experience as well as be deeply suspicious of their connection to the dominant American culture with its race and class biases.[7]

Part of the debate about the content of women's experience focuses upon the essentialist tendencies the category often exhibits. The universalist and essentialist aspects of women's experience create particular problems about which we gain insight from a scholar like Victor Anderson. In his book *Beyond Ontological Blackness*, Anderson demonstrates that in regard to black identity in the United States, the essentialist concept of ontological blackness distorts much of African-American life and experience. Extending his critique to the area of black and womanist theologies, he contends that by making oppression the defining experience of black men and women, a radical opposition to whiteness is created that, in effect, renders whiteness as necessary for black theology. The task of self-definition becomes bound to suffering and resistance rather than the promise of transcendence. Similar to Anderson's analysis of what is occurring in black and womanist theologies, an essentialist definition of women's experience as primarily linked to oppression (effectively functioning as a foundation for feminist theology), greatly weakens its own ability to transcend the culture and provide positive substance for women's identity. Because patriarchy

7. Thistlethwaite, *Sex, Race and God*, 91.

is the target of opposition, all elements identified as part of patriarchal tradition are rejected. In this sense, patriarchy functions determinatively (and negatively so) for feminist theology. Despite the poignant critique Anderson's position offers, it seems feminist theologians will continue to promote the category of women's experience as they seek to make women's voices heard. Perhaps there is a fear that if feminism diminishes the force of women's experience as a result of seriously considering the critiques against it, the political influence of women's identity will be lost as well.

Women's Experience at Work in Feminist Theology

Two significant branches of feminist theology illustrate our preliminary discussion. By examining them we shall try to clarify further the category of women's experience and how it operates by exploring the theology of religious experience and feminist liberation theology.

Women's Experience in a Theology of Religious Experience

Although religious experience is not the primary way feminist theologians speak of women's experience, there seems to be an underlying understanding of religious experience that influences much feminist theology. As Ruether explains, the patriarchal distortions of the Christian tradition have forced feminists to utilize the "primary intuitions of religious experience itself" as a theological resource.[8] Since feminist theology understands God as revealed through and present in oppression and the struggle against patriarchy, women's experience is closely related to what is revelatory of the divine, therefore, making religious experience an important aspect of women's experience. Moreover, since what we observe in feminist theologies of atonement is in many ways a theology of experience, it is helpful to consider in some detail aspects of a feminist theology of experience and the influence of Schleiermacher, the father of such theology. For the purpose of this thesis, the context for such a discussion is found in the work of Daphne Hampson, who emphasizes religious experience in her

---

8. See chapter 1, n. 14 above.

writing and whose post-Christian perspective provides unique insights into feminist theology.

Hampson explicitly makes experience the linchpin of her methodology. In her view, religion based upon human experience is a more ethical approach because it preserves the authority and autonomy of the individual in contrast to those religions that are based upon a revelation outside the self. Her position is very much dependent upon Schleiermacher's work, in which she finds useful the conception of the self in relation to that which is outside the self, as well as the understanding that there is no heteronomy in our relationship to God. Beginning with a belief in the possibility of an immediate awareness of God, Hampson incorporates actual evidence of religious experience, based upon research done by the Oxford Religious Experience Research Unit, as the basis of her method.

Hampson's approach reveals certain weaknesses to which a theology of experience is prone, such as a tendency toward pantheism and a danger of relativism. For example, Hampson represents God and the world as inter-related and describes an exclusively immanent rather than transcendent God, which leaves her particular theism vulnerable to pantheism because it is difficult to determine just where the world ends and where God begins. Furthermore, because Hampson's theism is based upon individual experience, there is a danger of relativism, in part because the notion of community and its relationship to experience is underdeveloped, which contributes to the sense that each particular context should create its own theism as Hampson herself has done. Hampson's flawed theology of experience places the individual human being at the center and considers God as known through the self.

However, we do not want to object too strongly to the category of religious experience and its value for the theological project, just as we do not want to object to the category of women's experience outright. The problem is not necessarily the category but the way in which it is used, and in Hampson's case, religious experience operates as an indubitable foundation, not unlike women's experience functioning as the authoritative foundation for feminist theology. Hampson's approach fails to provide a source of hope for genuine transformation and the means to live beyond the limits of our experience. Because the typical modern view, which maintains that there are certain truths or foundations on which to ground one's thought, appears incompatible with a relativist perspective, which accepts a variety of positions based on different sources, it may seem logically impossible that one could be both a relativist and foundationalist, yet Hampson exhibits tendencies toward both. Proudly admitting that she is a product of the Enlightenment, Hampson considers a foundation necessary in order to provide theology with credibility and reliability not unlike a scientific project. However, due to the fact that her "foundation" is grounded upon individual religious experience, relativism seems the likely outcome.

Women's Experience in Feminist Liberation Theology

According to feminist theology, women's experience of oppression is a predominant aspect of all women's experience in various forms and degrees. This emphasis is found most consistently in feminist liberation theology. Feminist liberation theologians seek to change unjust structures and distorted symbol systems and build new communities. Utilizing what is basically a method of correlation, the work of three important feminist liberation theologians, Letty Russell, Rosemary Radford Ruether, and Elisabeth Schüssler Fiorenza, emphasizes the need for liberation of women from oppression and has been formative in shaping feminist theology, regardless of the different approaches each brings to scripture.

Russell could be considered the more "biblical" of the three as she explicitly retains a positive role for scripture and Christian tradition in her work.[9] Like liberation theology, she includes experience as an important piece of the theological puzzle, recognizing the significance of context in the development of all theology. For Russell, the inclusion of experience makes theology more holistic. Experience is authoritative, but not a source independent of other resources such as scripture, tradition, and scientific knowledge. In somewhat of a contrast, Schüssler

9. Jones and Farley, *Liberating Eschatology*, ix. Jones and Farley note one distinguishing feature of Russell's work, that is, her reliance on scripture, identifying Russell as a feminist theologian who still finds the voice of God in the Bible. Jacquelyn Grant would agree, identifying Russell as a white feminist who gives the Bible primacy in theology (Grant, *White Women's Christ*, 118). Kathryn Greene-McCreight acknowledges Russell's focus on the Bible but does not include her in the category of biblical feminist, arguing that although Russell considers the Bible as witness to be her interpretive key, it is not the primary way she understands the Bible to function (*Feminist Reconstructions*, 147 n. 45).

Fiorenza begins with women's experience and evaluates texts and traditions usually considered normative in light of their liberative or oppressive potential. She roots an understanding of experience within a
community, "women-church" (*ekklēsia*), which provides the context for
biblical interpretation, concluding that only those texts that are nonoppressive have the theological authority of revelation. According to her, a
feminist liberationist exploration of Christian scriptures starts with an
analysis of women's experience rather than with biblical texts. The critical principle of Ruether's theology is the promotion of the full humanity of women. Those sources that promote the full humanity of women
remain viable and usable in feminist theology, thus in a sense creating a
new canon for theology. Despite the degree to which experience is authoritative in each system, all reflect a method of correlation that seeks
to correlate human experience to the biblical tradition in the sense that
they are developing a mediating or apologetic theology that attempts to
bring contemporary meaning to Christian doctrine.[10]

Such a correlationist approach is commonly associated with Paul
Tillich who attempted to connect religion and culture in the service of
theology. Whatever the particular flaws in Tillich's system, his effort to
create a mediating theology is important and a positive starting point
for feminist theologians who seek to make Christian doctrine more relevant to women's lived experience. However, regarding Christology, we
recognize the danger in a method of correlation whereby theology becomes merely an explication of symbols in the Christian message that
are adequate to the human situation. For instance, in Ruether's system,
Jesus resymbolizes the messianic prophet described as the paradigm of
liberated humanity. There is a stress on Christ's identity as that which
is continued in redemptive humanity and in the life of the community,
failing to identify Jesus as he is witnessed to in scripture, that is, as a

10. According to Greene-McCreight, Hans Frei sees the loss of narrative reading in
modern theology as related to the task of apologetic, which he describes as the "chief
characteristic of the mediating theology of modernity." Such an approach confuses the
logic of belief with the logic of coming to belief whereby the integrity of the Christian
narrative is in danger of being jeopardized (Greene-McCreight, *Feminist Reconstructions*,
14–15). It is interesting to note that Karl Barth describes Schleiermacher as being more
interested in apologetics than in Christian theology, which led him to be detached
from the essential theological task of proclaiming and interpreting Christianity (Barth,
Protestant Theology, 440–41).

savior who redeems humanity in a particular historical time and place. Jesus' unique role in Christianity is lost under such a scheme.

Tillich's method reveals similar problematic tendencies for Christology in that Jesus functions as a symbol. It is difficult to comprehend how Jesus as a paradigm or symbol is the key to reconciliation in the same way Jesus Christ as the unique savior provides the way for genuine transformation and redemption. The strength of the correlative method is in its attempt to mediate between religion and culture, revelation and experience, but such an approach reveals limitations in its failure to negotiate these competing sources. The emphasis upon culture and experience will lead to a more subjective view of atonement whereas concentrating upon religion and revelation will result in an objective focus. Perhaps it is impossible to give equal weight to theological sources, and one will take more priority than another; therefore the question becomes, which will take precedence and exactly how much? Feminist theologians have followed Tillich's lead by placing priority on the existential side of the equation, which, for feminists, is related to the issue of authority. In some sense, the method of correlation appears to boil down to an issue of who is the first speaker—God or humanity? In other words, how do revelation and human experience relate?

Women's Experience and Atonement Theology

The broader issues raised by the correlative method in feminist theology gain some focus by considering women's experience specifically within the context of feminist theologies of atonement. Chapter 4 detailed a few significant feminist views on atonement. First, there is a critical, yet popular, feminist position that argues that traditional atonement models in fact represent divine child abuse (e.g., Brock, Brown, and Parker). Such an approach claims that traditional models project a wrong view of authority and present suffering as something good, a view which is likely a reaction to a common, unsympathetic interpretation of Anselmian satisfaction theory. Brock develops a notion of salvation as an element of the "Christa/Community," which she contends is a more holistic, healing interpretation. Brown and Parker reject completely any notion of atonement that includes suffering, pain, or blood, and instead interpret salvation as living a life opposed to injustice and oppression. Mary Grey is slightly less antagonistic toward the traditional models, although she wants to move in a positive direction away from violent images and toward maternal imagery of birthing, which she finds more transformative. Grey recognizes that there will be pain, but like birth, there is creation of new life. This is the pattern of the world. Her position results in a rather panentheistic understanding where we are the "Body of Christ" sharing in the world's healing and creative resources. Alternatively, Ruether finds the question of Christ's maleness an important consideration in any talk of redemption. Returning to the Synoptic Gospels, she utilizes Jesus' message and practice as her starting point, maintaining that Christ's maleness is socially (though not theologically) significant in that he manifests the *kenosis of patriarchy* whereby the system of domination is overturned and social hierarchies are rejected. The relationship between the redeemer and the redeemed is paradigmatic, that is, Jesus is representative of a liberated community that continues Christ's identity, calling us to new dimensions of human liberation. Therefore, the face of liberated humanity is not only the face of Christ but also the face of liberating, healing encounters experienced in and through relationships.

In each of these feminist views on atonement, the category of women's experience determines the questions that are asked regarding the significance of Jesus. The cross is assessed primarily in terms of women's experience of oppression and the theological meaning of the cross is reinterpreted in light of these claims. We are again struck by the insight from women of color who lead us to ask: If white women's experience determines theological doctrine, then will Christian doctrine be inadequate because it fails to understand *women's* experience fully? Such critique is valid, yet somewhat troubling because it appears to lead to the development of Christian doctrine for each particular group. In other words, we have atonement theology based on particular women's experiences and hence theories of atonement that are applicable to specific groups of women. For example, womanist approaches like those of Kelly Brown Douglas and Delores Williams understand Jesus specifically in relation to *black* women's experience. Certainly it is reasonable that one theory or another will be more meaningful to particular groups; however, some models may appear normative at a level that transcends experience or judges it in different ways. Do we not need some (biblical) models that maintain a certain status regardless of experience? Furthermore, since the primary understanding of women's experience contains a strong and appropriate rejection of oppression, it leads to theories of atonement that neglect much of the Christian tradition and the biblical metaphors regarding the cross due to their oppressive nature. However, by excluding the violence and suffering of Jesus' death from any model of redemption, feminist theologians place more emphasis upon Jesus' life, a view which arguably lacks the power for transformation and redemption required of atonement theology as well as separates the person and work of Jesus Christ. Liberation becomes a result of human understanding and will to follow Jesus' vision or example, rather than a radical change of reconciliation in the world and ourselves.

Feminist theologian Kathryn Greene-McCreight has identified similar flaws in the feminist critique of "abusive" atonement models, attributing these to the fact that mainline feminist theologians do not work from a narrative approach to the Gospel stories.[11] Most feminist theologians take attention away from Jesus' crucifixion because they are interpreting the cross out of the larger framework of women's experience (of oppression). Because the cross is "really about something else," metaphors and symbols may be inserted that represent the "meaning" of the cross.[12] Greene-McCreight argues that a narratival approach would remedy such views as Delores Williams' because the New Testament emphasis on the once-for-all character of Christ's redeeming work would be understood.[13] Furthermore, a narratival reading that counters the "abusive" charge shows that the cross cannot be separated from the incarnation, and it follows that it cannot be separated from the doctrine of the Trinity. "That is, the cross may indeed be incomprehensible apart from its 'exegesis' within the context of a Trinitarian understanding of God's self-giving love."[14] Greene-McCreight's challenge is significant and highlights the weakness in a feminist approach to soteriology that

---

11. By mainline Greene-McCreight means the majority of feminist theologians who are usually members of mainline Protestant denominations or Roman Catholic. These are distinct from "biblical" feminists, which is the other category of feminists she identifies (*Feminist Reconstructions*, 38). Her understanding of a narrative approach is based upon the work of William Christian, George Lindbeck and Hans Frei.

12. Greene-McCreight, *Feminist Reconstructions*, 74.

13. Ibid., 75.

14. Ibid., 76.

fails to maintain the unity of Jesus' life, work, death, resurrection, and ascension.

The Subjective Aspect of Feminist Theologies of Atonement

Some feminist theologians note that the traditional atonement models have not been properly challenged over the centuries and are upheld by the church as somehow free from attack. However, many significant theologians, albeit male, have launched genuine critique against longstanding, traditional models, attempting to develop different models in response and these challenges have their weaknesses and opponents as well.[15] For instance, feminists are certainly not the first to identify an element of punishment in Anselm's theory, the notion that God is not free to forgive without punishment. It is often argued that Anselm's theory includes such a focus since he is concerned to account for the enormity of sin as well as to show the lengths to which God went in order to avoid punishing human beings. Some would contend that Anselm's reputation is perhaps a result of how his theory has been interpreted and used within Christian tradition rather than the actual model itself. In any case, it would be helpful for feminist theologians to more fully address this problem, asking which aspects of the Christian tradition perpetuate certain beliefs and practices associated with atonement theory that are not actually part of the theories themselves, but are rather a result of human failure to understand the true meaning of atonement. Likewise, Aulén's *Christus victor* model appears to be removed from its biblical and historical context and criticized by feminist theologians as a tool for oppressing battered women, rather than the theory being considered on its own merits in order to examine more closely how it has been interpreted historically and applied pastorally. All this is not to say that Anselm's or Aulén's models are immune to criticism but that perhaps some of the pastoral oppression which feminists rightly identify is due to a culture of patriarchy inherent within the church hierarchy itself, rather than

15. James Torrance mentions Barth, Rahner, Moltmann, Jüngel, and Balthasar as theologians in our own day who have recognized how Western theology has operated with a view of God more indebted to Aristotle than the New Testament, therefore drifting from a proper understanding of atonement. See Torrance, "Foreword," 7.

as a direct result of a particular theory of atonement. Granted, there are complex issues at work here, but a constructive feminist approach would be one that acknowledges that many important models of atonement predominant in the Christian tradition have been influenced by a culture of patriarchy, and examines how these particular models and metaphors are used within the church and interpreted throughout the church's history, in contrast to simply dismissing traditional models because of the ways they have been interpreted and used.

Admittedly, men develop most atonement theories, with women in only the past few decades putting forth models of redemption that include the particular concerns of half the human race. However, the question is: Are these feminist models helpful, and is their inclusion of, and indeed reliance on, the category of women's experience what other atonement models have been lacking? Are feminists able to present a better model for atonement because they include women's experience?[16]

The models for atonement that are predominant in feminist theology could be generally described as subjective theories rather than objective; in fact, they often explicitly reject an objective element of atonement. Feminist theologians are properly concerned to have atonement impact the lived experience of women, to make a difference in the here and now. This subjective emphasis is due in large part to making the category of women's experience a foundational aspect of feminist theology's methodological approach. Women's experience in relation to sin provides the window through which we understand feminist positions on redemption. How one interprets sin determines how one interprets redemption—*from* what do we need redeeming and *for* what are we redeemed? Generally speaking, feminists describe sin in terms of estrangement related to relationality, that is, there is a disconnectedness with others and with oneself. Sin in much feminist theology is described as a social evil whereby we have been socialized toward alienation and violence, with an emphasis not upon alienation from

16. Of course, the meaning of "better" is crucial. What are one's criteria for a good model of atonement? Is it that it is biblically accurate, theologically coherent, or more palatable to women? If the latter, then most feminist theologians would argue that they do present the better model. Once again, it seems to boil down to what is authoritative: scripture and tradition, or experience.

God, but rather, in terms of our relationship to others.[17] Therefore, the purpose of atonement is to restore mutuality in relationships. Because atonement is understood primarily in existential terms, a direct result of the predominating view of sin, feminist views of atonement appear overly subjective, lacking an objective element that explains atonement as that which occurs beyond human relationships and as also happens between God and humans on a larger scale. Granted, feminist theologians identify the need for relational reconciliation between the self, others, creation, *and* God, but such language is not necessarily intended to mean that human beings suffer from a state of original sin or alienation from our Creator as a result of human disobedience or willfulness. Moreover, the element of objective atonement that attests to the "bondage, pollution and disorder . . . encompassing all dimensions of human existence" is not adequately addressed by feminist theories of atonement.[18]

Similar to Schleiermacher and Tillich who draw attention to the subjective response of the believer, the subjective emphasis of feminist atonement models leads to an exemplarist view of redemption whereby Jesus is presented as a paradigm, and the cross, if retained as valuable, is characterized as a symbol, not a historical event that altered humanity's relationship to God. Jesus' life becomes a model of how we should act. His suffering and death are not examples to follow, although feminists do acknowledge that living a life in opposition to injustice and oppression could lead to suffering and death. Nevertheless, feminist theologies of atonement transfer the theological significance of Jesus' death and resurrection to his life and ministry. The first problem with such an approach is that Jesus is no longer unique. When he is understood as a model for living an exemplary life, the unique quality of Jesus as a divine-human person is lost.[19] Jesus becomes a martyr to follow or the inspiration for a liberated community. For Christians, the uniqueness of Christ as the God-man is of utmost importance, for there is no

17. Ruether, *Introducing Redemption*, 70–72. Ruether recognizes that Christianity is not entirely wrong in seeing sin in terms of pride, but argues that because this is understood vis-à-vis our relationship to God, it has failed to develop the implications of this teaching for our relations to others.

18. Gunton, *Actuality of Atonement*, 160.

19. Ibid., 159. Gunton, using what he describes as a "hackneyed illustration," asks: what distinguishes Jesus' death from that of Socrates?

atonement without the person and work of Jesus Christ who lived, died, and rose from the dead. Another problem is that the failure to see sin beyond the confines of women's experience leads to an incomplete view of sin. If sin is seen primarily in terms of the oppression women suffer under patriarchy, then there seems to be no opportunity for growth or transformation from the sin that women may still perpetrate.[20] By attempting to follow the model, vision, or paradigm of Christ, one is unable to bring about the healing that actually changes us in the core of our being, because not only does our condition as sinful human beings remain but also the justification of God in Christ that liberates us by the power of the Holy Spirit is not realized. Something is not right and we lack the ultimate means of making it so. Sin needs to be defined beyond the boundaries of women's experience because a theology of atonement grounded in such an approach leads to the neglect of the objective side of atonement, and in order to maintain the uniqueness of Jesus Christ as well as to address the gravity of human sin it seems that an objective aspect of atonement is indispensable.

Women's Experience and Revelation

Due to the subjective emphasis of feminist atonement models, feminist theology functions primarily with *example* models of atonement. We identify several difficulties in using the example model as the primary model for atonement. The first is that this model is never understood on its own, but it is defined in part by its relationship to other models. Because the example model is insufficient alone, we look toward scripture as an important source for understanding other models. Most feminists do engage the biblical texts at some level (e.g., Brock mentions Mark's Gospel, Grey identifies biblical imagery, Ruether utilizes the prophetic liberating tradition), however, regarding atonement, a wide variety of atonement metaphors in the Bible, for example, ransom, release, transformation, and reconciliation, are given little or no attention by feminists.

20. Greene-McCreight concludes that a "surprisingly objectifying and unqualified understanding of women's sin" has influenced feminist theology which maintains that women's sin is a response to the "oppressions of patriarchy, racism, and classism. Women's sin, in other words, becomes a passive reality" (Greene-McCreight, *Feminist Reconstruction*, 59).

A further difficulty is that the example model fails to account for humanity's inability to imitate the example of Jesus Christ (which is one of the main reasons we argue that feminist theologians do not take sin seriously). It is one thing to say that Jesus provides a model for relationships, a paradigm of liberated community, or a vision for ministry, but quite another to explain why we fail to follow such an inspirational model. We acknowledge that there has been an inherent problem that prohibits feminist theologians from fully addressing the subject of sin due to the fact that so often the traditional understanding of sin has made women scapegoats for evil and deserving of punishment through subordination to men. Therefore, when sin is discussed in feminist theology, it is usually characterized by patriarchy itself or as a result of patriarchy, whereby the oppressive behavior of men and women is a result of living under a whole system of domination of which men are the primary culprits. However, as Angela West notes, this cannot be an excuse for feminist theology to inadequately identify or address the issue of women's sin.

This leads to a third difficulty, that is, that the example model does not actually provide redemption. Even if feminist theology defines sin primarily as patriarchy or in terms of disconnectedness (rather than alienation from God), feminist atonement models do not provide the way forward. What do we do when we cannot live in new, transformed communities as equals? What do we do when women oppress other women because of race or class? What do we do when we fail to live as liberated humanity? Does the hope of transformation fade? The feminist views on atonement offer inspirational models and vision but do not adequately describe how we make such a vision part of who we are or what occurs when our attempts to live rightly fail.[21] These approaches do not explain why redemption so often is an elusive aspect of women's experience. It appears that the limitations of feminist atonement models are a result of the failure to address sin more comprehensively; therefore, in light of human frailty, such models provide a view of redemption that is only partial and sporadic in the sense that we human beings can participate in profound moments of liberation, but never

21. Ruether, *Women and Redemption*, 224. Ruether responds to such questions based on her understanding of an "ontology of primal 'origins'" whereby, although our nature is rooted in God, we tend toward oppression because of the perversion of the "life instinct" that tends toward self-aggrandizement.

bring about the sort of transformation of relationships between God, each other, and the world necessary for true salvation.[22]

The failure to take sin more seriously is related to the feminist position on revelation, by which we mean the knowledge of God gained from the Bible understood as primary witness to God's self-revelation in Jesus Christ. Let us revisit the work of two significant feminists and their understanding of revelation. Both Ruether and Schüssler Fiorenza function with a canon-within-a-canon and neglect some core themes of the New Testament, namely, the cross and resurrection, which are presented in scripture as the true source of liberating power.[23] Divine self-disclosure is found in women's experience rather than in the Bible, which seems to be the result of a particular view of authority rather than a genuine seeking of God's self-disclosure. Who or what is authoritative—God or experience? This approach appears to simplify what is a complex relationship between the divine and human, equating divine revelation with a simplistic authoritarianism. In contrast, Russell places her discussion of authority and power within the context of Christian faith and tradition, arguing that we gain an understanding of liberation from the Bible. As Christians, our authority is the Word of God, therefore, we have a different understanding of authority.

The Benefits of Women's Experience

We have outlined the general direction of feminist models of atonement, noting in particular the negative aspects of such views. However, it would be remiss not to consider the contributions of feminist versions of atonement examined in this thesis as well as feminist methodology

22. Instead of highlighting the problem of sin, Mary Streufert argues that because feminist theologians have struggled to articulate the divinity of Jesus Christ because of their criticism of sacrificial atonement theory, it has led to exemplary models of redemption. Streufert considers Schleiermacher's theology could aid feminist theology in constructing a more robust Christology that neither simply gives an example or teacher in Jesus nor ignores the problem of violent atonement (Streufert, "Reclaiming Schleiermacher").

23. To view the cross and resurrection as the true source of liberating power is understood in the context of the oneness of Jesus Christ's person and work, with the knowledge that God is the source of liberating power; God the Father through the Son in the Holy Spirit.

in general with the aim of identifying how they benefit theological reflection, particularly in the area of soteriology.

Correcting the Bias

It may seem rather obvious, but the essential role of experience in feminist theology is an important admonition that experience must be taken seriously in the work of theological reflection. Like the first liberation theologians who recognized that theology had been constructed by those living in the dominant West, feminist theologians identified that theology had also been constructed by *men* of the first world. "Rather than claiming a disinterest based on subject/object dualism [i.e., male scholarship], feminist scholarship values and seeks to articulate the personal bases of inquiry."[24] Such a perspective which acknowledges the part of human experience in theology and in the authority of the biblical text, in particular, demonstrates the reality that experience is not an external entity from which we are separate.[25] The concern is not so much to reinstate the role of experience as to correct a bias in the type of experience that shapes theological reflection.[26] One half of the human race has been ignored, their experience deemed of no value in the work of theological construction. Valerie Saiving made this issue more concrete by highlighting that the doctrine of sin, in particular, had been developed from a male perspective and placed severe limits on how much a woman could identify with such an understanding of sin. Due to her analysis of women's experience, Saiving was able to enrich our understanding of the doctrine of sin by taking it beyond the scope of male pride to the arena of female self-negation. Prior to Saiving's analysis general aspects of women's experience were not a factor in the construction of dominant views on sin, and women were left to adopt a perspective that did not fit their experience, thus making theology seemingly irrelevant to their lives. In addition, the entire concept of sin is deepened when the voice of women's experience is permitted to contribute to the process of theological reflection by providing layers of meaning previously unexplored.

24. Setel, "Feminist Insights," 39.

25. Ibid., 42.

26. Hellwig, *Whose Experience Counts?*, 11.

One can see the basic value of human experience, and specifically, women's experience, which Rebecca Chopp argues has benefited
Christian theology because it provides a vision of reality that centers
upon mutuality, celebrates corporality, and is directed toward the future.[27] Human experience is obviously an important source for theological reflection and part of taking experience seriously means that
one does not write theology in a vacuum (even if it were possible) or
pretend that one is doing so. Feminist theologians have reminded us
that there is no pure perspective from which we may construct theology. Experience must be taken seriously on personal terms, remember-
ing that no principle of general validity can be taken from it because, in
principle, things can always be different.[28]

The feminist effort to expose women's experience has taken particular shape in the area of oppression, therefore, one of Christian feminism's primary tasks, derived from authentic religious insight, has been
to expose "the idolatry of projecting onto God false dualisms or hierarchical arrangements between men and women, spirit and matter, and so
forth."[29] The assumption that maleness is co-extensive with humanness
underlies all manifestations of patriarchy, and it is this very exclusion of
female experience from our definition and understanding of humanity
that feminists identify as patriarchal oppression at its most potent.[30] By
examining and valuing women's experience, feminist theologians have
revealed the depth of oppression experienced by women as well as the
importance of acknowledging this aspect of their experience. Women's
experience of oppression under patriarchy throughout the history of
the church is a significant element of women's experience both past and
present. Liberation theologians draw attention to the fact that the voices
of the oppressed are basically ignored in theological doctrine, thus, feminist theologians note that, as part of the oppressed, the value of women's
perspectives is immense in God's kingdom. Those without a voice are
the ones God desires to support. It has been important for feminist
theology to stress that not only is all theology done from a particular
perspective—and women's perspective being no less relevant, to push

27. See Chopp, "Feminism's Theological Pragmatics," 252.

28. Heine, *Women and Early Christianity*, 6.

29. LaCugna, *Freeing Theology*, 2–3.

30. Hogan, *From Women's Experience*, 28.

for its inclusion—but also to reveal the particular aspects of women's experience of oppression and how it effects theological perspective.

A Reevaluation of Violent Atonement Imagery

Within this thesis we have concentrated upon the feminist emphasis on women's experience in relation to atonement theology. There is value in the feminist critique regarding the traditional understandings of atonement, especially those related to the substitutionary view and including aspects of violence against the Son. Feminists are not the first to question some of the more "distasteful" interpretations of atonement, which allegedly promote an image of a vengeful God who sacrificed his innocent child in order to pay the penalty for sin which God himself required. Such a view poses challenges to the basic view of God as loving and forgiving. The feminist critique stems out of an understanding of women's experience related to the notion of the scapegoat, whereby the traditional substitutionary atonement model perpetuates women's experience of oppression in the church in which women suffer as innocent victims at the hands of dominant men. Despite the fact that feminist theologians reject a traditional atonement model solely because of its incompatibility with women's experience, the positive effect of their position remains in that feminists have drawn attention to ways in which women's experience of oppression is perpetuated and devalued by noting the way atonement models are often interpreted and promoted in the church. Those aspects of atonement that offend particular feminist sensitivities provide an impetus for questioning and seeking a clearer understanding or better application of a specific model, but unfortunately women's views are often rejected, leaving them to accept a predominant, yet oppressive, position or leave the church. Feminist critique allows an opportunity for theological growth and depth, not a dismissal of women and their experience as it relates to one of the church's significant theological doctrines.[31] There is the possibility to

31. See Thompson, *Crossing the Divide* as an example of one feminist theologian's attempt to construct a feminist theology of the cross within the context of traditional Christian theology, specifically a theological framework based on Martin Luther. Thompson does not deny the reality of violence within the passion drama and provides a "cross-centered vision of vocation as friendship" as what it means to live as a follower of the crucified and risen Christ (139).

learn from one another by considering how personal experience and context affect one's understanding of theological doctrine. We may learn something new or gain an insight which, in the long run, allows us to better understand and embrace even our own models.

The feminist challenge to atonement theology has helped us consider the important function Christian doctrine has in the way men and women relate and how our understanding of God contributes to various roles we assume. Regardless of their rejection of traditional penal satisfaction or substitutionary atonement models, feminist theologians have identified the possibility that a certain interpretation of the model, in addition to practices based upon that interpretation, may lead to harmful relationships between men and women, and in the extreme case, physical abuse. Therefore, in this instance, the feminist critique has helped raise the important question of the relationship between Christian atonement theology and healthy human interaction.

Salvation's Subjective Aspect

The emphasis upon the subjective side of atonement is another strength of feminist theologies of atonement that is related to the fact that women's experience is the starting point. We have argued that the feminist focus upon experience leads to the development of atonement theology that emphasizes the subjective and neglects the objective element (which is ultimately a weakness that finally undermines the strength, to be discussed further). Nevertheless, maintaining a subjective element of atonement is critical to a proper understanding of atonement. As scripture has shown us, atonement is understood in *both* vertical and horizontal terms, therefore, sound atonement models should contain both aspects, and yet, the traditional models often emphasize the vertical relationship rather than the horizontal, unlike the feminist atonement models.

Throughout scripture we find that redemption has many layers of meaning, including the fact that God is concerned to effect our salvation in the here and now. Although salvation in the Bible contains an important eschatological component, the New Testament also emphasizes the present reality experienced by those who are shaped by Christ's rule. Jesus' many encounters with sick, lonely, and demon-possessed people demonstrate God's desire to change the present, physical reality of people's lives. In Acts there is a focus on salvation in the immediate present and Paul's epistles speak of the present experience of redemption which is grounded upon Jesus' work. Salvation throughout scripture is spoken of in many different terms, for example, salvation, redemption, rescue, save, and deliver, as well as in different tenses, including salvation in the present and in the future. Therefore, we must take seriously the subjective aspect of atonement, for indeed, God intends the experience of redemption to begin in our present lives. Our experience matters greatly to God and atonement models that concentrate on the vertical relationship between God and the world often minimize the importance of God's kingdom being established in the present time on earth. Each day we are able to experience as well as participate in God's rule, which includes manifesting God's redemption to those around us and to the creation. Such an understanding of salvation is a highpoint of feminist theology as it reflects God's loving concern about the physical reality of life on this earth.

Related to the strength of a subjective element in atonement theology is the notion that theology must be contextualized, that is, theology must be able to speak to us in our present context. An obvious example of this approach is found in Jesus himself, who told stories to those around in him in a language ordinary people could understand. The parables presented Jesus' message to his listeners on their own terms, in settings that related to their real lives. Generations of theologians since have learned that the most effective theology is one that mediates between God and humanity, allowing us to hear God in ways we can understand. The feminist emphasis on the subjective reveals the existential concerns of feminist theologians and their effort to contextualize theology. Likewise, the method of correlation is critical to feminist theology and it is not surprising that many feminist theologians utilize a correlation method as an attempt to bring God and human experience together. What makes feminists distinct is their effort to make the so-called contextual moment primary, compared to liberal-revisionist theologies, which usually include contextuality as third of several moments.[32] Feminists are determined to have theology fit the contemporary experience of women in order to make it meaningful for their lives, furthermore, Ruether argues that when the received in-

32. Fulkerson, *Changing the Subject*, 35.

terpretations of redemptive paradigms contradict experience, religious tradition falls into crisis. Religious symbols must speak to experience or otherwise be discarded or altered.[33] One might ask whether metaphors for salvation are, in fact, dead, because they no longer speak or because their meaning has been domesticated.[34] Whatever the feminist reply to such a challenge, it remains true that feminist theology emphasizes the importance of contemporary experience as a contextualizing resource for theology which contributes to its ongoing relevance.

The Shortcomings of Women's Experience in Feminist Theologies of Atonement

Despite the positive contributions of feminist theology, there are serious flaws to the methodology that warrant further consideration and limit the benefits of feminist atonement theology. The basic category of women's experience, its definition and use, repeatedly comes into question in addition to the tendency toward relativism, which is related to it and emerges from it. Finally, we shall reconsider the possibility of genuine redemption offered by the feminist atonement models, asking whether women, and men for that matter, are better off because of feminist theologies of atonement.

Content of Women's Experience Leads to Fragmentation

One of the drawbacks of feminist atonement theology takes us right back to our initial problem with the category of women's experience, that is, the content or definition of women's experience. Because there is not an understanding of women's experience that is representative or acceptable to all women, what we find is a tendency to ghettoize various Christian doctrines, including soteriology. That is to say, because some aspects of experience are unique to certain groups of women, atonement theology is developed in such a way as to address these particular experiences, leaving us with the likelihood of some women feeling excluded or unable to apply a specific emphasis to their own experience, which in turn may lead to the development of another viewpoint on

---

33. Ruether, *Sexism and God-Talk*, 16. See also chapter 3, n. 62 above.

34. Gunton, *Actuality of Atonement*, 50.

the doctrine to which these women can relate. For instance, womanists discard many elements of traditional atonement models as do white feminists, but for specific reasons related to black women's experience. Delores Williams ignores the blood and violence of Jesus' death, finding it completely at odds with black women's experience. Her disdain of any type of "surrogacy" model leads her to support a model of redemption that promotes Jesus' ministerial vision as a way toward liberation. However, what is totally rejected by a womanist like Williams is looked upon by Asian feminists as a source of identification and inspiration. Not that Asian feminists embrace the violence done to Jesus on the cross, rather, Asian women are able to identify with aspects of suffering Jesus experienced in life and death. Jesus' experience of pain and suffering is something to which Asian women relate, providing a source of encouragement because they know that Jesus understands their situation.[35]

An approach such as Williams' may not only lead to the diversity of atonement theology between women of various racial backgrounds but also contribute to a fragmentation between women and their own traditions. Womanist theologian Jacquelyn Grant highlights the value a suffering Christ has had for African-American women who identified with Jesus whose undeserved suffering and persecution culminated on the cross. These women recognized that Jesus was no mere man, but that he was also divine and this connected their suffering to God; a this connection is maintained throughout their religious life, reflected in their prayers and song traditions.[36] By ignoring the offensive nature of Jesus' death then, Williams risks alienating the very women whose experience she is trying to promote. If particular feminist views on atonement are given prominence to the neglect of more traditional models, there is the possibility that white feminist models will not only be at odds with womanist or Asian feminist models, for example, but that connections with women's own faith traditions will be lost or devalued. Womanists may dismiss Chalcedon as a significant source or norm for Christology, deeming it unnecessary as it fails to relate to black women's lives today,

---

35. The identification with Jesus' suffering, which Asian feminists recognize as part of Asian women's experience, does not necessarily translate into support for traditional models of atonement. However, it is distinct from some womanist views and positions such as Brown and Parker's, which refuse to acknowledge suffering and pain as in any way helpful for women.

36. Grant, "'Come to My Help,'" 67.

but in doing so they are rejecting centuries of Christian orthodoxy and risk losing important values of their own faith tradition.[37]

Fragmentation May Lead to Relativism

This brief comparison is just a glimpse into the potential fragmentation of atonement theology that can occur among feminist theologians. Certainly, specific groups of people will prioritize particular models and metaphors for salvation as they relate to their cultural experience. However, it is unclear what feminists, both white and those of color, intend by their various approaches. Do they consider a particular atonement model they find appropriate to the group of women they represent to be a model that other women should adopt? Do they intend that we merely be aware of one another's models and emphases? The former question is hardly relevant as most feminists are reluctant to appear in any way authoritarian whereby a particular position is pushed upon others.[38] The latter question is of more concern because it seems to represent what actually occurs. The impression one gets from feminist theologies of atonement is that one should adopt the model or metaphor that best suits one's experience. Perhaps there is some effort toward a more unified approach in white feminist atonement theologies; however, as these are based upon white women's experience, feminists of color seek to construct their own models which incorporate the unique aspects of their particular experience. We are left with a sense of fragmentation and what is essentially the ghettoizing of theological doctrine. Another term we might use is relativism, a common flaw of theologies of experience as recognized in Daphne Hampson's theism, for instance. The inherent danger of using women's experience and praxis as the primary theological sources is relativism.[39] If the center of theology is essentially

37. Douglas, *Black Christ*, 111.

38. The irony of the feminist position is that although most feminists would not identify one particular view as *the* view, there is no hesitation in clearly rejecting those traditional models which offend feminist experience (as well as encouraging other women to reject them). The reluctance to appear authoritarian stops when it comes to these traditional models.

39. Hogan, *From Women's Experience*, 170. Hogan notes that the radical relativism implied by the use of the categories of women's experience and praxis may be limited by the appeal to pragmatic, ethical foundations rather than to ontological ones, by placing the experiences of communities rather than individuals at the center of feminist theology, and by truly appreciating the embodied nature of all our knowledge.

the self, then the possibility for various concepts of God (and might we say atonement) are boundless.[40] Sarah Coakley poignantly describes the bind in which feminist theologians put themselves, noting that although relativism provides a sensitive viewpoint that acknowledges the contextually bound nature of all theological beliefs,

> the matter becomes more contentious philosophically . . . if what is implied . . . is not merely some principle of historical 'contextualization' of doctrine, but a true case of 'relativism', that is, the view that theological (or other) truths only *are* 'true' in virtue of, or 'relative' to, some specific 'context' or (female?) epistemological framework.[41]

This ghettoizing, relativism, or fragmentation appears to be a potential flaw of feminist theology for which there are basically two possible responses. The first is to provide a more inclusive definition of women's experience. If women's experience is the foundation of feminist theologies of atonement, and these theologies lead to fragmentation because the understanding of women's experience is somewhat different for each, perhaps we need a definition of women's experience with which more women can identify. Is there some basic common essence of women's experience that might serve us better? For instance, could we learn from Seyla Benhabib who wants to distinguish between substitutionalist and interactive universalism? She claims that the universalistic moral theories in the Western tradition are *substitutionalist* in that they define universalism by the experiences of a particular group of subjects, whereas "interactive universalism acknowledges the plurality of modes of being human, and differences among humans, without endorsing all these pluralities and differences as morally and politically valid."[42] Furthermore, we will recall the ongoing debate between essentialism and constructionism regarding the content of women's experience. Few feminists align themselves wholly with one side or the

---

40. See Hampson, *After Christianity*, 283. According to Hampson, a "theology of experience places the human self centre-stage." The starting point for such theology is our own awareness. This position leads to a relativism where interpretations of God vary with the experience of each individual (Hampson would likely disagree, asserting that there are some basic attributes that would be consistent with any understanding of God).

41. Coakley, "Response," 145.

42. Benhabib, "Generalized and the Concrete," 81.

other, applauding the constructivist critiques of gender while recognizing the need to maintain some universals. Diana Fuss describes one possible approach useful for anti-essentialist feminists who want to hold onto the notion of women as a group without submitting to the idea that it is "nature" which categorizes them. Her view is based on a Lockean distinction between nominal and real essence whereby the category of "women" is understood as a linguistic rather than a natural kind.[43] Fuss introduces the Lockean theory of essence to suggest that it is crucial to discriminate between the ontological and linguistic orders of essentialism.[44] The effort to develop an understanding of women's experience that contains some essential elements while allowing space for difference which would enable the category to function in a more inclusive way, is also illustrated by the placing of communal experience over that of the individual. Allowing the experience of the community to be primary is an attempt to avoid the relativism that may occur when individual experience is emphasized. Because we accept the claim that there are undeniable differences of race and class between women does not necessarily mean that we render any generalized view of women as groundless.[45] Whatever the approach, an effort to incorporate difference into our theology should still be encouraged. We may describe what is common, but not in order to negate difference, as in a patriarchal framework whereby difference is associated with difference from the norm and often implies inferiority and inequality. Moreover, it is the cumulative analyses rather than the scattered interpretations of different experiences which have the power to challenge the dominant discourse.[46] At the very least, feminists must examine the relativism that stems from individual experiences and be prepared to deal with it critically.[47]

43. Fuss, *Essentially Speaking*, 4. Real essence connotes the Aristotelian understanding of essence as that which is most irreducible and unchanging about a thing, whereas nominal signifies essence as a linguistic convenience, a classificatory fiction we need to categorize and label.

44. Fuss, *Essentially Speaking*, 5.

45. Dallavalle, "Toward a Theology," 544.

46. Zappone, "'Woman's Special Nature,'" 92, 95.

47. Lazreg, "Women's Experience," 56.

The Use of Women's Experience May Lead to Another Form of Oppression

An approach of redefining the content of women's experience may actually lead to more questions than it answers, therefore, another possible response to the fragmentation in feminist theology would be to consider how the category of women's experience is used. It is possible that the difficulties with the category lie more in its use as a foundation for theological method and exist separately from the limitations of its definition. The use of women's experience in feminist theology has led to its function as source and norm by which the categories of knowledge and revelation are judged. Some critics have pointed out that while it is beneficial to use women's experience as a source in feminist theology, when it is used normatively it fails to provide for self-criticism, thus opening feminist theology to "self-deception and a new kind of oppression."[48] The danger is women's experience becoming *the source* of knowledge and *the source* of revelation.[49] For instance, feminist theologian Mary McClintock Fulkerson does not object to women's experience as a category when it functions within a kind of consciousness-raising group, but she criticizes its use within academia because academic settings should be challenging the very production of knowledge.[50] Rather than our experience being shaped by knowledge of God and God's revelation, feminist theology has it reversed. Human experience brings a great deal to the process of theological reflection, but we must recognize the possibility for that same experience to be changed and transformed by theology as well. We do not accept what some consider a Barthian rejection of experience, where human experience is never in co-operation with the divine.[51] However, if women's experience defines the world,

48. Carr, "New Vision," 21.

49. For a helpful consideration of revelation see Gunton's *A Brief Theology of Revelation*.

50. Fulkerson, *Changing the Subject*, viii.

51. Barth, *Church Dogmatics*, I/1:228 According to Barth, even if the relationship between humanity and God is somewhat dialectical, self-determination is always subordinate to determination by God. Any co-operation would be viewed by Barth as semi-Pelagian. However, Barth maintains that this determination by God is not a removal of self-determination or a condition of complete or partial passivity and receptivity. The character of human experience of God is that of human self-determination. Then in what exists the experience of God? Barth says "acknowledgement" is key (233).

*"there is no independent criterion against which to test feminist construc-
tions of the world."*[52] Moreover, experience should not be determinative
of theology in the manner we have observed in feminist theologies of
atonement because, as we have seen, the doctrine of atonement becomes
rather limited in its scope. Just as we have considered the possibility
of expanding the definition of women's experience, perhaps another
way forward is revising the manner in which it is used in theological
method. Rather than being the source and norm for feminist theological method, might women's experience function more holistically in
relation to other significant theological sources such as scripture and
tradition? Let us utilize the value of women's experience in a way that
does not limit the breadth and depth of Christian doctrine, but rather
becomes an enriching element that expands traditional views.

In the area of atonement theology, scripture and tradition have
shown us multiple metaphors and models for understanding the cross
of Christ. These models are not primarily in competition with one
another but have provided the means for communicating the complex mystery of Jesus' death, with various models speaking loudly in
one generation and more quietly in the next. The richest understandings of atonement might actually be found in the interaction of these
longstanding, traditional models with contemporary perspectives on
the tradition. The relationship of the models with one another allows
us to begin to understand the depth of the atonement and to embrace
various significant interpretations of it at particular moments in time.
From the beginning, different explanations were given to deal with the
problem of the cross. In the Gospels Matthew saw Jesus' death as the
consequence of his proclaiming the reign of God; Mark understood it
as a ransom; Luke saw it as the fulfillment of prophecy; John focused on
the transcendental aspect; the writer of Hebrews wrote of Jesus as the
model of suffering and exultation. These oversimplified descriptions illustrate that every writer and evangelist had to work out an understanding of the mystery of the crucified Messiah.[53] Feminist Sallie McFague
recognizes atonement theology as one area of Christian doctrine that
illustrates the metaphorical theology she proposes because it allows for

---

52. Lazreg, "Women's Experience," 54.

53. Osiek, *Beyond Anger*, 67.

multiple models.[54] The problem comes, however, when one model is absolutized, such as satisfaction theory.

To some extent, the issue at this point becomes pastoral rather than theological. As various cultures, generations, and people groups prioritize particular models of the atonement, we must be prepared to listen and respect one another. We learn from one another's contexts and the theological perspectives inherent in each. This is not to attempt to answer the complex issue of how far one goes in accepting the differing viewpoint of another, for we are not attempting to determine criteria for truth in matters of atonement theology, but rather, are challenging what appears to be a relativism in feminist theologies of atonement whereby one group of women adopts a certain understanding of salvation as true over and against another group, based solely upon that group's particular experience.[55] Because one group of women concludes that a specific view is closer to the truth than another (because it better fits their experience), various models of atonement, including longstanding ones within the Christian tradition, are simply disregarded and tossed out of the theological discussion. For instance, McFague maintains that it is important for some to see Jesus as a parable and to deny his identity with God because their experience has been excluded due to Jesus' identity as male. In other words, McFague considers it appropriate to construct Jesus' identity in such a way as to ensure that it does not contradict or offend one's own experience.[56] But this is not the model the tradition, including the biblical text, has provided us. While we consider a genuine respect for particular contexts as part of being the church, we must still make an effort to find some normative metaphors for atonement in order to avoid relativism. The importance of context to theological metaphors is assumed, but we must recognize that context is not solely determinative because a model of atonement may force new meaning on our metaphors that we had not imagined.

54. McFague, *Metaphorical Theology*, 117. See also Driver, *Understanding the Atonement*, 16. Driver contends that no single term, image, or metaphor is capable of wholly containing the meaning of the atoning work of Christ.

55. Young, *Feminist Theology*, 236. Young argues that a norm outside the Christian tradition will lead to relativism.

56. McFague, *Metaphorical Theology*, 52.

Women's Experience, Sin, and Salvation

Whatever the weaknesses of the feminist approach to atonement presented above, these do not get to the heart of the matter, that is, the lack of the objective element of redemption in feminist theologies of atonement. The meaning of atonement is "at-one-ment"—the restoration of relationship between God and humanity who are estranged.[57] We have concluded that feminist models basically function as example models of atonement, and such a model, regardless of its positive aspects, does not provide the concept of genuine redemption that scripture teaches and feminists expect.

The feminist desire to avoid the objective aspect of atonement due to issues of authority and standard theological positions on sin, particularly related to women, is understandable. However, it is the utter seriousness of sin that compels us to seek a version of redemption that does more than alter the mind and will of the individual, but rather transforms particular hearts and minds, as well as the whole of creation.[58] In actuality, the "theological inadequacies of the feminist debate over the nature of women's sin in effect undercut the intentions of feminist scholarship to heal the wounds inflicted by sexism."[59] Feminist theologians should not be afraid to talk about sin because it is at the core of feminist theory, that is, feminists know the world is not as it should be.[60] Feminists have rightly addressed the fact of oppression, that women have been denied the right to flourish due to dynamic social and personal forces. That this oppression has occurred throughout centuries of patriarchal culture, particularly within the church, is one reason we know that the world is not right.

However, the very fact of racism is also a reminder that things are not as they should be, and indeed, not as they should be amongst women. One feminist claims that the rift between black and white femi-

---

57. Fiddes, *Past Event*, 3.

58. There is a radical distinction between a philosophy of life and the transformation of our hearts and minds by God—Jesus the example but not the Savior.

59. Greene-McCreight, "Gender, Sin and Grace," 415.

60. Jones, *Feminist Theory*, 112. Jones maintains John Calvin's understanding of "unfaithfulness" as a definition for sin. It is specific enough, but allows diversity which other terms do not. Hers is a helpful contribution to the important effort of finding resources within the tradition that feminists may accept.

nists is more than differences of experience, noting that most feminist approaches fail to attend to the depth of the rift or to acknowledge the root of the rift.[61] Might we say that racism is a significant symptom of the rift, but that our condition as sinful humanity is the source of it? The very fact of racism reveals the fact of sin. "White feminism has given insufficient attention to the Fall as a symbol of the depth of human intolerance for difference."[62]

Knowing how the traditional understanding of the fall has been used against women, feminist theologians avoid it and often dismiss the notion of original sin; however, the rejection of original sin as well as a lack of recognition of women's sin as part of human sin, leads feminists to explain redemption at quite a different level than is presented in scripture and taught in the tradition. The overemphasis upon subjective aspects of atonement leaves out the possibility of the world really being put right, except by the virtuous efforts of enlightened women (and men). Have we not learned that our high ideals and exercise of power of choice so often reveal stories of weakness, vulnerability, and pain, which our fantasies about the autonomous self can never explain?[63] Salvation must be, and is, more than a conversion of our minds and an affirmation of intrinsic human goodness because these cannot free us from the effects and implications of sin.[64]

The problems with the feminist subjective emphasis are very much related to an exemplarist view of Jesus. Not only do feminist views on atonement stress the subjective effect upon the individual, but they also hold an exemplarist view of Christ whereby the objective event of Christ's death is no longer, as in the traditional account, something that objectively changes the human standing before God. Certainly there are theological reasons for making Jesus an example, however, if sin is slavery then an example is not enough to save us; we need redemption.[65] Feminist theologians tend to concentrate on Jesus' life rather than his death, using his life and ministry as a model to follow. Whenever we

61. Armour, *Deconstruction, Feminist Theology*, 191 n. 26.

62. West, *Deadly Innocence*, 47.

63. Ibid., 134.

64. Ibid., 205.

65. Gunton, *Actuality of Atonement*, 158–59.

sever Christ's life from his death and resurrection our understanding of the objective and subjective aspects of salvation will be skewed.[66]

Ruether identifies a shift from seventeenth- to nineteenth-century views on redemption as from other-worldly to this-worldly, thus rejecting the notion that we are alienated from God and need a mediator to do the work of reconciliation. For Ruether, humans are in the image of God with an original goodness as part of their true nature, and Jesus becomes a "root story" for the redemptive process whereby his story models what we need to do.[67] Womanist Kelly Douglas would agree, arguing that Jesus' ministry is what matters and that because the Nicene Creed does not focus on Jesus' life, it has no bearing for womanists.[68] Such views fail to address two issues. First, that Jesus lost his life is a consequence of the vision he chose, therefore, should any who adopt such a vision be prepared to die? "The fact that the ministry and mission of Jesus led to his death dominates the narrative . . . so completely that no treatment of the Christian theology of salvation which wishes to be true to scripture is possible apart from it."[69] It is God who gives us the dream of justice, knowing that redemption does not come without suffering.[70] A typical feminist response to this line of reasoning would be to acknowledge that the cross is the extreme example of the risk involved in struggling against oppression, but that it is not redemptive in itself.[71] True, the cross is not redemptive in itself, but for its relationship to Jesus' life, death, and resurrection.

This raises another point: the separation of Jesus' life from his death, which occurs in much feminist theology, fails to ask the question of just who Jesus is. The dismissal of the Nicene Creed for its emphasis upon Jesus' death does not give much account to what the creed is

---

66. Rashdall, *Idea of Atonement*, 356. Following Harnack, Rashdall argues that Anselm's model was overly objective because he emphasized Christ's death over his life. A similar argument applies to feminist theologies of atonement, but in that case, the emphasis upon Jesus' life over his death leads us in the subjective direction.

67. Ruether, *Women and Redemption*, 275.

68. Douglas, *Black Christ*, 72.

69. Gunton, *Actuality of Atonement*, 158

70. Osiek, *Beyond Anger*, 72, 75, 83. See also Purvis, *Power of the Cross*, 89. Although her final conclusions are problematic, Purvis rightly argues that the cross can not be reduced to a symbol. For Purvis it represents a re-configuration of power that reveals the connection between love and suffering.

71. Ruether, *Introducing Redemption*, 102.

trying to say about Jesus. The question of who Jesus is and how Jesus understood himself directly relates to his death. If feminists see the cross as a possible end for those who seek reform from oppressive structures, what exactly do they mean?[72] It appears that by separating Jesus' life and work from his death and resurrection, feminist theologians have again allowed experience to function as the determinative norm for theological doctrine. The offensive aspects of Jesus' life must be rejected, just as the offensive elements of the biblical text. Rather than a canon within a canon, we seem to have a life within a life. This is not to say that every minute detail of Jesus' experience must fit our own in order to be meaningful, but his understanding of his mission and its relationship to his death should be taken seriously and viewed as part of a whole. Feminists praise Christ's life, but this life was an act of obedience to the Father in the power of the Spirit. The obedience extended to his death and was an obedience that was freely given. Feminist views do not take full account of the fact that Christ never acted on his own but (as part of the Godhead) in obedience to the Father. Are we to live like Christ but not with the same motivation as Christ, which is an obedient heart empowered by the Spirit? It appears that feminist theologians misunderstand who Jesus is.[73]

Conclusion: A Way Forward

It is in light of this dilemma that feminist versions of atonement, at least the predominant views outlined in this thesis, do not provide women or men with an approach to redemption that brings genuine liberation and healing. Such views seem to leave us with the nagging feeling that even our best efforts to live as Jesus lived will be unsatisfactory and result in an incomplete experience of liberation and transformation. Has feminist theology too quickly dismissed the traditional and biblical metaphors for atonement without attempting to reinterpret them in a way that is true to their original meaning and intent as well as reclaim them for a contemporary context? This is a task for feminist theology, specifically for those feminists who remain strongly grounded within the Christian tradition. We must revisit the models of atonement from

72. For example, Williams, "Crucifixion Double Cross?" 27.

73. Van Dyk, *Desire of Divine Love*, 146.

our roots and learn how they can speak to us now. It seems that a re-evaluation of our tradition is essential, particularly examining it on the basis of its own merits, without neglecting the issue of how tradition has used certain doctrines with deleterious effects.[74] Because the traditional models of atonement contain the needed objective element, they offer a perspective which is lacking in the feminist views.

Thus begins the way forward for feminist theologies of atonement, particularly a feminist theology that retains scripture and tradition as normative in some significant way. The purpose of this thesis is to consider the role of women's experience in feminist theologies of atonement and the implications for its use, rather than to develop another feminist model of atonement. However, through this process of examination we have identified four areas that may benefit future Christian feminist approaches to atonement models: (1) further addressing the content and definition of women's experience; (2) altering the use of women's experience; (3) employing a pastoral approach; and (4) giving serious attention to the gravity of sin and, hence, embracing both the objective and subjective aspects of atonement. Let us consider each of these in some detail.

Adequately Addressing the Content and Definition of Women's Experience

First, the content and definition of women's experience must be more adequately addressed, working to find some norms in order to preserve the political power of the category as well as to continue to provide the valuable contributions and perspectives of women for theological reflection. We must learn how to thematize women's experience, balancing the tension between essentialist and constructivist definitions. The positive aims of essentialism give women a voice where only men's stories have been heard, but in developing women's stories, the particularities of women's experiences have been neglected, for there is no generic woman.[75] It seems that feminists are somewhat "between

74. West, *Deadly Innocence*, 91. Dallavalle also challenges Catholic feminists to develop a sense of catholicity and engage their own rich tradition rather than be solely determined by justice issues ("Toward a Theology," 548).

75. Spelman, *Inessential Woman*, 159: "For essentialism invites me to take what I understand to be true of me 'as a woman' for some golden nugget of womanness all

a rock and a hard place" as Serene Jones has described it.[76] Feminist
theologians who build their projects upon universal, foundational rocks
construct Christian doctrine that is solid, strong, accessible, and visionary, although they may continue to struggle with women's experiences
that do not "fit" their generalized categories. Those feminist theologians
who avoid universalizing tendencies contribute a restlessness that lacks
constructive solidity, yet reflects a place of healthy instability. However,
due to the pragmatic demands for sturdy visions, these same feminists
will want more substance than their methods can provide.[77] Perhaps
the resources for defining women's experience lie in the work of other
feminists mentioned above, for example, Seyla Benhabib and her notion
of "interactive universalism" or Diana Fuss' use of Locke's category of
nominal essence. There are also possibilities in understanding experience from a communal standpoint as a corrective to the relativism
that can result from an emphasis on individual experience. Whatever
the approach, the issue of subjectivity seems to be at the core: how we
understand subjectivity in light of communities and individuals, race,
class, and gender distinctions, as well as how a myriad of factors contribute to the definition of our subjectivity (e.g., linguistic, sociological,
biological).

Despite the difficulties in understanding how to define women's experience, there do seem to be some concrete steps feminist theologians
could take in order to improve the situation. For instance, "women's
experience" is a term that is scattered throughout feminist theology, yet
is so infrequently clearly defined. Feminist theologians must continue
to make an effort to describe and clarify the category within the context
of their own work, in addition to explaining the standpoint from which
they approach the task of defining women's experience, realizing it is
an interpretation in need of interpretation.[78] By better understanding
the limitations of the category of women's experience within particular
feminist theological positions, it is possible, if not likely, that the category will become less volatile and oppressive to others.

---

women have as women; and it makes the participation of other women inessential to
the production of the story. How lovely: the many turn out to be one, and the one that
they are is me."

76. See chapter 1, n. 46.

77. Jones, "'Women's Experience,'" 178.

78. Scott, "Experience," 37.

Altering the Use of Women's Experience in Feminist Theological Method

The problems involved with generalized definitions of women's experience seem to be exaggerated by the use of women's experience as a foundation for theological method. In other words, it is one thing to provide a universalizing, albeit limited, definition of experience, but quite another to utilize it as a theological foundation. Such an approach moves feminist theology one step further on the path toward oppression, particularly in the case of white feminism. A universalizing definition of women's experience, combined with its foundational use, grounds the category more deeply in a method that neglects the variety of women's experience and is one reason for altering the use of women's experience from a foundation for feminist theology to a significant element in a correlative method that involves other sources. One possible scheme is found in the work of Susanne Heine who presents a two-stage approach that values what she terms the initial "irrational" element of the theological process as well as the use of reason. According to Heine, the process of reflection assists in detaching one from the immediate response, allowing evaluation of past eras based on their own terms and merits.[79]

Another helpful proposal would involve revisiting the tradition as a valuable resource for theological construction, including those elements that previous theologians considered to be important methodological components. Due to concerns over authority, feminist theologians have given little import to the value of traditional theological sources such as scripture and tradition, rather instead, focusing on women's experience and moral categories like justice. What results is a methodology that is correlative, but not adequately so, that is, due weight must be given not only to women's experience, but also to other valued theological sources in an effort to develop a holistic approach that emphasizes the functional relationship between these. In the case of feminist theologies of atonement, there must be a way to allow women's voices to speak, even speak loudly, without disallowing or diminishing the voices of scripture and tradition. This thesis demonstrates the problems that arise when women's experience is determinative of Christian atonement theology,

79. Heine, *Women and Early Christianity*, 46–47.

yet we still maintain the need to include the category in theological reflection. How the relationship between women's experience and other sources plays out is yet to be resolved; however, it would seem that there are a variety of possible ways in which women's experience could be incorporated into theological method and, in fact, be crucial to it, while still regarding other traditional theological sources as essential.[80]

Employing a Pastoral Approach to Difference

Within the context of atonement theology, feminist theologians need to employ an approach that acknowledges the particular milieus and priorities of women and incorporates a pastoral sensitivity that fits the feminist values of listening to and honoring the experience of others. While we attend to and respect one another's atonement models, we follow the biblical example of multiple metaphors for atonement as illustrated in the New Testament, which itself guards against the temptation to reductionism regarding atonement images. A mature Christian community will not limit itself to one, or even a few, images for atonement but is encouraged to grow into a "full-orbed vision."[81]

Although some images may be more central than others for one reason or another, these must not be interpreted in ways that "do violence to the so-called minor images."[82] An example of such an approach can be found in how different cultures adopt atonement imagery and the subsequent interaction between these cultures. For instance, African theologian Kwame Bediako sees the humiliated Christ as central to the redemptive metaphor in the African context. Within such a view, the African experience is validated and the *Christus victor* model of atonement takes on greater significance. A theology of the vernacular would have a redemptive metaphor for each context because metaphors, as feminist theologians note, must be relevant. However, Bediako argues

80. Although her work is in the area of feminist hermeneutics and biblical studies, Phyllis Trible is an example of a feminist who takes very seriously the role of women's experience and the place of scripture. Within feminist theology there may be informal approaches that incorporate and value a variety of sources (e.g., Letty Russell), but we have yet to find a more systematic proposal that accomplishes what we are suggesting here (in part because there is not a strong desire to do so among mainline feminists).

81. Driver, *Understanding the Atonement*, 246–47.

82. Ibid., 244.

that we do have a common humanity and as a result we share in one another's stories; Africa's story is our story, part of our historical consciousness.[83] It is in this spirit of shared human experience where we respect the particular contexts of each and learn to listen to and value the atonement metaphors each group finds valuable. Feminist theologians often neglect the inherited tradition of atonement theology, particularly those metaphors associated with the cross, and in the process, fail to exhibit the values of listening and respect which are part of the feminist view. The ability to deal with differences in theological contexts is an ongoing and complicated challenge, but we can see the value in attempting to make connections between different cultures, and thus, between various women's experiences, working to develop an atmosphere of respect in which we desire to learn from others, including those rooted in traditional contexts and metaphors. Because scripture gives us multiple models for atonement it seems appropriate that we contextualize atonement imagery, but we must listen to other models, past and present, and not merely exclude models because they do not fit our context. Such exclusion of traditional Christian theology can be dangerous in that one may be seduced into one's own "inviolable innocence."[84]

Taking the Doctrine of Sin Seriously

Finally, feminist theologians must take sin more seriously, thereby incorporating both the objective and subjective elements in a doctrine of salvation. Because the meaning of redemption within feminist theologies of atonement is at least partly based upon a deficient understanding of sin, we end up with models of atonement that fail to provide us with the resources for a genuine experience of redemption within ourselves and within our world. While the feminist views on atonement emphasize the subjective aspect, they remain lacking because the objective element has not been addressed. The inner change required in ourselves will not occur completely until the relationship between

83. Bediako, "Africa in the New World Christian Order."

84. Tanner, *Politics of God*, 253. Tanner notes that by "demonizing traditional Christian theology, one can be easily misled into thinking one need not be vigilant or on one's guard about the employment of one's own theological position the way those engaged in an internal critique should be."

God and humanity is restored.[85] Since feminist theologians have failed to see this, their models for atonement/reconciliation/redemption continue to need key elements. The distinctions of post-Christian Daphne Hampson's view of redemption are not significantly different from the Christian feminist views discussed in this thesis, thus, revealing the humanistic approach of both.[86] What should be considered the doctrine of sin is actually a weak anthropology whereby human nature is defined outside the context of the biblical narrative. The option to go beyond the scope of the biblical narrative to define humanity seems viable for post-Christians but "an odd move for those who are self-consciously Christian."[87] Hampson plainly places human beings at center-stage in her theistic program and designates salvation as "healing."[88] She understands the spiritual life to exhibit such ideals as compassion, honesty, integrity, order, attention, and self-realization.[89] The understanding of redemption presented in Hampson's model and the core values that follow are not dissimilar to what we find in the feminist models of atonement presented in this thesis. Therefore, it seems appropriate for feminist theologians to consider the fall and the possibility of original sin, in addition to developing interpretations of women's sin as they seek to present a more complete understanding of sin which would then lead to more of a balance between the subjective and objective aspects of atonement in order to provide Christian feminists with a genuine confidence in redemption.

It seems that "balance" is the key word in each of these: balancing the essentialist and constructivist tendencies in defining women's experience, finding the balance between sources in a correlative method, balancing the value of the various settings and viewpoints of women as we hold in tension multiple models of atonement, and placing in bal-

85. "Insofar as both mainline feminist theology and modern theology embrace the Enlightenment notion of the perfectibility of humanity, [the feminist] reaction to the doctrine of original sin is another example of feminist theologies' fitting into the larger pattern of modern theology" (Greene-McCreight, *Feminist Reconstructions*, 56).

86. Ibid., 132. Greene-McCreight argues that if mainline feminists were consistent, they would be closer theologically and ideologically to post-Christians like Daphne Hampson and Mary Daly. As it is they try to "redeem" Christianity and retain a mediating position.

87. Ibid., 62.

88. Hampson, *After Christianity*, 283.

89. Ibid., 259–60, 274.

ance the objective and subjective elements of atonement in an effort to provide meaningful models which reveal God's redemptive purposes.

Perhaps it is a tall order, but not beyond our reach. The Christian gospel is good news and a source of hope. Indeed, if Christianity is not good news for women, it is not good news for anyone.[90] Regardless of the work yet to be done, we have begun to identify the ways in which feminist atonement theology, and its use of women's experience, might be improved in such a way as to provide women with a model for redemption that takes seriously their experience and offers a genuine liberation from the oppression that characterizes it.

90. Soskice, "Turning the Symbols," 23.

Bibliography

Abelard (Abailard), Peter. "Exposition of the Epistle to the Romans (An Excerpt from the Second Book)." In *A Scholastic Miscellany: Anselm to Ockham*, edited by Eugene R. Fairweather, 276–87. The Library of Christian Classics. London: SCM, 1956.

Abraham, William J. *Canon and Criterion in Christian Theology: From the Fathers to Feminism*. Oxford: Clarendon, 1998.

Allik, Tina. "Human Finitude and the Concept of Women's Experience." *Modern Theology* 9 (1993) 67–85.

Alsford, Sally. "Sin and Atonement in Feminist Perspective." In *Atonement Today: A Symposium at St. John's College, Nottingham*, edited by John Goldingay, 148–65. London: SPCK, 1995.

Alston, William. *Perceiving God: The Epistemology of Religious Experience*. London: Cornell University Press, 1991.

Anderson, Victor. *Beyond Ontological Blackness: An Essay on African American Religious and Cultural Criticism*. New York: Continuum, 1995.

Anselm. *Cur Deus Homo*. The Ancient and Modern Library of Theological Literature. Edinburgh: John Grant, 1909.

Arellano, Luz Beatriz. "Women's Experience of God in Emerging Spirituality." In *Feminist Theology from the Third World*, edited by Ursula King, 318–38. Maryknoll, NY: Orbis, 1994.

Armour, Ellen T. *Deconstruction, Feminist Theology, and the Problem of Difference: Subverting the Race/Gender Divide*. Chicago: University of Chicago Press, 1999.

Aulén, Gustaf. *Christus Victor: An Historical Study of the Three Main Types of the Idea of the Atonement*. Translated by A.G. Hebert. SPCK Large Paperbacks 16. London: SPCK, 1970.

Baber, Harriett. "The Market for Feminist Epistemology." *The Monist* 77 (1994) 403–23.

Baillie, D. M. *God was in Christ: An Essay on Incarnation and Atonement*. New York: Scribner, 1948.

Barth, Karl. *Church Dogmatics*. Vols. 1/1 and 4/1. Translated by G. T. Thomson. Edinburgh: T. & T. Clark, 1936/1953.

———. *Protestant Theology in the Nineteenth Century*. Valley Forge, PA: Judson, 1973.

———. *The Theology of Schleiermacher: Lectures at Göttingen, Winter Semester of 1923/24*. Edited by Dietrich Ritschl. Translated by Geoffrey W. Bromiley. Edinburgh: T. & T. Clark, 1982.

Beardsworth, Timothy. *A Sense of Presence: The Phenomenology of Certain Kinds of Visionary and Ecstatic Experience, Based on a Thousand Contemporary First-hand Accounts*. Oxford: The Religious Experience Research Unit, 1977.

Bediako, Kwame. "Africa in the New World Christian Order." Presented for the Payton Lectures at Fuller Theological Seminary, Pasadena, California, October 12, 2000.

Belenky, Mary F., Blythe M. Clinchy, Nancy R. Goldberger, and Jill M. Tarule, editors. *Women's Ways of Knowing.* New York: Basic Books, 1986.

Benhabib, Seyla. "The Generalized and the Concrete Other: The Kohlberg-Gilligan Controversy and Feminist Theory." In *Feminism as Critique: Essays on the Politics of Gender in Late-Capitalist Societies,* edited by Seyla Benhabib and Crucilla Cornell, 77–93. Oxford: Blackwell, 1987.

Berger, Peter L., and Thomas Luckmann. *The Social Construction of Reality: A Treatise in the Sociology of Knowledge.* Garden City, NY: Doubleday, 1966.

Berkhof, Hendrikus. *Two Hundred Years of Theology: Report of a Personal Journey.* Translated by John Vriend. Grand Rapids: Eerdmans, 1989.

Berryman, Phillip. *Liberation Theology: Essential Facts about the Revolutionary Movement in Latin America and Beyond.* London: Taurius, 1987.

Boff, Clodovis. "Methodology of the Theology of Liberation." In *Systematic Theology: Perspectives from Liberation Theology,* edited by Jon Sobrino and Ignacio Ellacuria, translated by Robert R. Barr, 1–21. London: SCM, 1996.

Boff, Leonardo and Boff, Clodovis. *Introducing Liberation Theology.* Translated by Paul Burns. Maryknoll, NY: Orbis, 1987.

Boff, Leonardo. "The Originality of the Theology of Liberation." In *The Future of Liberation Theology: Essays in Honor of Gustavo Gutierrez,* edited by Marc H. Ellis and Otto Maduro, 38–48. Maryknoll, NY: Orbis, 1989.

Bradley, Ian. *The Power of Sacrifice.* London: Darton, Longman & Todd, 1995.

Briggs, Sheila. "A History of Our Own: What Would a Feminist History of Theology Look Like?" In *Horizons in Feminist Theology: Identity, Tradition and Norms,* edited by Sheila Greeve Davaney and Rebecca S. Chopp, 165–78. Minneapolis: Fortress, 1997.

Brock, Rita Nakashima. "And a Little Child Will Lead Us: Christology and Child Abuse." In *Christianity, Patriarchy, and Abuse: A Feminist Critique,* edited by Joanne Carlson Brown and Carole R. Bohn, 42–61. Cleveland: Pilgrim, 1989.

————. *Journeys By Heart: A Christology of Erotic Power.* New York: Crossroad, 1988.

Brown, Joanne Carlson. "Divine Child Abuse?" *Daughters of Sarah* 18:3 (1992) 24–28.

Brown, Joanne Carlson and Parker, Rebecca. "For God So Loved the World?" In *Christianity, Patriarchy and Abuse: A Feminist Critique,* 1–30. Edited by Joanne Carlson Brown and Carole R. Bohn. Cleveland: Pilgrim, 1989.

Camp, Claudia V. "Feminist Theological Hermeneutics: Canon and Christian Identity." In *Searching the Scriptures. Volume One: A Feminist Introduction,* edited by Elisabeth Schüssler Fiorenza, 154–71. London: SCM, 1993.

Carr, Anne E., and Elisabeth Schüssler Fiorenza, editors. *Motherhood: Experience, Institution, Theology.* Edinburgh: T. & T. Clark, 1989.

Carr, Anne E. "The New Vision of Feminist Theology." In *Freeing Theology: The Essentials of Theology in Feminist Perspective,* edited by Catherine Mowry LaCugna, 5–29. San Francisco: HarperSanFrancisco, 1993.

————. *Transforming Grace: Christian Tradition and Women's Experience.* San Francisco: Harper & Row, 1988.

Chodorow, Nancy J. *Feminism and Psychoanalytic Theory.* New Haven: Yale University Press, 1989.

Chopp, Rebecca S. "Feminism's Theological Pragmatics: A Social Naturalism of Women's Experience." *Journal of Religion* 67 (1987) 239–56.

————. *The Power to Speak: Feminism, Language, God.* New York: Crossroad, 1989.

Christ, Carol P. "Embodied Thinking: Reflections on Feminist Theological Method." *Journal of Feminist Studies in Religion* 5 (1989) 7–16.

————. "Spiritual Quest and Women's Experience." In *Womanspirit Rising: A Feminist Reader in Religion,* 2nd ed., edited by Carol P. Christ and Judith Plaskow, 228–45. San Francisco: Harper & Row, 1992.

Chung, Hyun Kyung. *Struggle to Be the Sun Again: Introducing Asian Women's Theology.* Maryknoll, NY: Orbis, 1990.

Clague, Julie. "BISFT Interview with Dr. Daphne Hampson." *Feminist Theology* 17 (January 1998) 39–57.

Clayton, John P. *The Concept of Correlation: Paul Tillich and the Possibility of a Mediating Theology.* Berlin: deGruyter, 1980.

Coakley, Sarah. "Response." In *Swallowing a Fishbone? Feminist Theologians Debate Christianity,* edited by Daphne Hampson, 145–49. London: SPCK, 1996.

Code, Lorraine. *What Can She Know? Feminist Theory and the Construction of Knowledge.* Ithaca, NY: Cornell University Press, 1991.

Collins, Patricia Hill. *Black Feminist Thought: Knowledge, Consciousness and the Politics of Empowerment.* Edited by Kay Deaux, Myra Marx Ferree, and Viginia Sapiro. Perspectives on Gender 2. Boston: Unwin Hyman, 1990.

Cone, James H. *A Black Theology of Liberation.* 20th anniversary edition. Maryknoll, NY: Orbis, 1986.

————. *God of the Oppressed.* New York: Seabury, 1975.

Cooey, Paula M. *Religious Imagination and the Body: A Feminist Analysis.* Oxford: Oxford University Press, 1994.

Copeland, M. Shawn. "Journeying to the Household of God: The Eschatological Implications of Method in the Theology of Letty Mandeville Russell." In *Liberating Eschatology: Essays in Honor of Letty M. Russell,* edited by Serene Jones and Margaret A. Farley, 26–44. Louisville: Westminster John Knox, 1999.

Culpepper, Emily Erwin. "Contemporary Goddess Thealogy: A Sympathetic Critique." In *Shaping New Vision: Gender and Values in American Culture,* edited by Clarissa W. Atkinson, Constance H. Buchanan, and Margaret R. Miles, 51–71. Ann Arbor, MI: UMI Research, 1987.

Dallavalle, Mary A. "Toward a Theology that is Catholic and Feminist: Some Basic Issues." *Modern Theology* 14 (1998) 535–53.

Daly, Mary. *Beyond God the Father: Toward a Philosophy of Women's Liberation.* Boston: Beacon, 1973.

Davaney, Sheila Greeve. "Continuing the Story, But Departing the Text: A Historicist Interpretation of Feminist Norms in Theology." In *Horizons in Feminist Theology: Identity, Tradition and Norms,* edited by Sheila Greeve Davaney and Rebecca S. Chopp, 198–214. Minneapolis: Fortress, 1997.

————. "The Limits of the Appeal to Women's Experience." In *Shaping New Vision: Gender and Values in American Culture*, edited by Clarissa W. Atkinson, Constance H. Buchanan, and Margaret R. Miles, 31–49. Ann Arbor: UMI Research, 1987.

————. "Problems with Feminist Theology: Historicity and the Search for Sure Foundations." In *Embodied Love: Sensuality and Relationship as Feminist Values*, edited by Paula M. Cooey, Sharon A. Farmer, and Mary Ellen Ross, 79–95. San Francisco: Harper & Row, 1987.

————. *Theology at the End of Modernity: Essays in Honor of Gordon D. Kaufman.* Philadelphia: Trinity, 1991.

Davis, Caroline Franks. *The Evidential Force of Religious Experience.* Oxford: Clarendon, 1989.

Douglas, Kelly Brown. *The Black Christ.* Edited by James H. Cone. The Bishop Henry McNeal Turner Studies in North American Black Religion 9. Maryknoll, NY: Orbis, 1994.

Driver, John. *Understanding the Atonement for the Mission of the Church.* Scottdale, PA: Herald, 1986.

Dyrness, William A. *Learning About Theology from the Third World.* Grand Rapids: Zondervan, 1990.

Elliott, Terri. "The Making Strange What Had Appeared Familiar." *The Monist* 77 (1994) 424–33.

Feuerbach, Ludwig. *The Essence of Christianity.* Translated by George Eliot. London: Harper & Row, 1957.

Fiddes, Paul S. *Past Event and Present Salvation.* London: Darton, Longman & Todd, 1989.

Fiorenza, Francis Schüssler. "The Crisis of Hermeneutics and Christian Theology." In *Theology at the End of Modernity: Essays in Honor of Gordon D. Kaufman*, 117–40. Edited by Sheila Greeve Davaney. Philadelphia: Trinity, 1991.

Fiorenza, Francis Schüssler. *Foundational Theology: Jesus and the Church.* New York: Crossroad, 1984.

Fulkerson, Mary McClintock. *Changing the Subject: Women's Discourses and Feminist Theology.* Minneapolis: Fortress, 1994.

Fuss, Diana. *Essentially Speaking: Feminism, Nature and Difference.* London: Routledge, 1989.

Gerrish, B. A. *A Prince of the Church: Schleiermacher and the Beginnings of Modern Theology.* London: SCM, 1984.

Gilligan, Carol. *In a Different Voice: Psychological Theory and Women's Development.* Cambridge: Harvard University Press, 1982.

Grant, Jacquelyn. "'Come to My Help, Lord, For I'm in Trouble': Womanist Jesus and the Mutual Struggle for Liberation." In *Restructuring the Christ Symbol: Essays in Feminist Christology*, edited by Maryanne Stevens, 54–71. New York: Paulist, 1993.

————. *White Women's Christ and Black Women's Jesus: Feminist Christology and Womanist Response.* Edited by Susan Thistlethwaite. American Academy of Religion Academy Series 64. Atlanta: Scholars, 1989.

Grant, Judith. *Fundamental Feminism: Contesting the Core Concepts of Feminist Theory.* London: Routledge, 1993.

Greene-McCreight, Kathryn. *Feminist Reconstructions of Christian Doctrine: Narrative Analysis and Appraisal*. New York: Oxford University Press, 2000.

——. "Gender, Sin and Grace: Feminist Theologies Meet Karl Barth's Hamartiology." *Scottish Journal of Theology* 50 (1997) 415–32.

Grey, Mary C. *Redeeming the Dream: Feminism, Redemption and Christian Tradition*. London: SPCK, 1989.

Gunton, Colin E. *The Actuality of Atonement: A Study of Metaphor, Rationality and the Christian Tradition*. Grand Rapids: Eerdmans, 1989.

——. *A Brief Theology of Revelation*. Edinburgh: T. & T. Clark, 1995.

——. *The Christian Faith: An Introduction to Christian Doctrine*. Oxford: Blackwell, 2002.

Gutiérrez, Gustavo. *The God of Life*. Translated by Matthew J. O'Connell. Maryknoll, NY: Orbis, 1991.

——. *A Theology of Liberation*. Translated by Sister Caridad Inda and John Eagleson. Rev. ed. Maryknoll, NY: Orbis, 1988.

——. *We Drink From Our Own Wells: The Spiritual Journey of a People*. Translated by Matthew J. O'Connell. Maryknoll, NY: Orbis, 1984.

Hampson, Daphne. *After Christianity*. London: SCM, 1996.

——. "A Reply to Angela West." *Scottish Journal of Theology* 51 (1998) 116–21.

——. *Swallowing a Fishbone? Feminist Theologians Debate Christianity*. London: SPCK, 1996.

——. *Theology and Feminism*. Oxford: Blackwell, 1990.

Harding, Sandra. "Why has the Sex/Gender System Become Visible Only Now?" In *Discovering Reality: Feminist Perspectives on Epistemology, Metaphysics, Methodology, and Philosophy of Science*, edited by Sandra Harding and Merril B. Hintikka, 311–24. Dordrecht: Reidel, 1983.

Harnack, Adolph. *History of Dogma*. Vol. 4. Edited by T. K. Cheyne and A. B. Bruce. Translated by William McGilchrist. 3rd German ed. Theological Translation Library 11. London: Williams & Norgate, 1899.

Hart, Trevor A. "Anselm of Canterbury and John McLeod Campbell: Where Opposites Meet?" *The Evangelical Quarterly* 62 (1990) 311–33.

Hartsock, Nancy C. M. "The Feminist Standpoint: Developing the Ground for a Specifically Feminist Historical Materialism." In *Discovering Reality: Feminist Perspectives on Epistemology, Metaphysics, Methodology, and Philosophy of Science*, edited by Sandra Harding and Merrill B. Hintikka, 283–310. Dordrecht: Reidel, 1983.

Hays, Richard B. *The Moral Vision of the New Testament: Community, Cross, New Creation*. Edinburgh: T. & T. Clark, 1996.

Heim, S. Mark. "Saved By What Shouldn't Happen." In *Cross Examinations*, edited by Marit Trelstad, 211–24. Minneapolis: Fortress, 2006.

Heine, Susanne. *Women and Early Christianity: A Reappraisal*. Translated by John Bowden. Minneapolis: Augsburg, 1988.

Hellwig, Monika. *Whose Experience Counts in Theological Reflection?* Milwaukee: Marquette University Press, 1982.

Heron, Alasdair I. C. *A Century of Protestant Theology*. Cambridge: Lutterworth Press, 1980.

Hesse, Mary. "How to be Postmodern Without Being a Feminist." *The Monist* 77 (1994) 445–61.

Heyward, Isabel Carter. *The Redemption of God: A Theology of Mutual Relation.* London: University Press of America, 1982.

Heyward, Carter. *Saving Jesus From Those Who Are Right: Rethinking What it Means to be Christian.* Minneapolis: Fortress, 1999.

———. "Suffering, Redemption, and Christ: Shifting the Grounds of Feminist Theology." *Christianity and Crisis* 49:17/18 (December 1989) 381–86.

Hilkert, Mary Catherine. "Experience and Tradition—Can the Center Hold?" In *Freeing Theology: The Essentials of Theology in Feminist Perspective*, edited by Catherine Mowry LaCugna, 59–82. San Francisco: HarperSanFrancisco, 1993.

Hogan, Linda. *From Women's Experience to Feminist Theology.* Sheffield: Sheffield, 1995.

hooks, bell. *Feminist Theory from Margin to Center.* Boston: South End, 1984.

Hopkins, Jasper. *A Companion to the Study of St. Anselm.* Minneapolis: University of Minnesota Press, 1972.

Houts, Margo G. "Atonement and Abuse: An Alternate View." *Daughters of Sarah* 18:3 (1992) 29–32.

James, William. "The Will to Believe." In *Classical and Contemporary Readings in the Philosophy of Religion*, 3rd ed., edited by John Hick, 196–212. Englewood Cliffs, NJ: Prentice Hall, 1990.

Johnson, Elizabeth A. "Redeeming the Name of Christ." In *Freeing Theology: The Essentials of Theology in Feminist Perspective*, edited by Catherine Mowry LaCugna, 115–37. San Francisco: HarperSanFrancisco, 1993.

———. *She Who Is: The Mystery of God in Feminist Theological Discourse.* New York: Crossroad, 1992.

Jones, Serene. *Feminist Theory and Christian Theology: Cartographies of Grace.* Minneapolis: Fortress, 2000.

———. "'Women's Experience' Between a Rock and a Hard Place: Feminist, Womanist and *Mujerista* Theologies in North America." *Religious Studies Review* 21:3 (July 1995) 171–78.

Jones, Serene and Farley, Margaret A. *Liberating Eschatology: Essays in Honor of Letty M. Russell.* Louisville: Westminster John Knox, 1999.

Jüngel, Eberhard. *Justification: The Heart of the Christian Faith.* Translated by Jeffrey F. Cayzer. Edinburgh: T. & T. Clark, 2001.

Keightly, Georgia Masters. "The Challenge of Feminist Christology." In *Horizons on Catholic Feminist Theology*, edited by Joann Wolski Conn and Walter E. Conn, 37–60. Washington, DC: Georgetown University Press, 1992.

Kelsey, David H. *The Fabric of Paul Tillich's Theology.* Yale Publications in Religion 13. London: Yale University Press, 1967.

Lazreg, Marnia. "Women's Experience and Feminist Epistemology: A Critical Neo-Rationalist Approach." In *Knowing the Difference: Feminist Perspectives in Epistemology*, edited by Kathleen Lennon and Margaret Whitford, 45–62. New Haven: Routledge, 1994.

Lindbeck, George A. *The Nature of Doctrine: Religion and Theology in a Postliberal Age.* Philadelphia: Westminster, 1984.

Longino, Helen E. "In Search of Feminist Epistemology." *The Monist* 77 (1994) 472–85.

Lorde, Audre. "The Master's Tools Will Never Dismantle the Master's House." In *Sister Outsider: Essays and Speeches*, 110–113. Trumansburg, NY: The Crossing Press, 1984.

Luscombe, D. E. *The School of Peter Abelard: The Influence of Abelard's Thought in the Early Scholastic Period.* Edited by M. D. Knowles. Cambridge Studies in Medieval Life and Thought, 2nd ser., 14. Cambridge: Cambridge University Press, 1969.

Mackintosh, H. R. *The Christian Experience of Forgiveness.* London: Nisbet, 1927.

Macquarrie, John. *Twentieth-Century Religious Thought.* 4th ed. London: SCM, 1988.

Maitland, Sara. "Ways of Relating." *The Way* (February 1986) 124–33.

Martin, Francis. *The Feminist Question: Feminist Theology in the Light of Christian Tradition.* Edinburgh: T. & T. Clark, 1994.

McClendon, James Wm., Jr. *Systematic Theology: Doctrine.* Vol. 2. Nashville: Abingdon, 1994.

McFague, Sallie. *The Body of God: An Ecological Theology.* Minneapolis: Fortress, 1993.

———. *Metaphorical Theology: Models of God in Religious Language.* London: SCM, 1982.

McGrath, Alister. "The Moral Theory of the Atonement: An Historical and Theological Critique." *Scottish Journal of Theology* 38 (1985) 205–20.

McIntyre, John. *St. Anselm and His Critics: A Re-Interpretation of the* Cur Deus Homo. Edinburgh: Oliver & Boyd, 1954.

McIntyre, John. *The Shape of Soteriology: Studies in the Doctrine of the Death of Christ.* Edinburgh: T. & T. Clark, 1992.

McKelway, Alexander J. *The Systematic Theology of Paul Tillich: A Review and Analysis.* London: Lutterworth, 1964.

Megill-Cobbler, Thelma. "A Feminist Rethinking of Punishment Imagery in Atonement." *Dialog* 35:1 (1996) 14–20.

Megill-Cobbler, Thelma. "Women and the Cross: Atonement in Rosemary Radford Ruether and Dorothee Soelle." PhD diss., Princeton Theological Seminary, 1992.

Mondin, Battista. *The Principle of Analogy in Protestant and Catholic Theology.* The Hague: Hijhoff, 1963.

Morgan, Sue. "Race and the Appeal to Experience in Feminist Theology: The Challenge of the Womanist Perspective." *Modern Believing* 36:2 (1995) 18–26.

Mouw, Richard J. Response to Johanna W. H. van Wijk-Bos, "The Shadow of a Mighty Rock." Unpublished paper for the American Academy of Religion Annual Meeting. New Orleans, November 1996.

Narayan, Uma. "The Project of Feminist Epistemology: Perspectives from a Nonwestern Feminist." In *Gender/Body/Knowledge: Feminist Reconstructions of Being and Knowing*, edited by Alison M. Jaggar and Susan R. Bordo, 256–69. New Brunswick, NJ: Rutgers University Press, 1989.

Nelson, Lynne H. *Who Knows: From Quine to a Feminist Empiricism.* Philadelphia: Temple University Press, 1990.

Niebuhr, Richard R. *Schleiermacher on Christ and Religion.* Edited by John McIntyre and Ian T. Ramsey. London: SCM, 1964.

O'Neill, Mary Aquin. "The Nature of Women and the Method of Theology." *Theological Studies* 56 (1995) 730–42.

Oduyoye, Mercy Amba. "Reflections from a Third World Woman's Perspective: Women's Experience and Liberation Theologies." In *Feminist Theology from the Third World*, edited by Ursula King, 23–35. Maryknoll, NY: Orbis, 1994.

Olsen, Glenn W. "Hans Urs von Balthasar and the Rehabilitation of St. Anselm's Doctrine of the Atonement." *Scottish Journal of Theology* 34 (1981) 49–61.

Ormerod, Neil. "Quarrels with the Method of Correlation." *Theological Studies* 57 (1996) 707–19.

Osiek, Carolyn. *Beyond Anger: On Being a Feminist in the Church*. New York: Paulist, 1986.

———. "The Feminist and the Bible: Hermeneutical Alternatives." In *Feminist Perspectives on Biblical Scholarship*, edited by Adela Y. Collins, 94–104. Chico, CA: Scholars, 1985.

Pears, Angela. "Women's Experience and Authority in the Work of Elisabeth Schüssler Fiorenza." *Modern Believing* 36:3 (1995) 16–21.

Plantinga, Alvin. "Reason and Belief in God." In *Faith and Rationality: Reason and Belief in God*, edited by Alvin Plantinga and Nicholas Wolterstorff, 39–77. London: University of Notre Dame Press, 1983.

Plaskow, Judith. *Sin, Sex and Grace: Women's Experience and the Theologies of Reinhold Niebuhr and Paul Tillich*. Washington, DC: University Press of America, 1980.

Plaskow, Judith, and Carol P. Christ. *Weaving the Visions: New Patterns in Feminist Spirituality*. San Francisco: Harper & Row, 1989.

Polanyi, Michael. *Personal Knowledge: Towards a Post-Critical Philosophy*. London: Routledge & Kegan Paul, 1958.

Proudfoot, Wayne. *Religious Experience*. Berkeley: University of California Press, 1985.

Purvis, Sally B. *The Power of the Cross: Foundations for a Christian Feminist Ethic of Community*. Nashville: Abingdon, 1993.

Rashdall, Hastings. *The Idea of Atonement in Christian Theology: The Bampton Lectures 1915*. London: MacMillan, 1919.

Reno, R. R. "Feminist Theology as Modern Project." *Pro Ecclesia* 5 (1996) 405–26.

Rich, Adrienne. *Of Woman Born: Motherhood as Experience and Institution*. London: Virago, 1979.

Riley, Denise. *"Am I That Name?" Feminism and the Category of "Women" in History*. London: Macmillan, 1988.

Ruether, Rosemary Radford. "Feminist Interpretation: A Method of Correlation." In *Feminist Interpretation of the Bible*, edited by Letty Russell, 111–24. Philadelphia: Westminster, 1985.

———. "The Future of Feminist Theology in the Academy." *Journal of the American Academy of Religion* 53 (1985) 703–13.

———. *Introducing Redemption in Christian Feminism*. Sheffield: Sheffield Academic, 1998.

———. "Is Feminism the End of Christianity? A Critique of Daphne Hampson's *Theology and Feminism*." *Scottish Journal of Theology* 43 (1990) 390–400.

———. *Sexism and God-Talk: Towards a Feminist Theology*. London: SCM, 1983.

————. *To Change the World: Christology and Cultural Criticism.* New York: Cross-road, 1981.

————. *Womanguides: Readings Toward a Feminist Theology.* Boston: Beacon, 1985.

————. *Women and Redemption: A Theological History.* Minneapolis: Fortress, 1998.

Russell, Letty M. "Authority and the Challenge of Feminist Interpretation." In *Feminist Interpretation of the Bible,* edited by Letty M. Russell, 137–46. Philadelphia: Westminster, 1985.

————. *Household of Freedom: Authority in Feminist Theology.* Philadelphia: Westminster, 1987.

————. *Human Liberation in a Feminist Perspective: A Theology.* Philadelphia: Westminster, 1974.

Saiving, Valerie. "The Human Situation: A Feminine View." In *Womanspirit Rising: A Feminist Reader in Religion,* 2nd ed., edited by Carol P. Christ and Judith Plaskow, 25–41. San Francisco: Harper & Row, 1992.

Schleiermacher, Friedrich. *The Christian Faith.* Edited by H. R. Mackintosh and J. S. Stewart. Translated by D. M. Baillie et al. 2nd German ed. Edinburgh: T. & T. Clark, 1976.

————. *On the Glaubenslehre: Two Letters to Dr. Lücke.* Edited by James A. Massey. Translated by James Duke and Francis Fiorenza. American Academy of Religion Texts and Translation Series 3. Chico, CA: Scholars, 1981.

————. *On Religion: Speeches to its Cultured Despisers.* Edited by Karl Ameriks and Desmond M. Clarke. Translated by Richard Crouter. 2nd ed. Cambridge Texts in the History of Philosophy. Cambridge: Cambridge University Press, 1996.

Schneiders, Sandra M. "The Bible and Feminism: Biblical Theology." In *Freeing Theology: The Essentials of Theology in Feminist Perspective,* edited by Catherine Mowry LaCugna, 31–57. San Francisco: HarperSanFrancisco, 1993.

Schner, George. "The Appeal to Experience." *Theological Studies* 53:1 (1992) 40–59.

Schüssler Fiorenza, Elisabeth. *Bread Not Stone: The Challenge of Feminist Biblical Interpretation.* Edinburgh: T. & T. Clark, 1990.

————. *In Memory of Her: A Feminist Theological Reconstruction of Christian Origins.* 2nd ed. New York: Crossroad, 1994.

————. *Jesus: Miriam's Child, Sophia's Prophet. Critical Issues in Feminist Theology.* New York: Continuum, 1994.

————. "The Politics of Otherness: Biblical Interpretation as a Critical Praxis for Liberation." In *The Future of Liberation Theology: Essays in Honor of Gustavo Gutiérrez,* edited by Marc H. Ellis and Otto Maduro, 311–25. Maryknoll, NY: Orbis, 1989.

————. *Searching the Scriptures: A Feminist Commentary.* Vol 2. New York: Crossroad, 1994.

Scott, Joan W. "Experience." In *Feminists Theorize the Political,* edited by Judith Butler and Joan W. Scott, 22–40. London: Routledge, 1992.

Segundo, Juan Luis. *The Liberation of Theology.* Translated by John Drury. Maryknoll, NY: Orbis, 1976.

Setel, T. Drorah. "Feminist Insights and the Question of Method." In *Feminist Perspectives on Biblical Scholarship,* edited by Adela Y. Collins, 35–42. Chico, CA: Scholars, 1985.

Sikes, J. G. *Peter Abailard*. Cambridge: Cambridge University Press, 1932.

Snyder, Mary Hembrow. *The Christology of Rosemary Radford Ruether: A Critical Introduction*. Mystic, CT: Twenty-third Publications, 1988.

Sobrino, Jon. Preface to *Systematic Theology: Perspectives from Liberation Theology*. Edited by Jon Sobrino and Ignacio Ellacuria. Translated by Robert R. Barr. London: SCM, 1996.

Solberg, Mary M. *Compelling Knowledge: A Feminist Proposal for an Epistemology of the Cross*. Albany: State University of New York Press, 1997.

Soskice, Janet Martin. "Turning the Symbols." In *Swallowing a Fishbone? Feminist Theologians Debate Christianity*, edited by Daphne Hampson, 17–30. London: SPCK, 1996.

Spelman, Elizabeth V. *Inessential Woman: Problems of Exclusion in Feminist Thought*. Boston: Beacon, 1988.

Stanley, Liz and Wise, Sue. *Breaking Out: Feminist Consciousness and Feminist Research*. London: Routledge & Kegan Paul, 1983.

Stewart, Carlyle Fielding, III. "The Method of Correlation in the Theology of James Cone." *Journal of Religious Thought* 40 (1983–84) 27–38.

Streufert, Mary J. "Reclaiming Schleiermacher for Twenty-first Century Atonement Theory: The Human and the Divine in Feminist Christology." *Feminist Theology* 15:1 (2006) 98–120.

Swinburne, Richard. *The Existence of God*. Oxford: Clarendon, 1979.

Tanner, Kathryn. "Incarnation, Cross, and Sacrifice: A Feminist-Inspired Reappraisal." *Anglican Theological Review* 86 (2004) 35–56.

———. *The Politics of God: Christian Theologies and Social Justice*. Minneapolis: Fortress, 1992.

Thislethwaite, Susan Brooks. *Sex, Race and God: Christian Feminism in Black and White*. London: Chapman, 1990.

Thomas, George F. "The Method and Structure of Tillich's Theology." In *The Theology of Paul Tillich*, edited by Charles W. Kegley and Robert W. Bretall, 86–105. New York: Macmillan, 1952.

Thompson, Deanna A. *Crossing the Divide: Luther, Feminism, and the Cross*. Minneapolis: Fortress, 2004.

Tillich, Paul. *The Courage to Be*. New Haven: Yale University Press, 1952.

———. *Systematic Theology*. Vol. 1. London: Nisbet, 1953.

———. *Systematic Theology*. Vol. 2. London: Nisbet, 1957.

———. "What Is Wrong with the 'Dialectic' Theology?" In *Paul Tillich: Theologian of the Boundaries*, edited by Mark Kline Taylor, 104–16. Minneapolis, Fortress, 1991.

Tolbert, Mary Ann. "Defining the Problem: The Bible and Feminist Hermeneutics." *Semeia* 28 (1983) 113–26.

Tracy, David. *Blessed Rage for Order: The New Pluralism in Theology*. London: University of Chicago Press, 1996.

Torrance, James B. "Foreword" in *John McLeod Campbell on Christian Atonement: So Rich a Soil*, by George M. Tuttle. Edinburgh: Handsel, 1986.

Van Dyk, Leanne. *The Desire of Divine Love: John McLeod Campbell's Doctrine of the Atonement*. Edited by William L. Fox. Studies in Church History 4. New York: Peter Lang, 1995.

————. "Do Theories of Atonement Foster Abuse?" *Dialog* 35 (1996) 21–34.

————. "Vision and Imagination in Atonement Doctrine." *Theology Today* 50:1 (1993) 4–12.

Van Wijk-Bos, Johanna W. H. "The Shadow of a Mighty Rock." Unpublished paper for the American Academy of Religion Annual Meeting. New Orleans, November 1996.

VandenBerg, Mary. "Redemptive Suffering: Christ's Alone." *Scottish Journal of Theology* 60 (2007) 394–411.

Watson, Francis. *Text, Church and World: Biblical Interpretation in Theological Perspective*. Edinburgh: T. & T. Clark, 1994.

Weaver, J. Denny. *The Nonviolent Atonement*. Grand Rapids: Eerdmans, 2001.

Weingart, Richard E. *The Logic of Divine Love: A Critical Analysis of the Soteriology of Peter Abailard*. Oxford: Clarendon, 1970.

Welch, Claude. "Paul Tillich and Theology of Correlation." In *Religion*, edited by Paul Ramsey, 249–59. The Princeton Studies: Humanistic Scholarship in America. Englewood Cliffs, NJ: Prentice-Hall, 1965.

West, Angela. *Deadly Innocence: Feminist Theology and the Mythology of Sin*. London: Cassell, 1990.

————. "Justification by Gender—Daphne Hampson's *After Christianity*." *Scottish Journal of Theology* 51 (1998) 99–115.

Williams, Delores S. "A Crucifixion Double Cross?" *The Other Side* 29:5 (1993) 25–27.

————. *Sisters in the Wilderness: The Challenge of Womanist God-Talk*. Maryknoll, NY: Orbis, 1993.

Wilson-Kastner, Patricia. *Faith, Feminism, and the Christ*. Philadelphia: Fortress, 1983.

Wolterstorff, Nicholas. *Faith and Rationality: Reason and Belief in God*. Edited by Alvin Plantinga and Nicholas Wolterstorff. London: University of Notre Dame Press, 1983.

Wondra, Ellen K. *Humanity Has Been a Holy Thing: Towards a Contemporary Feminist Christology*. Lanham, MD: University Press of America, 1994.

Woodhead, Linda. "Spiritualising the Sacred: A Critique of Feminist Theology." *Modern Theology* 13 (1997) 191–212.

Young, Pamela Dickey. "Diversity in Feminist Christology." *Studies in Religion/Studies Religieuses* 21:1 (1992) 81–90.

————. *Feminist Theology/Christian Theology: In Search of Method*. Minneapolis: Fortress, 1990.

Zappone, Katherine E. "'Woman's Special Nature': A Different Horizon for Theological Anthropology." In *The Special Nature of Women?*, edited by Anne E. Carr and Elisabeth Schüssler Fiorenza, 87–95. Concilium 6. London: SCM, 1992.

Index